Mermaids are Real

THE
MYSTIQ PRONG

Bo Wu

Cover Design & Formatting by Damonza.com

Prologue

Joe Fisher looked in his boat's cooler box. Three shrimp sat on ice. "That ain't enough for an appetizer. Not gonna pay the bills with this haul."

Joe lifted his cap with one hand and wiped his forehead with a red handkerchief he pulled from his back pocket with the other. Several blonde curls dangled around his eyebrows until he pushed them back with the inside brim of his hat. He dug into his front pocket and pulled out his phone. Joe's big callous hands made the phone look like a playing card. His wife picked up on the second ring.

"Hey, dear," said Joe.

"Everything OK?" asked Rita.

Rita wedged the phone between her head and her shoulder while she kneaded the bread dough for dinner rolls due at the evening's city council fundraiser. The Mayor wanted to draw more tourists to the tiny beach town of Beech Mill, and everyone knew Rita's food was a sure way to put people in a good mood.

"I'm gonna make another run this afternoon. I won't be home 'til late tonight. I got skunked this morning," said Joe.

"Well, make sure you wash that skunk off before you come in the door tonight," said Rita. She said it with a smile. She said everything that way.

Joe laughed. "See you tonight, dear. Good luck with the town dinner."

"You know me, hon. Dinner will be the talk of the town tomorrow," said Rita.

"I'm a lucky man," said Joe.

"I'm luckier. Go git'em," said Rita.

She lifted her head and held out her arm. The phone slid off her shoulder and down her arm onto the prep table in her catering company's kitchen. A strand of black hair with a streak of white from the flour fell into her face. She huffed and shot it back over her head without a second thought and continued kneading.

Whitecaps started clapping against the side of the Rita I an hour later. One minute Joe Fisher bent over untangling a hung line on the rear of the boat, and the next he was rubbing the top of his head wondering where his hat had flown off to.

He turned back to the shore and saw a faint blip from the lighthouse through the sheets of water now pouring down around his head. "Scratch that. I guess I'll be home early, then."

Joe scrambled to winch in the nets when he caught sight of a few fins in the water.

A hollow thump from below rattled throughout the hull. He was too deep to run aground. Another bump followed soon after.

Something's underneath the boat, he thought.

That's when the fins caught his eyes again circling, bobbing up and down.

"Dolphins bob. Sharks glide," he mumbled to himself.

As he moved his gaze around, he noticed a solid stream of fins bobbing up and down, about twenty feet away, completely surrounding his vessel.

Just past the circle of dolphins, he saw a larger fin gliding along the surface. He glanced toward the stern of the boat and saw another slicing through the water. Behind him, on the leeward side of the boat, he saw another and another.

At first glance, Joe thought, *Those dolphins are guarding the boat.*

He looked out again.

Nah, man. Dolphins don't do that... do they? he thought, wiping the water out of his eyes with his forearm.

Joe shook his head and cleared the thought, then caught sight of his faded blue and red Fisher and Son cap floating within reach. "My lucky cap!"

As soon as he bent down to snatch it, the starboard side of the boat lifted out of the water with so much force he fell back before he fell forward. The back of his head smacked the deck, and he kissed the water belly-flop-style. Joe's head spun furiously, but he remained conscious.

The first body swept his leg and pulled him under hard.

Joe scrambled for the surface. Before he got there, a tail caught him on top of the head and pushed him back down a few feet. Panicked voices called out from every direction.

"We can't hold them off! There are too many," said one.

"Quick! Get him out of here!" said another.

"Reinforcements are on the way!" barked someone else in the distance.

As Joe started to panic, a smooth body came rushing under his belly. He threw his hands around it, and they both burst through the surface.

Joe's waterlogged clothes pulled him down as much as he struggled to kick and swing his arms to stay afloat. Something swept under him again and yanked him downward. Then, a single arm clenched him around the waist and thrust him upward with so much power his thighs nearly left the water. He had just enough time to cough and take a deep breath when he saw the most gorgeous blue eyes he'd ever seen staring at him. The sapphire eyes locked on Joe's.

"Benji... My Benji... Please... Safe... Please... Hide..."

Despite her state of confusion and the noise of the storm, her voice mesmerized Joe.

He tried grabbing hold of the woman, but he just flailed his arms instead.

The woman's arm held Joe tight around the waist.

He gasped for air as her nails pierced his side just before they both went down again.

Joe closed his eyes.

The woman screamed so loud it sent shivers through Joe's skin. Then, her grasp around his midsection disappeared with a jerk.

When Joe opened his eyes, a murky carbonated red engulfed his head. High pitch screams, clicks, and whistles from every conceivable direction added to the confusion.

He gave a big push downward with both arms to get back to the surface. When he got there, a corner of the overturned boat caught him on the right temple.

Darkness followed.

The sound of the rubber squeaking as he shifted his legs helped Joe realize he was sprawled out in the life raft.

"What the hay?" he muttered while his hand reached for his head.

Opening his eyes took every bit of energy he could muster. Joe looked up at the star-sprinkled sky and smiled back at the Cheshire Cat of a moon shining down on him. He raised his wrist in front of his face and lit up the screen on his watch.

"10:00 pm. Yep. Gonna be late, dear."

Five little fingers grabbed Joe Fisher's chest.

"WHA......!"

Joe jerked his head over and stared at a little green bundle stuffed inside a sea turtle shell. The smallest arm he'd ever seen jutted out and clenched his t-shirt.

Joe Fisher pulled some random things out of the ocean before, but the little bundle next to him definitely ranked number one.

A few splashes of water around the life raft pulled his attention away from the baby in the turtle shell. A circle of bobbing fins moved at a mechanical pace around the raft.

He looked back at the shell and started talking to himself.

"How was your day, dear? Oh, just dandy. I ended up in my life raft with a baby stuffed turtle shell being guarded by a pod of dolphins. I lost my boat. Not sure how you do that, but I did. Just a typical day on the water. You know?"

The events of the last several hours were slowly refocusing in his memory when his head nearly split open from the short, rapid pulse of a Coast Guard siren. The sound of the motors running in the water reverberated through the rubber life raft and massaged Joe's headache into crevices of his brain he didn't know existed.

"Joe? Joe Fisher?" sounded a voice over a bullhorn. "Joe is that you? Are you alright?"

Joe jutted his arm up into the air with thumb raised. The searchlight illuminated his gesture, and the ocean swallowed the shadow. A round of clapping erupted from the boat.

"We got him, boys," called the voice behind the bullhorn.

The crew hoisted Joe and the baby boy out of the life raft and wrapped them both in blankets.

Joe held the baby in his arms.

The captain approached him with a blank face.

"Thanks, Rich. I never thought I'd need you boys' help," said Joe.

"Me neither," said Rich.

Rich took a sip of his coffee. "Cup 'o Joe?"

"Hardy har, Cap'n. All I ask is that you get me home to my wife."

Rich put his hand on Joe's boulder of a shoulder while shaking his head. "Joe," he said looking at the floor. "Rita was in an accident tonight."

Kutawiki Okimboo

(swearing turtle)

HEY, FISHBOY. PSST, fishboy! Hey. Hook me up with some food. No. No. Don't hook me up. I mean... I need some food. Hey, I saw your eyes dart over here. I know you hear me, said Butterbean.

A spitball ricocheted off the back of Benji Fisher's head and stuck to the bookcase where Butterbean's fishbowl sat. Benji turned his test paper over and slammed his pencil down with a huff.

"Is everything OK, Mr. Fisher?" asked Mrs. Sanchez.

Mrs. Sanchez taught U.S. History. She peered at Benji over her purple reading glasses. A number two pencil stuck out of the bun in the back of her head like a helicopter rotor.

"Yes, Mrs. Sanchez. I'm finished," said Benji.

"I'm sure you are. There's no need to broadcast it to the rest of the class, Mr. Fisher," said Mrs. Sanchez.

I need some food, fishboy! Nobody fed me this morning. You do realize fish need food, right? I can't eat these glass marbles down here. And I'm not hungry enough to recycle yet, which by the way, someone needs to clean this place, too, said Butterbean.

Mrs. Sanchez scanned the room once more for wandering eyes. Before she returned to marking papers from the previous class, Benji threw up his hand.

"Yes, Mr. Fisher?" said Mrs. Sanchez over her reading glasses with a mild tone of annoyance.

"Since I'm finished, can I feed Butterbean and clean out his bowl?" asked Benji.

"Since you're finished, you can be quiet and let the others work in peace. Put your head down and sleep if you want, but don't drool on your paper," snapped Mrs. Sanchez.

Half the class snickered. The other half looked around at their neighbor's paper during the disruption.

"Eyes to yourself, Mr. Biggums," called Mrs. Sanchez.

Benji pulled a sweatshirt out of his backpack and balled it up on his desk for a pillow. He leaned over and put his head down exposing the back of his Fisher and Son t-shirt. A blue hook with a cartoon shrimp dangling from it faced Charley Goodstone.

"Cute shirt, fishboy," whispered Charley.

Benji ran his hands over the birthmarks on the side of his neck then buried his head in his sweatshirt to clear all the commotion going on around him.

"What's the answer to number twelve, fishboy?" whispered Charley.

"Mount Everest," whispered Benji.

Charley scribbled away on his paper.

Fishboy! I need food. I don't care what that four-eyed bug of a lady said. I'm hungry. I think my stomach is going to implode at any second. Food! Food! Food! said Butterbean. The goldfish started doing barrel rolls. *I'm dying. Oh, I'm dying.* Butterbean swam to the top of the bowl, turned his tail toward the class, and splashed Benji with water.

Scooter Biggums rapped his pencil on his desk over and over and over again.

Lisa Kamenski smacked on her gum.

Charley Goodstone worked up a double-barrelled spitball as wet and nasty as rainforest monkey poop.

"What's the answer to number fifteen, fishboy?" said Charley.

"Leave me alone," whispered Benji.

He put his face in his crumpled up sweatshirt, and Charley lit him up. The spitballs landed with a *SMACK*. One of them lodged between Benji's left ear and the side of his head. The second one hit him right in the middle of the neck. Benji shot up in his seat. When he did, the spitball on his neck oozed down his back.

That's when Benji Fisher lost it.

A head-rattling shriek crippled every eardrum in the classroom. Most of the class threw their hands over their ears.

A few of them, including Stuart Biggums and Charley Goodstone, hit the floor and shot under their desks.

Butterbean's fishbowl exploded into a thousand pieces. Water washed down the bookcase and sloshed on the floor. Butterbean yelled the whole way down. The fish hit the floor with the same sound as the last spitball hitting Benji's neck. *Oh, no. Oh, god! Help me! I'm dying. I can't breathe! (cough...cough) Save me, fishboy. Please! I'm too pretty to go out like this. Too young!*

Benji took a deep breath. All the muscles in his face pinched toward his nose. His balled up fists clenched his jeans at the thighs. He slowly opened his right eye, then the left, as he scanned the room.

Half the class stared up at him from their desks, blank expressions plastered across their mugs.

Benji's desk had turned over. His chair toppled over behind him and wedged against Charlie's desk. Benji stood in the middle of a puddle of water with a flopping fish and two of his whimpering classmates at his feet.

Benji bent down and scooped up Butterbean. He cut his outer palm on a piece of glass and winced.

Benji looked around the room then stopped when his eyes scanned Mrs. Sanchez's desk. He walked over with the fish in his hands.

Butterbean hollered for his life. *Please. Please. Don't let me go out like this.*

Benji plopped the fish into a mason jar Mrs. Sanchez used for drinking her filtered water. A drop of blood fell in with the fish, and the history teacher's head clunked on top of the test papers she had been marking. Her arms sprawled out, sending a few of the exams flying into the air.

Benji turned around and looked at his classmates. A few of them still had their faces covered on their desks. The others looked at Benji with their mouths wide open, eyes the size of truck tires.

Benji slowly backed out of the room, then turned and sprinted down the hall toward the infirmary.

* * * *

"Ok, kiddo, you know the drill," said Joe Fisher.

"Questions?" said Benji.

Joe came up with the game a few years ago to buy himself some time between the onslaught of 'whys' and also to try and tire his son out with questions of his own. Neither worked, but the game lasted, nonetheless.

One person starts with a question. The other person answers and then follows with one of their own. It turned out to be a good way to keep things from getting too lopsided. Either person could throw in the towel after five who, what, when, why, or wheres. Another game wasn't allowed for thirty minutes.

"Yep," said Joe. "You got any coins?"

Benji shoved his left hand into his pocket and pulled out a bubblegum wrapper. The gauze on his right hand kept him from digging in the other pocket. He patted it and shook his head.

"Shoot! Me neither. Rock, paper, scissors," said Joe.

Joe looked at Benji's hand as they both slid into the pickup truck. The driver's side door creaked as it opened and closed.

"Looks like you've had an interesting day. 1-2-3," said Joe.

"You could say that. Rock beats scissors," said Benji.

"I got to keep some change on me. You always win."

Joe put the truck in drive, and they rode out of the school parking lot.

The principal and school secretary stood inside the door talking up a storm.

Benji gave his dad a sly grin.

"You know something I don't?" Joe asked.

"Maybe," said Benji.

"You askin' first?" said Joe.

"Yeah, I'll go first," said Benji.

"The ole diversion tactic. I gotta stay sharp today. Lead on, chief."

Benji faced straight ahead, peeking out of the corner of his eye.

The twisty swamp road leading back toward town monopolized Joe's attention.

Mahloowoo, thought Benji.

Joe scrunched his brow and looked over at Benji.

Benji kept his head pointed straight. Out of the corner of his eye, he saw Joe focus on the road again.

This time he thought harder.

Mahloowoo.

Joe jerked his head toward Benji.

Can you hear me, Dad?

"What kind of… That's not my question. Of course, I can hear you. Wait a second. You asked me that with your mouth closed. Where did you learn that?"

Benji shrugged his shoulders and kept his lips sealed with a slight grin on his face.

Well?

"That's pretty cool. Who taught you that?" asked Joe.

No one. I thought maybe you could do it too. Can you?

"I've seen that on TV, but I don't know how to throw my voice. We should get you one of those puppets. We can order one tonight. You need to figure out what kind of character you want to practice with, though."

I'm not using my voice.

"I bet Miss Wendy can help you make one if you ask her."

Dad! I'm not using my voice to talk.

"What the……?"

"Don't swear, Dad."

A chill ran down Joe's spine. His shoulders nearly slammed into his earlobes, and his neck disappeared for a few seconds. "I didn't swear."

"Yeah, you did. You said …"

"Ship."

Benji snorted then yelled, "Look out for that turtle."

Joe yanked the wheel toward the right. His front wheels straddled the turtle. The back driver's side wheel clipped the turtle's shell and sent the reptile spinning off the road.

Ahhhhhhh! Watch where you're going you big…

Joe looked in the passenger side mirror. "Did I...?"

"No, Dad. You scared him pretty good, though. I heard him swearing at you from the ditch."

Joe pulled over. Half the truck sat in the bike lane. The other half rested on the slope of the ditch.

"You heard the turtle what?" asked Joe.

"I heard him swearing at you," said Benji.

Joe laughed. "You heard a turtle swear?" He laughed again as he rested his head on his white-knuckled hands gripping the steering wheel. "You heard a turtle swear," he whispered. Joe shook his head left and right turning the steering wheel slightly as he did. "My son hears turtles swear."

A rap on the window sent Joe's head rocking even faster. "Please tell me that's not a talking bird," he said peering at Benji.

"It's Andy."

"The deputy?"

Benji nodded.

"Just as bad."

Andy pushed his sunglasses up the bridge of his nose and rapped on the window again. "Joe, you ah 'ight? Joe?"

Joe rolled down window with the wrench he fastened to the bolt after the plastic knob broke off.

"I'm fine. Benji and I were just..." Joe looked at Benji with a 'help me' look in his eyes.

Spider.

"Spider in my lap, Andy. Scared the buhjeezus out of me."

The deputy got excited. "Big 'un?"

"Thing was big as a softball, Andy."

"Man, oh man!"

Joe lifted his head and held his hands apart. "This big."

"Ooh wee! You git'em?"

Joe looked at Benji, his eyes as big as silver dollars. "Well?"

Benji snickered and covered his mouth with his good hand. His stomach shook a few times before he got the words out. "Yes, sir. I shooed him out the window. He's probably halfway up one of those trees by now," Benji said, pointing his thumb toward the ditch.

Andy looked over the bed of the truck into the woods lining the ditch and started to giggle. "One time, when I had ole Fred in the back for sleeping in the park, a bumble bee got in and buzzed him a couple of times. He was a' hootin' and a' hollerin' up a storm. 'bout made me wet myself." Andy put his thumbs inside his belt buckle and shook as he laughed. "I can imagine that spider did the same to y'all two."

"Yeah, it got lively in here for a second. I guess that's why you stopped," said Joe.

"Yeah, I saw. Spider or not, be careful, Joe. You were zig zaggin' all over the place. Mighta' hit someone had they been…"

Joe drooped his head and closed his eyes.

"Aw, man. Sorry 'bout that Joe, I didn't mean nothin' by it. I was jus' watchin' out for you. You know what I mean?"

"It's OK, Andy. I know." Joe reached for the keys. "We ok to go, Andy?"

"Yeah, Joe. You're good. Be careful now, and watch out for them spiders," said Andy with a nervous laugh. The deputy patted the hood of the truck with his palm and motioned forward.

They pulled up to the house, and Joe slumped down in his seat. He sputtered out what was in his lungs, making his lips bounce up and down, then pulled his hat back over his head. "Where were we on our questions?"

Benji shrugged. "I lost count when Andy showed up."

"Me too, but I don't think Andy had anything to do with it."

They met up at the front of the truck, and Joe threw his arm over Benji's shoulder. The two of them walked through the back yard under the dogwood tree then split the two cypress trees guarding the entrance to the dock Joe's father built. Low tide exposed a few of the knobby roots from the cypress trees on the bank. Water bugs danced on the surface. A few minnows snapped at the insects from below.

They both slumped down on the wooden bench at the end of the dock.

Joe reached under the seat and pulled out a beer and a soda from a cooler. "They're probably still cool. Oops. Wrong one. Hand that over. You still got a few years before you can have that one."

They snapped the tops and both took a big gulp.

Joe and Benji threw their arms over the back rail at the same time and got their hands tangled up. Once they figured out whose arm went where, Joe piped up, " 'right then. How long…?"

"For a while now."

"Before we move forward, let's take a few steps back. I'm still not sure what's going on, so for the time being, let's not get inside Dad's head anymore. Cool?"

"Ok, Dad."

"How long have you been able to do this?"

"As long as I can remember."

"Why…," stumbled Joe.

"My turn," said Benji.

"Oh yeah."

"Does this make me weird?"

"Benji, you're twelve years old. You're a senior in high school. You're also nearly as tall as I am, and I'm six foot five. You're the best surfer in the area, and… well, you're just different, son. That's not a bad thing; it's just the truth. Excluding all that and answering your immediate question, it's not something I can do or anyone else I know can do, but let's not go calling it weird. OK?"

"Fair enough."

"My turn."

Joe held out his fist then started extending fingers as he counted. "From what I gathered earlier, you can hear my…"

"Not just you."

"Wait for me."

"Sorry. I wasn't in your head. That was me…"

"Jumping the gun? Putting words in my mouth? You're not the only one who can do that one," said Joe as he poked Benji in the shoulder.

Benji shot soda out his nose.

"So, you can shoot soda out your nose. You can hear my thoughts. You can also talk to me without actually talking. You can hear turtles swear. Am I missing anything?"

"Well, yeah. I can hear other animals, too, not just turtles."

"Of course you can. Just hearing turtles *would* be weird," Joe said with a wink.

"Ha ha. I can talk with them the same way I talked to you in the car. That's weird, right?"

"Different. Does anyone else know?

"Uh…"

"You're not showing off at school are you?"

"No, Dad. You're skipping me again. My turn."

"Oops."

"What do you think of Miss Wendy?" said Benji.

"Woah now! Where did that come from? That's not my question. Hold on." Joe took a gulp of his beer and then a second to compose himself. "She's your teacher. She's a nice woman. She's a good teacher, from what you say. She…"

"That's not what I mean, Dad. Do you like her?" said Benji.

"Like I said, she's your teacher. Let's just keep that one where it's at for the time being," said Joe.

"Everyone knows I don't need any help getting A's Dad. It's OK if you like her. She's not really my teacher anyway. Not at school at least."

"My question. Last one was…" Joe massaged his stubbly chin. "…does anyone know? Yeah. Yeah. Let's keep this between us for now. Beech Mill is a small town. People here like simple living. Simple lives. This is a step above simple. I'm sure you've looked online, read everything you can get your hands on."

"Yeah."

"Well? What did you find?"

"I'm telepathic."

"Meaning?"

"I can talk to you without actually talking. I can 'think' to you is a good way to describe it. I can hear what you're thinking, too."

Benji cleared his throat and fumbled with the can in his hands.

"I'm also telekinetic, a little."

"What's that last one?" said Joe rubbing his forehead.

"I can only do it with liquid, right now."

"Do what?"

Benji rocked back and forth on the wooden bench. He steadied himself then leaned back and extended both arms. His free hand hovered over the soda can. He snapped his finger over the hole, and a stream of soda shot out. He moved the can to the left as the stream arched and caught it as the liquid came back down.

"I'll be," muttered Joe. His face lit up with a twinkle of adolescence. "Do it again."

Benji snapped his fingers twice this time and caught one after the other as they came back down.

"It's gonna lose all the fiz, Dad."

"We got more in the cooler," said Joe as he patted Benji on the arm and nodded toward the can again.

Benji snapped his fingers twice more.

The first board on the dock creaked, and they both jerked their heads around.

"Man!" cried Benji as the soda soaked his leg.

"No sneakin' up on you boys. Huh?" said Miss Wendy.

Joe hired Miss Wendy the year before to keep Benji interested in studying. She tutored him after school in college-level math and science. She also watched him surf after he finished his lessons.

"That's a redneck security system, right there," said Joe nodding at the creaky board.

Miss Wendy smiled. "Planning on taking over the world out here?"

"One can at the time," said Benji. "Come on out."

Dad, can you hear me?

"Yeah," muttered Joe.

Close your mouth.

"Thanks. There's a time and place for that trick. But I don't want you in here anymore," whispered Joe as he tapped his temple. "OK?"

OK, Dad.

"I'm supposed to be tutoring someone out here right now," said Miss Wendy.

"Shoot!" said Benji.

"While you two have been all buddy buddy out here on the dock, I've been hearing rumors at school that Benji was in a fight. Then I heard he wasn't. Then I heard it was a freak accident involving a sonic boom. Then I heard... I don't remember what else. I left school and headed home where

I was supposed to meet someone I know," she said with her hands on her hips, her head cocked to one side.

"This afternoon got a little lively," said Benji.

"I've been trying to call for the last hour," said Miss Wendy.

Both of them patted their pockets.

"The car," said Joe.

"My school bag," said Benji.

"Boys," she shrugged. "So, I guess Trigonometry is out this afternoon?"

"Yeah, I think we can hold off on that until tomorrow," said Joe.

Miss Wendy stood there drenched in the orange-pink hue of the late afternoon sun.

Joe and Benji stared at her like they had lost their senses.

"I'm not playing your question game today. Somebody needs to tell me what happened," said Miss Wendy.

"Yeah, I am still waiting," said Joe.

"You've been together all this time, and you don't know?" she said as she stared Joe down with pouty lips.

"We've had some… uh… other things to discuss. It's been a weir… I mean… it's been an interesting afternoon," said Joe.

"I told him," said Benji.

Joe looked at Miss Wendy then they both jerked their heads toward Benji.

"Good," said Miss Wendy.

"You told *her*?" said Joe.

Miss Wendy raised her eyebrows then walked to the end of the dock.

"It's about time," she said in a soft yet irritable tone. "And?" she raised her voice a few notches looking at Joe.

"I'm still processing," said Joe. "Wait a minute, Benji. You said nobody else…"

"Technically, I never answered that question."

"You told her before me?" said Joe. His voice softened and almost quivered.

"I'm a woman, Joe," she said.

"And what does that mean?" stammered Joe.

"Compassionate. Understanding. Patient. I'm also an interested third party he trusts. I'm also cuter than you. Should I go on?" said Miss Wendy.

"Nah. I understand. You definitely got me in the cute department, but I can be pretty compassionate, too. I mean, I was worried about that turtle today, right?"

Benji snorted.

Miss Wendy looked at Joe like he was half-crazy.

"Sorry, Dad," said Benji.

Joe looked out over the water.

A mullet broke the surface and sent ripples toward the dock.

A seagull squatting on one of the dock pilings stood up and squawked then sat back down eyeing the three of them for scraps of food.

"I heard Charlie Goodstone blabbing to his father in the hall. I want to hear what happened from you," said Miss Wendy.

"What did Charlie say?" said Benji.

"Don't you worry about what that... that boy said. I don't believe a word that comes out of his mouth. Nobody else does either," said a flustered Miss Wendy.

"Unless he's threatening to beat their lunch money out of them," said Benji.

"Come on, son. Stop stallin'," said Joe.

Benji shoved his left hand into his pocket and dropped his head. He paced on the end of the dock while Miss Wendy and Joe stared at him. "We had a history test today in Mrs. Sanchez's class. I finished early and put my head down. As soon as I did, Butterbean started buggin' me about...."

"Butterbean?" asked Joe.

"That's the goldfish in Mrs. Sanchez's class," said Miss Wendy.

Joe interrupted Benji several times before the entire story came out, but, for the most part, he sat there taking it in with Miss Wendy playing translator and mediator.

"The fish calls you fishboy?" said Joe.

"He got that from Charlie Goodstone," said Miss Wendy shaking her head.

"Cause I'm a fisherman?" said Joe.

"And my last name's Fisher. And the birthmarks on my neck look like gills," said Benji.

"Oh, he's original," said Joe

"Charley's not the brightest bulb, Dad," said Benji.

"The two of them were driving me up the wall. Bean in my head and Charlie in my ear. All the while, the rest of the class scribbled away on their papers. A scraped chair here. A cough there. A cleared throat here.

"I kept looking at the clock wishing the time away. I did my best to block it all out. I had a lid on it for a while. I even handled the first spit-ball alright."

Joe snorted, and Miss Wendy cut him a look that made him stop immediately.

"I'm not too sure what happened next. I don't think I yelled, but every-one covered their ears. Next thing I know, Bean's bowl shatters, and he's flopping around next to the bookcase. I scooped him up, cut my hand on a shard of glass, and ran to Mrs. Sanchez's desk with him in my hands. As soon as she saw the blood, she passed out. I dropped Bean in her jar of water and ran out the door to the infirmary to tell them about Mrs. Sanchez and get my hand wrapped up."

"And you got in trouble?" said Joe.

"No. I didn't really do anything, or I don't think I did anything. The whole thing just creeped everyone out. I told the principal I felt lightheaded and if I could get a hold of you, I wanted to go home."

"You said you didn't think you yelled," said Miss Wendy.

"I remember I clenched my eyes and jaw and thought 'Stop it, Charlie!'"

"Charlie told his father you yelled so loud and high-pitched that the glass broke and scared everyone in class. I heard the noise on the other side of school. Some of the other teachers mentioned it possibly being a sonic boom from the Marine base," said Miss Wendy.

"Scooter Biggum's glasses shattered, too. I saw them on the way out the door. I couldn't have broken the glass, right?"

"Benji, I heard Lisa and Stuart talking beside Charley's father. They both said you stood up with your head cocked and your mouth wide open," said Miss Wendy.

Joe glanced at the soda can in Benji's hand then looked away quickly.

Benji caught his dad's eyes, raised his eyebrows, and shrugged his shoulders. "Maybe I did."

"But you're ok?" asked Miss Wendy looking at his hand.

"That?" he said raising his bandaged hand. "It's a sympathy bandage, honestly, but now that you mention it, I'm starving."

"There's a pizza on the kitchen counter," said Miss Wendy.

"Woah!! Best teacher of the year award right here, folks," said Benji with his hands in the air and fingers pointing down on Miss Wendy. "Wup! Wup!!" he yelled as he sprinted down the dock and flew through the back door.

"I hope you're not mad, Joe," said Miss Wendy, sitting down on the bench next to him.

"Mad?"

Joe reached under his seat and pulled out a beer.

"Mad?"

He popped the top and handed it to her.

"I'm lucky you're around. Benji's lucky you're around. We're both lucky."

"Tomorrow's going to be a rough day for him," she said.

"He's tough. We've done a good job of teaching him how to handle himself. Let's get some pizza before the little monster eats it all."

"In a minute. I bought two. The other one is still in my car," she said reaching for his hand.

Joe flinched a little then blushed.

"Sorry, Joe. If I waited for you, we'd both be retired by the time you made a move on me."

They sat watching a group of pelicans in formation swoop over the inlet in front of them.

"Would you look at that," said Joe.

Three dolphins surfaced off the end of the dock and cleared their blowholes. They bobbed up and down for fifty feet then disappeared again.

He's ready, said Eeke.

They're both ready, said Zeke.

Octavius will be the judge of that, said Mai. *He'll want to hear about this, immediately.*

Λ

Zouleaki Shazfoopi

(flying shorts)

EACH TIME BENJI caught a wave, his movements synced perfectly to the classical music Miss Wendy played on her phone. Benji took the last wave fifty yards down the beach. A dolphin raced ahead of him in the curl of the wave; another followed on the back side.

Miss Wendy sat on a beach towel thinking what it would be like to be in Benji's head for just a few minutes. None of the recent events fazed him. He was just a kid on a lacquered piece of foam riding waves.

"Hey, kiddo," said Miss Wendy. "You caught me spacin' out."

Benji wedged his board in the sand and plopped down next to her. "I do that pretty often out here. That's what it's for, right?"

"Nice work out there."

"Thanks. Waves are pretty small today, but I had good company." He smiled at her and then nodded toward the ocean. Two fins bounced up and down on the back side of the breakers. "Present company included, of course."

"Your Dad taught you well." Miss Wendy smiled then broke off for a moment as she listened to the sand shushing a wave. "Do you ever feel like they follow you?"

"Who?"

"The dolphins. Every time you're in the ocean, they're not far off. It's like they come to play with you. You should be a marine biologist or a trainer," said Miss Wendy.

"They don't need training. They're super smart. You should hear them yapping."

"What do they say?"

"A lot of it I don't understand. They talk about places I've never heard of and other dolphins, I guess. I did hear them talking about finding pirate gold one time."

"Well, now. That's something we all understand. You might have found yourself the first talking metal detectors. You need to introduce yourself."

"That'd be something else to find a boat full of gold, wouldn't it?" said Benji.

"That would be pretty high on my list of awesome things to happen," she said. "Speaking of something else, your birthday is tomorrow. I hear your Uncle Bill and his band are going to be in town performing on the pier. How does a party sound?"

"It's always a party when he's around," said Benji.

"Anyone special you want to ask to come along?" asked Miss Wendy.

"Not really. That's where everyone in town hangs out anyway, so I don't really need to, do I?" said Benji.

"No special lady friends?"

"Ha! Any girl that I might have been able to bribe is long gone after that fishbowl incident."

"They'll come around. Anything special you want? Are you sure you don't need a new wetsuit? I've never seen anyone sit there all day, even in the Spring, without at least a shorty."

Benji outgrew his first wetsuit in six months and after repeated protests never wore another.

"Nah. Don't get cold."

While the two of them sat there exchanging small talk, Charley Goodstone, Benji's antagonizing red-headed neighbor, strutted over the dunes with a couple of his lackeys. They walked by pointing and laughing. Charley yelled out "Hey, fishboy," as he and his cronies made their way to the water.

"Eat it, Big Red," said Benji.

"Don't pay him any attention," Miss Wendy quipped as she shot the crew a menacing look.

"Pretty hard. He lives right across the street. Here comes his famous sign-off."

Without missing a beat, Charley saluted Benji with his favorite finger before taking off full speed into the ocean. The blubber around his belly giggled with each stride.

"Someone needs to teach that kid a lesson," Miss Wendy snarled.

"I got a few good ideas brewing," said Benji.

"Definitely not you, and you can put a lid on any of those ideas. He's not worth the trouble."

Benji stroked his chin like he was thinking of something devilish, and Miss Wendy playfully smacked his arm.

"Ow!"

"Grab your board. Your dad called earlier. He's running late and asked me to take you home tonight."

Miss Wendy rustled Benji's wet hair then headed up the wooden walkway leading back to her beach house.

As Benji stood up to grab his surfboard, Charley screamed then disappeared underwater. Benji straightened up and kept his eyes on the spot where Charley disappeared. Charley jumped back up, grabbed a mouth full of air, then dropped out of sight again. Benji ran down the beach and dove through the first wave.

Charley popped his head above water as soon as Benji went under and barked out a set of orders at one of his lanky buddies. The little minion swam in Charley's direction. They exchanged some heated words then both stuck their faces in the water like they were looking for something.

Benji swam underwater until he caught sight of Charley's fat feet shuffling sand back and forth. Benji lost half the air in his lungs when he noticed Charley standing there minus the shorts he had gone in with.

Two dolphins surrounded Charley. One of the dolphins had his head between Charley's legs. The other floated in front of the bully chanting. "Do it, Eeke! Do it!"

"You sure?"

"Do it! Spout 'im! Spout 'im, Eeke," said Zeeke.

The dolphin between Charley's legs lifted his head up a few inches, opened his blowhole, and shot a blast of air between Charley's butt cheeks that lifted the boy a good twelve inches. Charley's yell carried into the water causing Benji to laugh.

"Ahem," a voice cleared beside Benji's head.

Benji's entire body froze, his arms and legs spread eagle six inches above the sand. Benji's eyes slowly pulled his head in the direction of the voice.

A dolphin stared at him with a pair of red trunks in her mouth. She spit them out with a wink and swam off with a cocky swat of the tail. A purple octopus sat wrapped around her dorsal fin glaring back at Benji. The blast of water from the dolphin's tail nearly knocked Charley over, and the naked boy let out another yelp.

The other two dolphins circled Charley then raced by Benji.

Benji's eyes shot wide open, and he coughed out the rest of the air in his lungs. He grabbed Charley's shorts and shot to the surface for air.

Benji popped up a few feet from his neighbor and pushed the water off his face with his free hand. Charley squealed again when he saw Benji, then quickly regained his composure.

"Was that you, fishboy?" said Charley.

"Missing something, match head?" Benji held Charley's red shorts with a sly grin.

"Give me those, freak."

"What's the magic word?"

"Let me see…Abraca… EAT IT! Give me my shorts, fishboy!"

Benji faked a toss over Charley's head, and when the bully's hands went up in anticipation, Benji slung the shorts at his neighbor, plastering his face with a sloshing 'SPLAT' right between the eyes.

Charley used a few choice words telling Benji what he could do and where he could go.

Benji swam back to the beach. He walked past Stuart Biggums rustling through a backpack.

"You should put your buddy in a life jacket," said Benji.

Stuart gave Benji a distasteful look. "Don't scare those fish off with your freaky scream. They look like the only friends you've got."

"They're mammals. They make better friends, and they're a lot more intelligent than some people I know," said Benji as he bent down to pick up his board. "I'd rather be out there with them any day."

As Benji bent over, Stuart pushed him over his surfboard.

"My dad says you owe me a new pair of glasses." Stuart laughed his way back into the waves to join Charley and the rest of the crew in his duct tape-mended glasses.

Benji sat beside his board with his arms propped over his knees staring at the gang in the water for a minute then walked calf-deep into the waves to wash off the sand.

On his way back out of the water, something slippery shot out from under Benji's right foot. Despite growing up by the ocean and having a fisherman for a father, stepping on something unexpectedly that feels like a frisbee-sized goober never ceased to send a chill up his spine.

Benji laughed as he put his hand on his chest hoping to slow his pulse. He wriggled his toes and saw something glimmering where the stingray shot off. A little, clear-blue sphere twinkled back at him.

A seagull drifted down and landed ten feet from the water's edge where the little treasure sparkled. The seagull eyed Benji and then the shiny object.

"A pretty little keepsake all for you," hissed a voice.

Benji's head darted left to right. A stingray circled his feet and then fluttered away.

Benji's curiosity spiked, and he bent down for a closer look. A shell whizzed over his head and skipped into the sand a few inches from where the seagull stood. The startled bird spread its wings and took flight immediately. Benji looked back through his legs and saw Charley standing in waist deep water with a devilish grin on his pale, freckled face.

Benji ran his foot over the marble-like object then nudged it with his big toe. It was the size of a small fishing bobber, but clear; a tablespoon of seawater molded into a bubble.

Benji held it up to the last bit of daylight still lingering in the cloudless sky. His eyes swam through the current swirled in the tiny ball.

Miss Wendy called him from the walkway. Benji pocketed his treasure and grabbed his board on the way back up the beach before hustling over the rickety wooden walkway.

"What was that all about?" asked Miss Wendy, nodding toward Charley and his friends.

"They were asking about some surfing lessons," said Benji.

"I guess you said no," she said with a look of mild irritation as she stared at Charley bouncing around in the water. "Let's go get you some meat on those bones. How's Chinese sound?"

"Are you picking up on my mind reading talents?"

*　*　*　*

A swarm of chatter broke out under the waves.

"When's he coming back? I want to talk to him," said Eeke.

Eeke was the youngest of three bottlenose dolphins. The white star between his blowhole and his eyes distinguished him from his brother. Eeke joined his siblings on the detail to look after Benji a year ago. He passed all his skills test for a scout with flying colors, and since his brother and sister already had the patrol, he stepped up as first in line to take up the duty when another dolphin was requested to watch Benji.

"You'd talk to the pilings on the pier if they listened," said his brother Zeeke. "I can't wait to run with him like Mom and Dad used to do with his father. Bet he's faster, too. Have you seen those feet? They'll make killer fins when he figures out what he's really supposed to be using them for."

"You ought to ask him when he's coming back. Based on all the chatter you two do when he's around, I'd be shocked if he doesn't know our whole family tree, the history of Aquari, and the fact that mahloowoos do smell underwater," harped Mai.

Mai loved her brothers more than life itself. Having them by her side while they guarded Benji made her beyond proud. Both of her brothers enjoyed cutting up more than any other mammal or fish she knew, but they'd rarely been caught doing so. They were as slippery as their skin.

"I got the red-headed kid good, didn't I?" said Eeke.

"You did," said Zeeke.

Zeeke was a whiz at trading when they found things in the ocean. He turned tin cans into homes for hermit crabs and transformed a half-broken javelin into a new nose for a wounded swordfish once, each time for more than enough pirate gold to bribe other patrol members to let the three of them out to explore at night.

"But are you supposed to be hassling the Topsiders?" said Mai.

"You didn't hear what they said about Benji. You showed up just in time to see the part you weren't supposed to see," said Zeeke.

"What they said about Benji or to Benji is not your concern. Both of you know better than to meddle with the Topsiders," said Mai.

"You snagged the bully's shorts, and you spouted him," lectured Octavius from atop Mai's back. "I sense some unsettling developments in Aquari. We need your attention on Benji and his safety. Leave the red-headed kid to his own devices."

Octavius was an octopus. He arrived outside Beech Mill earlier that morning to carry out a special assignment. Octavius was purple for the time being. Depending on how he felt or if he needed to disappear, he could be any color of the rainbow or any combination, too. Today he felt regal. Purple it was.

"I'll turn a blind eye today, but don't get involved with the Topsiders again," said Octavius.

"Sorry," said Zeeke.

"Me too," said Eeke.

Octavius froze and turned silver. A tentacle shot away from Mai's body and snatched a baitfish.

"Were you able to talk to Joe this morning… or more importantly was Joe able to hear you?" Zeeke asked looking over his sister's head at Octavius.

"We saw Joe today," mumbled Octavius with half a fish in his mouth. "Most Topsiders hear what they want to hear, but Benji's guardian wants to know just as much as Benji deserves to, not just for himself but for Benji, too. I believe Joe knows in his heart that Benji has a place here. Joe was chosen for a reason."

"You did talk to him. That's what took you and Mai so long today," said Eeke.

"Looks like we got back just in time to stop any more mischief," said Mai.

Zeeke hung his head in embarrassment. "When do you think Joe will tell him?"

Octavius looked away from Zeeke without answering and finished the rest of his snack.

"Do you think Benji will come?" said Eeke.

"When Benji does find out, I think he will come," said Octavius.

Mai interrupted the three of them, "Well, the sooner he finds out and decides, the better for us all."

"We have to be at the docks in three hours," said Octavius.

"I thought we were finished for the night," said Zeeke.

"You *were* able to talk to Joe this morning," said Eeke. "I knew it!"

"Sweet!" bellowed Zeeke.

"You'll find out soon enough," said Octavius.

Mai gave a quick swipe of her tail heading away from the shore. The other two followed quickly behind chattering the entire way back out to sea.

Kulinki Nomba

(talking fish)

BENJI WALKED OUT on the back porch and threw an arm over his dad's shoulder.

Joe twitched.

"Easy, Dad."

"You got me, kid. I was just thinking."

"I thought I smelled something burning," Benji said with a smirk. "How was work today?"

Joe gave Benji a crooked smile. "Today was… interesting, wise guy."

Never once had Joe ever muttered anything remotely mundane or anything that resembled, 'Just another day at the office.' To Joe each day was an adventure; each day was something new out on the ocean.

Benji held out both his hands, palms down. "Pick one."

Joe pointed at Benji's right hand.

Benji turned his hand over and opened his fingers revealing a fortune cookie.

"Almost forgot," said Joe.

"I ate mine already," said Benji.

"Any sage advice?"

"Always eat cake from a fat baker."

Joe smiled. "That's pretty good advice."

Joe cracked his open. "Lucky numbers: three, nine, twenty-three, forty-two, and eighty-five."

"You want a drum roll?" Benji crossed his arms. "What's it say?"

"A stranger comes bearing news." Joe crumpled the paper and put it in his pocket. "A few hours late."

"Huh?"

"Let's take a ride. Meet me at the truck."

Joe walked back inside and grabbed a cold beer from the refrigerator.

Benji met him around the side of the house, and they both hopped into the rusty blue truck.

Joe took a long, deep breath through his nose.

Benji gave his dad an odd stare then shrugged his shoulders as Joe backed out of the driveway.

"See anything cool today, Dad?"

"I saw a lot cool. I saw a few weird, and in the process experienced something I never imagined out on the water, unless you count the day you…"

"The day I what?"

Joe kept quiet until they pulled into the parking lot at the docks.

The gravel crunched under the tires. The fishy salt air of the marina crept in through the front windows.

As soon as Joe put the truck in park, he pulled the beer from the seat between them, popped the top, and took a big swig. He let an exhausted, satisfied gasp then looked at Benji.

"You're starting to worry me, Dad."

"Come on. The most interesting discussions happen on a boat. After today, there's no arguing that."

"You boys takin' a late evening cruise?" A neatly trimmed white beard followed the sturdy voice through a cloud of pipe smoke hanging beside one of the pier pilings.

"Melvin," sighed Joe. "Thought, I'd bring the man out here for a little one on one father-son talk."

"No better place for that to happen," said Melvin.

"My words exactly," said Joe shaking Melvin's hand.

"Been a while, Benji," said Melvin. "How's everything?"

"Pretty good."

"Stayin' out of trouble?" asked Melvin.

"Tryin' to."

"You need to get out more," chuckled Melvin. "Joe here says you got a birthday comin' up."

"Yes, sir. Thirteen tomorrow."

"Well, now. I smell trouble brewing already."

"Easy Melvin. We've had a nice clean streak so far. Let's keep it that way, 'right?" said Joe.

"We all believe in him."

Melvin stuck out his big callous paw.

Benji grabbed his hand.

Melvin hooked his middle two fingers with Benji's. Their index and pointer fingers wrapped up and over the back side of each other's hand. Melvin gave Benji a wink, and then his eyes disappeared behind another puff of smoke. "Remember that, pup."

Benji jumped onto the boat with his dad and looked back toward the dock.

Melvin limped back toward the loading dock and turned down the adjacent pier to check on the other boats.

Benji scratched his head. "That's a funny handshake ole Melvin's got."

"How so?"

"That two finger grab."

"Maybe that's a birthday thing where's he's from."

"Where is Melvin from?"

"I'm not sure where he's from, but he's spent most of his time in and around the Caribbean. We're lucky we got him, though. He's a good dockmaster."

Joe leaned on the ladder heading up to the captain's deck.

Benji leaned against the inside of the hull.

Joe took a swig of beer and looked around the boat.

Benji got a little nervous with the silence and blurted out, "My birthday isn't prompting any grown-up speeches is it, Dad? We have the internet. I got all the bases covered."

Joe spit out his beer as the words left Benji's mouth. "You what?" he said with a high pitched reply.

"I mean... I... I know about the bases. No need for a 'birds and bees' talk, Dad" stammered Benji.

Joe half-snorted, half-laughed and messed his hand through Benji's windblown hair. "You ever wonder why you long for the ocean as much as you do?"

"It's in my blood. Same as you, right? We're Fishers."

"That's true in both instances, I 'spect. No one at school ever mentioned anything about you being a baby with me out on the ocean?"

"Nothing that would strike me as anything you're fishing for," said Benji.

Joe walked back to the stern, turned around and stood motionless staring into the cabin.

Benji put his hands in his pockets to conceal his nervousness and fumbled with the little bubble he found earlier on the beach.

Joe pointed down into the cabin at a gigantic hollowed sea turtle shell. "Do you know when I found that?"

"That old turtle shell?" said Benji as he pulled the bubble out and rolled it around in his palm. "Not a clue."

"I found that the day you came into my life. That was the same day the Rita I sank," said Joe shaking his head. "That turned out to be an eventful outing."

Benji scuffed his soles on the deck. "Pretty big," he said tossing the little bubble up and down in his hand.

"Big enough for a baby boy," said Joe.

"Looks like you could fit two of them in there with room to spare," said Benji.

"Well, I only found one."

"Huh?" said Benji as he snatched the bubble out of midair.

"That's where I found you, son."

Benji bit his bottom lip. His next question fell innocently out of his mouth. "What was I doing in a turtle shell, Dad?"

"I have no idea, or I had no idea. I still don't have any idea. I heard a story today and..." fumbled Joe.

"Who put me there?"

"Well..."

"Did I fall out of the boat?"

"You were never in the boat, Benji."

Benji squinted his eyes and scrunched his nose as he tried to process Joe's words.

"Here's where it gets interesting," said Joe. He fixed his eyes on Benji and summoned all the courage he had in him. Bringing in a five hundred pound tuna, or a ton of shrimp single handed was as routine as brushing his teeth. Talking about the mystical experiences surrounding Benji's arrival ended up being a little more difficult.

"Even more so than finding me in a turtle shell? I think we're already at interesting, Dad. I haven't been this challenged since Miss Wendy started tutoring me trigonometry this year," said Benji.

"Afraid so."

Joe took a deep breath and then everything from the very beginning started dribbling out of his mouth.

"My wife, Rita, and I couldn't have kids. We tried everything. Went to see doctor after doctor, but they couldn't help. We gave up a year or two before she died.

"The night you showed up is the same night she died. I had a bad haul in the morning and decided to make another run late that afternoon. If I had known it was going to get as nasty as quick as it did, I would have made a beeline toward the docks. My dad used to tell me, 'If a frog had wings, he wouldn't bump his butt when he hopped, either.' But if I had gone back, you wouldn't be here."

"But Rita might," whispered Benji.

Joe patted Benji on the back. "There's no tellin', and I can't change that. Knowing what I know now, I wouldn't change a thing, Benji."

Benji looked up at Joe out of the corner of his eyes and gave him a weak grin.

"She wouldn't either, son. If she's looking down on us, which I know she does from time to time, I can tell you she's just fine with swapping spots with you. I'm proud of you, and even though she's not here with us, I can tell you that she is, too. I can feel it."

Joe told Benji the story of the storm and the events that brought the two of them together almost thirteen years ago.

Benji threw both his arms up and clasped them behind his head. He looked up into the starry night and got lost for a minute. "I don't know what to say, Dad. I mean, do I even call you that anymore?"

"You better believe it, mister. I'd call you a liar if you said anything else."

"Then what does that have to do with anything? I mean, it doesn't change anything does it?"

"It doesn't change anything up to this point, and it doesn't change anything going forward, not as far as I'm concerned. But I don't believe we're the only ones concerned. In fact, I think a lot more people are concerned than just you and me. I think someone wanted you hidden. Not a bad place to hide though, is it?"

"You mean Beech Mill or in the turtle shell?"

Joe laughed. "I was thinking with me here in Beech Mill."

"I can't think of many other places I'd rather hide if that's what you call the last thirteen years."

"You're still twelve, kiddo," said Joe as he nicked Benji on the shoulder. "There's a lot more out there, Benji, but you're right. Beech Mill isn't a bad little place to call home."

"But you think this isn't my home."

"It's your home if you ask me. It's your home if you ask you Miss Wendy. It's your home if you ask the people in town, but as far as the rest of them goes, I don't believe they agree."

"The rest of who?"

Joe pulled his cap off his head and used the brim to scratch his head. "About six months before I found you, a pod of dolphins started following me out to the ocean and back every day. At the time, it was the strangest thing I had ever seen. It felt like I was being…"

"…watched?"

"…looked after," said Joe with a low voice.

"That's how I feel when I'm surfing."

Joe nodded his head silently. "Ever since then, I feel like I have been looked after out there." Joe motioned with his hand out onto the water. "I feel like both of us have. I've seen the company you keep out in the waves when you're surfing. It's not what most people would call normal."

"What is normal?" said Benji.

"Good point, but the connection you have with the animals out there is definitely different. That doesn't make it not normal. Normal's what you're used to, and I think you and I have a few things going on that a lot of other people may not be used to."

"I'm not sure what's real and what isn't right now. I don't even know who I am."

"You're my son, and I'll die fighting anyone who says otherwise. If you tell yourself something over and over again, after awhile, it becomes the truth. Right or wrong, real or not, that's what I've believed for the last twelve years. You came into my life when I needed you the most. And I think that goes both ways.

"But I also know a few things about your past that you have a right to know. There are others out there that know more than I can tell you."

Neither of them said a word. They both looked around the boat and into the distance for something their minds could grasp. The silence didn't want to break. It wasn't uncomfortable but stood its ground.

"Dad?"

"Yeah, son?"

"When I asked you about your day today, you said it was interesting… just interesting. You've never said your day was just interesting. As long as I've known you, you've always shared something with me you saw out there on the ocean. What you just told me didn't happen today."

"No, it didn't."

"Was that like a warm-up lap or something?"

Joe took a sip of his beer and cleared his throat. "Something."

"So, what happened today?" said Benji.

Joe didn't know how else to say it, so he just blurted it out. "I talked to an octopus straddling the back of a dolphin this morning." Joe looked down at his feet, moving them back and forth like a nervous kid confessing an act worthy of punishment.

"And?"

Joe shot Benji two darting eyes. "I'm not crazy?"

"I saw them in the surf this afternoon," Benji said with a smile, now knowing he wasn't completely alone in another world he had somehow known always existed. "Sounds like they've been on tour today."

Joe took a deep breath and used it to bring his head back up. He stopped fidgeting with his feet and put his arm around Benji.

"You ok, Dad?"

"I can't begin to explain any of this, but if I am crazy, at least I'm in good company," said Joe.

"Thanks," Benji said as he elbowed his dad in the ribs.

Joe stomped his right foot on the deck of the boat three times.

A gentle splash of water and several gasps of air echoed between Joe's boat and the one next to it.

Benji walked over to the side of the boat and saw eight glimmering eyes staring at him in awe. Each of them doubled in size when they saw him; a slow gasp snuck out of each of their mouths.

"It's him," whispered Eeke.

"You've seen him every day for the last… how many months?" said Zeeke

"Yeah, but now it's different. He knows we're here," said Eeke in astonishment.

"I've known you were there for a long time now," said Benji.

An oblong body slowly emerged around the extra pair of eyes over Mai's head, and Benji stared at a large purple octopus.

"Thanks," said Joe nodding at Octavius. "I planned on driving myself straight to the nuthouse if you hadn't shown up."

Octavius nodded back at Joe.

"Where are your manners, you three? Benji, my name is Octavius. These three are your scouts. This is Eeke, Zeeke, and Mai," said the octopus as he gestured with a tentacle toward each of the dolphins.

"Nice to meet you, Benji," said Zeeke.

"You're awesome on that surfboard, Benji," said Eeke.

Mai stared at Benji and gently nodded her head with a silent smile.

"You're the three that follow me when I'm surfing," said Benji.

"He recognizes us," said Eeke with a proud nod of his head.

"I recognize your voices," said Benji.

"See! I told you guys to keep your mouths shut when we're on patrol," said Mai. She dipped her snout in the water and splashed both of them.

"Benji, Joe told you about your arrival in Beech Mill. You have more questions. I have more answers," said Octavius.

"You could hear us talking?" asked Benji.

"Boats are giant speakers. We hear everything," chirped Eeke.

"I'm not sure where to start," said Benji.

Judging from what he heard since Benji and Joe arrived on the boat, Octavius decided subtlety wasn't needed. "Benji, you are a mermaid. Sorry…" Octavius cleared his throat. "…merman."

Benji's eyes could not have any gotten wider. His lips parted slightly to acknowledge the last bit of sense leaving his head. He put his hands in his pockets and looked at Joe for a reply.

Joe shrugged his shoulders and rocked on his heels.

Benji looked back toward Octavius and nodded for him to continue.

"Technically, you are a Mystiquarien, but I thought the sound of mermaids at your age would be more enticing."

"I'm a….?"

"You are a child of the sea. Actually, you are one of the last of your kind," said Octavius.

"But there are more?" asked Benji.

"Yes, there are. Just like there are different sizes, shapes, and colors of Topsiders. The same exists underwater. Your species, Mystiquarien, is capable of living on land and water. You have special abilities you may not have imagined even your wildest dreams," said Octavius.

"I hear voices. All kinds of animal voices," said Benji.

"Ain't it cool," said Zeeke.

"There's much more," said Octavius.

Benji's natural state of inquisitiveness kicked into high gear. "Then, how come when I am surfing I can't breathe underwater when I come off my board."

"Joe told you earlier what he told himself about you. What he said to himself each day and what he now and has for a long time believed in his heart, that you are his son.

"The same is true with you, Benji. Although you never had to tell yourself that you are one of them, you grew up being a Topsider. In your mind, there is no question that you are, except something deep inside of you has always pulled you toward the ocean. Something deep inside you has pulled you toward home. You never knew what it was, but you knew you didn't fully belong up there. No matter how strange you think you are up there, you are very special someplace else. That someplace is Aquari, your true home."

Benji and Joe continued staring at Octavius.

"You were born in Sanjowqua. A protected…"

"San… who?"

"Sanjowqua. You may know it as the Bermuda Triangle," said Octavius.

"The place where everyone goes missing?" said Benji.

"Yes. That is the place. That is where we live. That is one of the places Aquarien similar to you live," said Octavius.

"Well, you could probably tell me right now that pigs fly, and I would believe you, but if there are other mermaids out there, how come I'm not talking to any of them? Why am I talking to three dolphins and an octopus?" said Benji.

"Based on that comment, I gamble that you will take my word for it," said Octavius.

"Hmm. What's it like there?" said Benji.

Eeke spoke up. "It's one of the most beautiful places you've ever seen."

Mai gave Eeke a hard stare, and Zeeke pulled in a mouthful of water and shot a stream at his younger brother's head.

"What? It is!" scrambled Eeke.

"Go on, Eeke," said Octavius.

Eeek gave his sister a nervous glance then began again with his head slightly bowed, "It's the best place in the world to live. Well, I haven't been Topside, but…"

"Eeke, stay on point," said Mai.

"Sanjowqua is everything you could ever ask for. There are white sand islands that stretch as far as the eye can see. The islands float and have massive reefs underneath them.

"The Shequarien, the mermen and mermaids, have homes in little floating island bungalows all throughout.

"The coral is beyond your dreams beautiful because the Shequarien and water fairies take good care of it. There's every kind: brain coral, bubble coral, sea fans, and anemone in every nook and cranny. Some of them glow at night and turn the ocean into a glittering wonderland.

"There are sunken pirate ships and old world war boats. We've explored a lot of them, but the Topsiders like to leave their boats with us for some reason, so there are more waiting."

"They also like to leave their garbage," said Zeeke.

Mai cleared her throat. Zeeke got quiet, and Eeke veered back on subject.

"When we're not on duty or training, we hunt, we explore, and at night we share stories from the day and have competitions around Waputu Wamkala."

"Waputu Wehkiki?" said Benji.

Eeke snickered. "Wehkiki is us: dolphins. Waputu Wamkala is the center of Sanjowqua. Poseidon's Trident is stored inside."

Joe took off his cap and wiped his brow with his forearm.

"The Shequarien have learned how to farm underwater. They grow fresh mangoes, coconuts, pineapples, and every kind of tropical fruit you can imagine. I'm personally not a fan, but Sanjowqua's vegetable gardens will make your head spin.

"The Shequarian hunt with us, and they guard Sanjowqua against outsiders. And for someone that's bored with school like you, they absorb history and theories through the halls of Waputu Wamkala. There's enough inside those bubbles to keep your mind busy until... well, way after you're dead."

"How'd you know I was bored at school?" chirped Benji.

Eeke bowed his head again when he realized he probably said more than he should have.

"We are telepathic, Benji. We can read unguarded thoughts and feelings," said Octavius.

"I know what telepathic means. I don't appreciate having my thoughts invaded." Benji looked at the four of them wondering what else they knew.

Joe cleared his throat and tapped his temple.

"Ohhhh. Well, that was like me just learning and stuff... I mean... Sorry, Dad," said Benji.

Eeke and Zeeke both snorted into the water.

"We can teach you how to protect those thoughts," said Octavius.

"Why are you showing up here today? Why do you want me to come 'home' with you?" said Benji.

"Sanjowqua is in trouble. All of Aquari is in trouble. For centuries, we have lived a life of peace in the oceans, far removed and hidden from the Topsiders. As the Topsider population has exploded, we have experienced devastating destruction caused by the pollution that flows into our waters. This has caused major divisions among our kind."

Octavius paused. Benji didn't say a word, so the octopus resumed.

"Mystiquarien like you, your parents, and their friends were driven from Sanjowqua years ago. Your parents and their kind were hunted and forced into hiding by another powerful Aquarien. Your parents believed harmony and peace with the Topsiders is the key to the future. They were in favor of breaking centuries of silence and anonymity for helping the Topsiders understand the perils of their abuse above and below the water.

"The leader of the Donquarien, the eastern branch of Aquarien, led a revolt against your parents and the rest of your kind. You were lucky to get out alive," said Octavius.

"I'll second that," said Joe.

"If we continue to do nothing, life in the ocean will perish. We need your help," said Octavius.

"How do you expect me to save all of this? I'm just a twelve-year-old kid, or merman, or Aquarien, or whatever you say I am," said Benji.

"The same way we accomplish anything in life. One step at a time. You're not expected to save Aquari by yourself, and we're not expecting it to be done tomorrow," said Octavius.

"Well, that's good news." Benji sat there waiting for more from the octopus. The three dolphins merely stared at him with hopeful eyes. "When do you need me to come?"

"Soon," said Octavius.

"How soon?"

"The sooner, the better. Your location has been a secret, but it won't remain so. Most of those involved in your parent's death were apprehended, but the knowledge of your escape is known to all of Aquari.

There have been sightings of trouble from the same group that attacked your parents, and we fear your exact location may be compromised."

"So you want me to go deeper into the ocean where it's supposedly not safe for me to be? I'll take my chances up here."

"You know as well as I do that you cannot stay away from the ocean. You are also not the only one at risk. You also risk Joe's safety by staying," said Octavius.

"Wait a second. Don't use me as bait here. Benji needs to do what he wants to do without any baggage from me hanging over his head," said Joe.

"What does this Don-thing want with my dad?"

"It's more than Joe. The fate of all the Topsiders is at risk. As one of the last Mystiquarien, you are the key to establishing relations with the Topsiders. If the Mystiquarien line is terminated, hope of peace with the Topsiders falls even further away.

"The Donquarien will stop at nothing to make sure the Topsiders pay for their abuse of Aquari. They do not seek peaceful actions. There are tools in Aquari that can destroy Topside if they fall into the wrong hands."

"What are they going to do? Have sharks attack people at the beach?" asked Benji.

"Shark attacks would be one way of having fun with the Topsiders. Imagine a world where the land that you know no longer exists," said Octavius.

"Like a great flood?" said Benji.

"Not like a great flood. It will be a great flood if they have their way. The land that Joe's home sits on would no longer exist. Nor would any other land you have ever seen."

"Gouguon, the Donquarien who killed your parents, is still imprisoned, but those who are loyal to his cause do not waver in their goal. He is still handing out orders and controlling those sympathetic to his cause despite imprisonment. He knows where you were last seen."

"How do we get to Sanjowqua?" said Benji.

"We have means of transportation for the majority of the journey, which doesn't take that long, plus we're pretty good in the water, as you will be when you learn how to maneuver without a surfboard."

Eeke winked at him enthusiastically.

"I need to think this over," said Benji.

"That is expected," said Octavius.

"So what now?" said Benji.

"We give you the time you need. The decision is yours Benji, but know that the implications of that decision affect more than you can, at this point, even imagine," said Octavius.

"No pressure, though," snorted Benji.

Joe let out a stiff, nervous laugh.

Octavius extended one of his tentacles, unfurling it until a shiny gold coin lay exposed at the very end. He sat the coin on the side of the boat, and the tentacle slowly retreated.

Benji and Joe eyed the gold coin in awe.

"When you are ready, toss the coin into the ocean, and we will make plans to bring you home safely," said Octavius.

"That's it?" said Benji.

"Unless you are ready to come now, or if you have more questions," said Octavius.

Benji gave Octavius a blank stare.

"I take it that you do not have any more questions," bowed Octavius.

Zeeke winked at Benji. "See you soon."

"Wait," said Benji.

"What is it, Benji?" said Octavius.

"What's *mahloowoo* mean?" asked Benji.

Eeke and Zeeke both snorted into the water and sprayed the side of the boat. Mai turned her head. Both she and Octavius stared down the younger dolphins.

"Really? That's the first word he picks up from you guys? My two genius brothers," said Mai shaking her head.

"Eeke, would you like to share with Benji what a mahloowoo is?" said Octavius.

Eeke lifted his body parallel to the surface and squeezed one eye. He let out a gentle sigh along with half a dozen bubbles from his underside.

"Ah, man," complained Zeeke as he ducked his head under the water.

Octavius and Mai both shook their heads again.

"A simple definition would have been sufficient Eeke," grumbled Octavius.

"Sorry," said Eeke. "It's a fish fart."

"I put two and two together," said Benji waving the air around his face.

And with that, the four animals slipped their heads below. Three swells popped up from the dolphins' tails pushing them away. Water sloshed gently against the boat marking their departure.

Benji closed his eyes for the first time in what felt like a week. When he opened them again, he stared out over the bay. The water shimmered in the moonlight. He walked over to the side of the boat and ran his fingers over the gold coin.

"Dad?"

"Yeah?"

"What am I supposed to do?" asked Benji as he picked up the coin and rubbed it between his fingers.

"As your dad, my job has been to prepare you for what lies ahead, and that scares me. One: because you are twelve. And two: I can't even fathom what's ahead. If you were to come and work with me, for example, I could give you pointers and help you along the way. Even if you go off to school next year, I can kind of give you some guidance when you need it. I got nothing on this one, Benji.

"I'm going to feel uncomfortable with either decision you make. Knowing what I know now, how can I hold you back? But not knowing any more scares me. It's your decision, Benji. This choice will change your life. There are two doors open right now. You have to choose one of them to walk through."

"Can't I just stand still?"

Joe laughed. "Don't let life pass you by, son. There are no mistakes. There are just roads you know now that you didn't know before."

"OK, but that doesn't help much."

"I understand, son. Our lives are molded by the decisions we make. I can't tell you what to do. I can't decide for you. That is your responsibility now."

"But... I'm only twelve."

"You were thirteen a few minutes ago," Joe chuckled.

"Haha."

Joe's eyes got watery, and he put both his arms around Benji. The two of them patted each other on the back then climbed back on the dock and walked silently toward the truck.

The ride home was quiet except for the wind blowing through the two front windows. Joe and Benji slung their arms out into the cool breeze and surfed their hands on the wind whipping by.

"Good night, Dad." Benji walked into his bedroom and closed the door behind him, kicked off his shoes, and slumped onto his bed with his feet on the floor; his elbows resting on his knees; face in his palms.

He lifted his head out of his hands and ran his fingers along his thighs feeling something in each pocket. He slipped his hands inside and pulled the clear bubble out first.

Benji's mind raced as he rolled the bubble around in his palm.

Did that just happen, he thought.

He placed the marble-sized ball on his nightstand and dimmed the light.

Benji laid back in bed and slipped his hand back into the other pocket. He pulled out the coin and flipped it over and over in his palm. The gold glimmered in the speck of moonlight coming through the blinds.

One side sported a Trident with the word Aquari stamped on the bottom. He spun the coin around in his fingers, and on the other side, a pair of dolphins jumped out of the water from opposite sides of the coin. Each head crossed the other's back forming an 'X'.

He slipped the coin back into his pocket and stared at a photo Miss Wendy took of him surfing. It turned out so good she made a poster out of it, and he taped it to the ceiling. In the photo, a dolphin's head pierced the curl of the wave a few feet ahead of him with what looked like a huge grin on his face. Two other fins raced behind him. Benji smiled as he realized his answer for Octavius had been staring him in the face each night as he slept.

He closed his eyes, but all they did was move furiously behind his eyelids. His brain churned into overdrive. *What do they look like? How many of them are there? Do they sleep underwater? How am I supposed to breathe underwater? What is this place called Sanjowqua? Are the girls pretty, or do they look like fish? Why didn't any mermaids come to see me tonight?*

Those and a million other questions swam inside his head.

Finally, the weight of it all put the brakes on his thoughts, and he drifted off to sleep with his hand gripped firmly on the golden coin inside his pocket.

Chunomba Makawindi

(shark party)

BENJI HEARD A voice call his name and turned over in bed. The slow moaning call of each syllable "Ben… ji," froze his neck and shook his shoulders. He slid his sneakers on and walked out of the house. The crickets and bullfrogs started singing for him as soon as he hit the side porch. His eyelids wanted to be together, but his feet pushed them further apart with each step in the dew-soaked grass. He had to get to the beach. He had to get in the ocean.

She called him. "Ben… ji. Ben… ji," she sang.

Benji jumped on his bicycle and pedaled down the street over the inlet bridge. Cresting the bridge, he looked down at the porch lights that accentuated little pastel patches of the beach houses scattered across the island below.

As soon as his tires hit the crushed oyster shell driveway of Miss Wendy's place, Benji jumped off his bicycle. The momentum carried the bike forward until the front tire wedged into the boxwoods that wrapped around the house. He headed straight for the shed and grabbed his board.

The voice called his name. "Ben… ji. Ben… ji." It lured him.

Three-foot shooshing waves disappeared into the beach sand.

Benji duck dove through the first set with ease. Once he paddled past the breakers, the voice stopped. He sat there straddling his board looking in every direction.

He slid off his board head first and sunk like a rock. When his momentum slowed, he kicked both legs simultaneously and went down further. The moon's rays sliced through the water around him. He flared his arms and floated upright, above the darkness that loomed at the tips of his toes.

Benji closed his eyes and floated; his ears primed for the sound of the voice that carried him out into the water in the middle of the night. The motion of the ocean rocked his body and soothed his mind.

His eyes began twitching behind his eyelids, and as he opened them, two others stared directly into his; beautiful black pools that sparkled in the moonlight reflecting off of them.

Benji threw his arms to the side and swung them in a circular motion, propelling himself backward.

The distance unveiled a girl floating in front of him. "Ben… ji," she whispered.

Her eyes locked on his. Her long black hair billowed around her head like wisps of smoke from a campfire. Her angular face sported sharp cheekbones. Her uniqueness pulled on his intrigue.

Benji stared. The kids at school did the same. Maybe this is how they felt when they saw him; studying something different from themselves.

Benji swung his arms again and moved further away. The light played tricks on his eyes.

Her lean silvery body shimmered the same as the water around her. One minute her figure appeared clear as day. The next, she disappeared into the water surrounding her. Her cloud of black hair ebbed and flowed with the push and pull of the waves above them. From the waist down, a silvery-blue tail sparkled in the moonlight. Light silver dominated the tops of her thighs and shins. Where the ankles stopped, and feet usually would have begun, a blue-green fin fanned out a foot and a half in each direction moving the water around her with grace and power. Water swirled off the tips in little liquid tornados.

The girl raised one hand and gave Benji a slight wave. A translucent webbing connected each finger to the next and stretched slightly as she moved her digits back and forth.

Her lips remained sealed, but Benji noticed a smile creep upon her face. She looked behind her, then beckoned him forward.

Benji pushed his arms through the water to advance slowly. As he did, he noticed the same webbing between his own fingers. *That's cool,* he thought.

The girl pushed her tail gently and began moving backward.

Benji looked down in astonishment. His own legs merged into one. A silver tail started just below his navel. He moved it with a clumsy thrust and wobbled in the water.

Something latched onto Benji's leg. He tried to thrust forward, but the grip on his tail tightened. He twisted to break free and woke up with a gasp.

Uncle Bill held on to his leg at the foot of the bed. "Jeez, Benji. You almost knocked me out with those fins of yours."

"Wha...?" Benji threw his hands down on the bed as he sat up staring at his size twelve feet.

"Some dream, huh? Girl from school?" said Uncle Bill with an up-all-night-look in his eyes.

Benji looked around his room while Uncle Bill fidgeted with some fishing line in his hand.

"What are you doing here, Uncle Bill?"

"Good to see you, too."

"Sorry. I'm not used to being restrained in my sleep."

"Yeah, well, it was either that or catch a foot to the head."

"I had a gig not far up the road last night. Left and went to the beach to watch the sunrise. Came over here when I thought everyone would be awake. You're last. Here you go, sunshine," said Uncle Bill tossing Benji the line he held in his hands.

"What's this?"

"Saw it on your nightstand when I came in earlier. Never seen anything like it. Thought I'd get crafty while I waited for you to wake up. Your dad isn't the only one who's handy with fishing line."

Uncle Bill had fashioned a tiny net that encased the bubble-ball

Benji found on the beach and tied it to a strap of leather from one of the kitchen drawers.

"Man, that's awesome! Thanks."

"Yep. Happy Birthday. Got any special requests for your birthday tonight?"

"Not really, but can I get one for this morning?"

"No more sleepy, pal. Waves look good. I already have my board in the van. I want to see the fish whisperer at work today. You teach me how to catch waves this morning, and I'll teach you how to land a date at the show tonight. Deal?"

"Sounds good," Benji said, as he jumped out of bed knowing he would be in the ocean in a matter of minutes. "Do you mind tying this on for me?"

"My pleasure, dear."

Benji punched his uncle in the shoulder and turned around.

Uncle Bill winced. "Getting stronger, kid."

Benji wrapped the necklace around his neck, and Uncle Bill fastened it for him. The two of them walked out of the room joking with each other and met Joe in the kitchen. The stove top fan whirled at high speed. An open top trash can sat beside Joe. Eggshells nearly spilled over the sides.

"Happy Birthday to you. Happy Birthday to…"

"Dad! I just woke up," Benji said with his hands muffling his ears.

"Yeah. No offense, bro, but that was pretty heinous. Guess I got all the vocal talent in the family," smirked Uncle Bill.

"Ha ha. Is this your idea of breakfast?" Joe held up a fast food bag with his fingertips.

"Breakfast of champions," said Uncle Bill, flexing his biceps.

Joe smirked and tossed it in the trash. "I'm whipping up a special birthday breakfast. Uncles can join in if they're not wise guys."

They all sat down to a hearty breakfast of shrimp omelets and blueberry pancakes. Benji told his uncle about the waves lately, and Uncle Bill shared his stories of life on the road. Uncle Bill took one of his stories past the setting of the grimy bar and Joe immediately interrupted.

"How about these omelets? Fresh shrimp, compliments of the chef," said Joe, holding up his fork in one hand and the knife in the other.

Benji scarfed down his breakfast and looked at his uncle. Uncle Bill rubbed his stomach and stared at the ceiling knowing the delay drove Benji crazy. Benji clamped both hands around the arms of his chair ready to catapult himself from the table and out to the van. "Ready?"

"Aren't we supposed to wait thirty minutes for our food to digest?" joked Uncle Bill.

"It will take you that long to get a wetsuit on over all the pancakes you just shoveled down your throat."

"Ooh hoo hoo. In that case, I think it's more like an hour," Uncle Bill said with a sly grin.

"Now you're just being mean," said Benji.

"True, but it's funny watching you squirm over getting in the surf," said Uncle Bill.

Uncle Bill put his head down, pushed back from the table, and jumped out of his chair.

"Last one to the van has to wax my surfboard," Uncle Bill said halfway out of the kitchen.

"Son of a gun!" Uncle Bill bellowed as he jammed his toe on the door between the kitchen and the hall leading to the side door. Benji casually walked to the van and opened the door to the passenger side as Uncle Bill hobbled out on one foot with a very red and crooked looking pinky toe.

"A little salt water will do it some good. Oh, and some elbow grease from waxing your surfboard," said Benji.

Joe stood on the side porch. "I'll meet you guys in an hour. Need to run a few errands this morning."

Uncle Bill limped to the van, and they took off to the beach.

Benji shot in the water before his uncle found his wetsuit from under all the junk piled in the back seat.

When he finally paddled out to meet Benji, Uncle Bill looked around and saw the dolphins surrounding them. "You got more friends in the water than I do on land."

"Me too," Benji said as he cocked his head thinking about the words that just left his mouth.

The two of them traded waves all morning. When Uncle Bill wasn't riding his own, he watched Benji and his entourage with admiration.

Joe joined them an hour later while Miss Wendy sat on the beach taking photos. Miss Wendy packed a picnic, and they sat in the sand catching up for lunch. Uncle Bill threw chips behind Benji when he turned his head so seagulls would swoop down and annoy him. After lunch, Uncle Bill left to go set up for his evening gig at the pier, and Benji swam back out to ride the waves with Joe.

After a day on the beach, Joe, Benji, and Miss Wendy walked a few blocks down to Main Street to grab a spot for music and food.

Spring blossomed in every azalea bush surrounding the big flag pole in the middle of the square. Tourists bumbled down the sidewalks and crisscrossed Main Street, bouncing from one shop to the next.

Children whined as they walked into some of the shops and grinned on the way out of others holding oversized lollipops and wearing brown rings of fudge around their lips like medals of honor.

Seagulls swooped down, snatching hush puppies and other leftovers some of the tourists took out of the restaurants in paper napkins to feed to the flying hobos.

On the boardwalk, several restaurants hovered over the canal separating them from a small barrier island. Vacationers pumped coins into tower viewers trying to steal a glance at the wild horses grazing on marsh grass. Glass flooring in a few restaurants attracted guests when the food wouldn't do.

Joe stopped at an open tiki bar right beside the pier where Uncle Bill's band had set up. *The Strummin' Bums* belted out beach tunes, and several couples already swung in each other's arms.

A rusty-looking seagull flew down on the counter of the tiki bar and startled everyone before the barman shooed him away. Benji watched the bird circle overhead hoping for some food then make a beeline toward the far end of the canal. A commotion from the direction the seagull flew off to pulled Benji out of his seat to go check it out.

"I'm going to see what all the fuss is about," said Benji.

"No problem. We're going to grab a cocktail and dance a little. Meet us back here after the next song, and we'll decide where we want to eat. You have some presents to open," Joe said with a nod at the bag beside Miss Wendy's legs.

Benji headed up the boardwalk and turned onto an adjacent dock to his uncle's band. He walked out to the end and surveyed the beautiful spring day. Uncle Bill saw him, gave him a thumbs up, then quickly turned his attention to a cute brunette dancing near Joe and Miss Wendy.

When Benji reached the end of the dock, he caught the sight of everyone's interest. A flock of hundreds of seagulls dive-bombed a school of fish at the far end of the canal. The bait ball had turned into the inlet and now worked its way toward him.

Benji dug into his pocket and pulled out the gold coin Octavius gave him the night before. He turned it over in his hand several times then looked back toward the party.

"Here we go."

He flipped the coin in the air and counted the rotations. One-two-three-four. He caught it between his thumb and forefinger and slung it out over the canal. The coin skipped six times and plunked into the water.

Benji waited for a flash of light or a tunnel of water to emerge in the canal, something mystical.

Nothing happened.

"I'm ready!" he hollered.

Nothing happened.

Maybe it's like snail mail, he thought.

Benji folded his arms in frustration. The tips of his sneakers hung off the edge of the dock. The untied laces on his right shoe reached toward the water begging for a dip. He looked down at his reflection. The bubble necklace his uncle made for him captured the sunlight and sent it back out in a dozen different directions.

A single seagull circled above. A small 'plop' on the back of the head terminated interest in his new necklace.

That's good luck, right? Benji huffed as he thought that was just an excuse people used to make themselves feel better about being pooped on by a bird and stop others from laughing at the fact it just happened.

The boards of the floating dock creaked behind him. The dock dipped and swayed with added weight.

"I guess it's your lucky day, lanky," called a familiar voice.

Benji knew that voice all too well. It spewed out of the last person he wanted to see in the waning hours of a perfectly good birthday.

Charley and his weasel-faced cronies waddled towards him. Charley sported a grin as wide as his waist. Stuart Biggums wore a new pair of turtle-shell glasses.

"Thought you were pretty funny yesterday, huh?" said Charley.

"Just returning what wasn't mine," said Benji.

Benji stood six inches taller than Charley, but the red-headed terror easily outweighed him.

"You left this behind, fishboy," said Charley as he gave Benji a hearty shove in the chest.

Benji stumbled back throwing out his arms to keep his balance. He managed to slap his left hand on a piling that shifted his fall just enough to avoid a two-thousand-pound great white shark barrelling out of the water.

Half of the pier where Benji stood seconds before shot up twenty feet in the air. The side of a rocket-sized great white skimmed his right thigh. The shark's blunt pectoral fin caught Benji's legs behind the knees and sent his feet flying toward the clouds along with hundreds of splintered pieces of the floating dock.

A purple tentacle slithered out of the water and wrapped around a cleat used to secure a fishing boat still milling about on the ocean. Seven more tentacles shot up out of the water in pursuit of the flying boy. Three of them managed to latch onto Benji's arm and yank him back down.

Charley threw his arms up in the air knocking Stuart Biggum's new glasses into the canal.

The horrified look on Charley's face ended up being the last thing Benji Fisher saw of Beech Mill that day.

Benji plunged into the water amidst white water, bubbles, and broken pieces of the dock. Five tentacles fastened to the three already around Benji's arm and each of the hundreds of suckers stuck to him with no intention of letting go.

An angular face outlined with black, wavy hair appeared before Benji. Her striking appearance nearly wiped away the sense of urgency in her pursed lips. She slapped a hand down on each of his cheeks and squeezed his face together so his lips poked out. She planted her lips squarely on his and inflated Benji's chest with the warmest most pleasant breath he'd ever taken.

Benji immediately got light-headed; his eyes felt droopy. Anxiety and adrenaline caused by a shark exploding through the dock and nearly swallowing him whole, plus an octopus ripping him into the water where the monster came from subsided. The kiss made everything OK.

Benji gave the woman a goofy smile. *You got black hair. I likey the blackey hair. It's preddy. Like night time,* he thought.

"Poetry's not his thing," snorted a male voice under Benji.

Benji's head darted around looking for faces to assign to the voices.

"You may have gone overboard, Meena," said Octavius.

"Pardon me! Stakes are just a little higher than normal at the moment," she said.

Both of her hands quickly left Benji's cheeks and darted out to the arm where Octavius attached himself. "Ready, Jaylon?" said Meena nodding down toward Benji's other arm.

Jaylon grabbed Benji's dangling hand. "Yes, please."

They tugged Benji's arms over his head and took off through the water nearly leaving his head stuck at the scene of the kiss. He went from floating spread eagle to super-sonic speed in seconds.

Benji flew backward. With his drunken eyelids heavy and half-closed, he looked back at his legs whipping back and forth. His pivoting hips made his legs and feet look like a rag doll being dangled from a Formula One race car. Benji let out a contented giggle.

Despite the speed at which bubbles whizzed by his temples, everything behind Benji moved in slow motion. His two escorts pulled him directly under the boardwalk that extended over the canal, using the pilings and docked boats as cover. The wooden posts cast eerie shadows throughout the water around him. Benji zipped by them so fast he couldn't have counted them if he had used multiples of five, maybe ten.

A pack of voices echoed from the inlet.

"Case the boardwalk," called a bull shark.

"They can't hide in there forever," said another.

"One of you double back and cover the other end of the docks," called the great white.

Benji tried to pull his arms toward his sides and use the momentum to prop his head up a bit, but the force of being pulled backward made that impossible.

He stared at his bumbling feet over the tops of his eyelids and started humming. *I'm un-der the wa-ter. Swim, swam, swum, swim-ming all a-long in the o-cean.*

He blew bubbles and watched them disappear between his legs.

"Octavius. Put a stop to that, please," called Meena.

Octavius slithered up Benji's arm and slid a purple arm over his head. The top of the tentacle changed colors rapidly, and the suckers on the bottom massaged Benji's temple. Benji let out a small hum, and his eyelids flirted with each other. Calmness crept in throughout his entire body, leaving him as useful as a chair without a seat.

Three rows of razor sharp teeth attached to a hammerhead shark suddenly appeared a few feet from his dangling legs.

"Company!" called Octavius. "Pick it up a notch."

Benji's chin bounced off his chest. His eyes shot open, and he stared down the grimacing shark's mouth.

Hey, sharky sharky.

The top and bottom rows of jagged teeth crashed together as the shark chomped at Benji's legs.

"He wants him alive!" grumbled a voice off to the right of the hammerhead.

Benji looked off to the side and saw the great white out in the canal. The enormous shark followed on the outskirts of the dock.

"They're his feet. He doesn't need them to breathe," growled the hungry-looking hammerhead.

"True," huffed the great white.

Benji's eyelids shot wide open.

The pair of hands pulling him backward through the water clamped down harder.

The untied shoelace on his right shoe fluttered up and down faster than hummingbird wings. Benji dug the tip of his left shoe into the heel of the right and pushed the sneaker toppling back into the shark's mouth. One of the ends of the lace snagged the first row of the hammerhead's teeth. The shoe bucked up and down in the cavern of a mouth rattling the tongue that looked so eager to taste Benji's sockless toes. The sneaker tugged hard on the lace from a gust of water that shot in through the heel and inflated the toes, yanking out a few teeth and sending them all barrelling down the dark pit of the hammerhead's throat. The shark coughed twice and fell behind. Benji watched the shark shake its head. Frustrated wrinkles appeared around the bridge of its broad nose.

"Nice work, Benji," prodded Octavius.

"Get out of the way. I'll take care of it," snorted the great white as he cruised up behind the hammerhead.

Benji's leg nicked one of the barnacle-covered pilings, and a thin line of blood streamed out through his tattered jeans. He looked at the cut in his leg then saw the great white lick his lips. The enormous fish darted under the docks, throwing boats from side to side. The tight quarters slowed the mammoth creature down, and two smaller bull sharks flew by him on either side.

"He's mine," grumbled the great white with renewed vigor.

The docks above lifted and parted when the huge fish cruised underneath. Pilings, plastic pontoons, and boats crashed against the bulkhead and into some of the restaurants above. Feet plunged into the water as a crowd of people on the docks fell amongst the chaos. A pair of legs and a billowing sundress danced in the mayhem like a pink and yellow jellyfish.

Benji and his companions shot out from under the docks, and he watched more pilings explode into toothpicks. The two bull sharks got caught under the falling debris the great white left in his wake.

"Two down," yelled Octavius, "but the big guy is on a mission."

The increased ferocity of the shark caught Octavius' attention, and he scrambled down Benji's side toward the gash. Each arm slithered steadily down Benji's body until the octopus reached the bloody calf and wrapped himself around the wound. The blood no longer streamed into the ocean, but the taste of it lingered in the great white's mouth.

Out of nowhere, Jaylon called out, "Benji! You OK?"

Really, thought Benji. *I got kissed by a beautiful woman who is towing me through the water. I'm being chased by a great white bigger than most boats. An octopus is playing nurse on my leg. AND somehow I don't even care about any of it. Yeah. I'm great.*

"Save that thought until we're safe," called Jaylon. "Heck of a way to bring him back, huh, Meena?"

Huh? thought Benji.

"We knew it might go down today, Jaylon," struggled Meena.

"Yeah, and by the look of that great white, we're close to it being finished," said Jaylon.

"I got an idea," said Meena. "Go hard straight. When I say 'break' you let go and roll left. Then come back to center as soon as you do."

"What? Are you crazy?" said Jaylon.

"Trust me," said Meena.

"You're usually right," said Jaylon.

Usually? I don't like those odds right now, thought Benji.

They shot through the inlet; the barrier island on Benji's left. The docks of Beech Mill appeared smaller and smaller with each flutter of Benji's feet. The jet streams on either side of his hips synchronized perfectly and mellowed out his figure-eight movements until he moved seamlessly through the water. He had nothing on either side of him to gauge how fast they traveled, but his body told him he'd never been this fast in, on, or above the water.

"The big guy is closing in," called Octavius.

The great white's mouth opened. Each row of teeth glimmered and shone ready to close the deal.

"Break!" called Meena.

The grip on Benji's right hand disappeared, and at the same time, his body rolled over. The cloud-speckled sky vanished, and the fading sun winked good-bye. Clear blue turned navy, and then the white sand of the ocean floor brightened his view.

BONG!!!!

A metallic gong reverberated through the water. Benji tightened his shoulders with a shudder. He kept rolling over until he found himself swirling through the ocean on his back again and his right hand met up with Jaylon's.

"Good idea," said Jaylon.

"You couldn't have timed it any better," said Octavius.

"I have my moments. That ought to buy us a few minutes from the big guy," boasted Meena.

Silver dolphins streaked past them headed in the opposite direction.

"There goes the cleanup crew," said Jaylon.

A large metal buoy slowly disappeared in the distance. The great white floated beside it.

The hammerhead and bull sharks shot past either side of the buoy. The dolphins intercepted all three of them with swift bottle-nosed strikes to the sides. The sharks seized up and doubled over from the impact.

Benji still raced through the water, but the pace slowed enough for him to look over his shoulder.

"How you doing back there, pup?" said Jaylon.

Benji stared for longer than he thought. He looked at the man's face and then slowly trailed his eyes down to a sharp silvery tail.

"Benji?" said Jaylon.

Benji tried to verbalize the words. Nothing but a garbled collection of bubbles escaped his mouth.

"You'll have a hard time doing it that way down here, Benji. Think about," said Jaylon.

Think about it?

"Yep, you got it. Not so loud, though. We're going for stealth mode. No need to broadcast it to the whole ocean," said Jaylon.

"I thought you said he was up on the basics, Octavius," said Meena.

Octavius watched Benji sputtering his lips like a motorboat and shook his purple head. "Meena's kiss turned out to be a little more than he could handle."

"That's what I've been saying for years now. There's your proof," said Jaylon, winking at Meena.

Meena shot him a condescending look.

Benji had to think about whispering each word as he materialized it in his head. "Uh... I'm... in... one... piece,... but... I'm... being... towed... through... the... water... by... a... couple... of... mer... maids."

"One! One mermaid and one Man! Mer. Man."

"Sorry."

"Or… dude. Call me Jaylon, and that's a fair assessment considering the circumstances."

I… agree, Benji thought back toward Jaylon quietly.

Benji looked over his left shoulder and caught a glimpse of the mermaid towing him on the other side. She looked like the one from his dream.

She's beautiful, he thought.

"Haha. Busted, Benji," said Jaylon. "She's with me, by the way."

"Huh?" said Benji. A mouthful of bubbles shot to the surface again.

"Meena just heard that. We all did. Don't worry. You'll get the hang of it," said Jaylon.

Benji's cheeks blushed. He caught a faint smile stretch across Meena's lips.

Octavius made his way back up to Benji's shoulder. Benji saw Octavius' eyes move down to his neck. One of the octopus's tentacles shot out immediately and wrapped around the bubble necklace Uncle Bill made. Benji's neck stung as Octavius snatched the necklace off his neck and released it into their wake.

"Wai…" A faint semblance of a word bumbled out of Benji's mouth with a whole lot more bubbles than sense.

"Think it, Benji," said Octavius.

"Wait a minute!" said Benji.

"Where did you get that?" demanded Octavius.

"I found it on the beach. My uncle made it into a necklace for a birthday gift. You can't…"

"That's how they found you. That 'gift' almost killed you," said Octavius.

Benji watched the necklace flutter out of sight toward the bottom of the ocean. "What was it?"

"It's a jambuku. They're found in pairs. Whoever has the other one knows exactly where you are and what you are doing. They can be used for safety, but in your case, they can also be used for spying," said Octavius.

"Who…"

"Whoever planned the attack today," said Jaylon.

"Pretty gutsy to try it in broad daylight, too," chirped Meena.

Benji let out an exasperated breath. He tilted his head back toward the sky and noticed the surface getting farther and farther away.

"Why would someone want to attack me? I'm just a kid from Beech Mill," said Benji innocently.

"Someone wants to keep it that way," said Jaylon.

"Is it the same person that killed my parents?" asked Benji.

"We'll get to that once you are safe," said Octavius.

"Where's safe?" asked Benji.

"Sanjowqua," said Octavius proudly.

Kushaburuki Balakwi

(swimming chameleon)

AFTER THE SCARE in the canal, Benji counted his toes then double-checked his calculations.

His new companions kept their brisk pace out into the open ocean. The setting sun cast a pink tinge that glittered on the surface. Orange rays of light fell through the water flickering off his escorts' tails.

"OK, you two," said Octavius. "Hold up here for a minute."

Jaylon and Meena let go simultaneously and turned over to face him. Benji stared. Two mermaids, or one mermaid and a merman/dude floated in front of him.

Jalyon stood a foot taller than Benji. Meena hovered over Benji by six inches.

"Is everyone this tall... or long?" asked Benji.

In Beech Mill, Benji easily towered over most of the grown-ups.

"They're about average, Benji," said Octavius.

"My father is a little taller than me. My mother is a little shorter than Meena," said Jaylon.

"Mine died thirteen years ago," said Meena.

Neither of them was what Benji expected, not that it was a bad thing. The imagination can conjure up a hefty dose of add-ons that don't necessarily belong in the real world... where mermaids exist.

"I think proper introductions are past due," said Octavius.

One of Octavius' tentacles slithered up Benji's neck and wrapped gently around the top of his head. Octavius turned Benji's head to the left. "Benji, this is Jaylon."

"Benji." Jaylon drifted over and grabbed Benji's hand. He hooked his middle two fingers with Benji's, and they wrapped their index and pinky fingers around the back of each other's hands. Then they both clasped their free hand over the other. "You've done that before, pup."

Melvin, thought Benji.

"Who?" said Jaylon.

"Nuh… nothing. I… I catch on fast," stumbled Benji. "Nice moves back there, by the way."

Jaylon's speckled silver tail started a few inches below his rib cage. His thighs stretched forty inches around, thick and muscular. Seeing him in action earlier, Benji knew the sharp, silver tail fin helped Jaylon with agility and speed.

Jaylon's bulbous chin made Benji smile each time he looked at his face. Jaylon wasn't funny looking, just fun-looking. Jaylon wore his platinum-blonde hair tied tight behind his head. A six-inch ponytail dangled between his shoulder blades. Jaylon's skin stretched tight across his muscles with long thick veins swirling around the upper and lower arms.

Octavius turned Benji's head to the right. "And this is Meena. I believe you have already exchanged greetings."

Benji blushed.

Meena shot Octavius a menacing glance and nodded her head at Benji.

Meena floated ten feet in front of Benji. Her jet-black hair morphed in the water like a creature with a mind of its own. Meena's midnight black eyes pierced the distance between the two of them. Benji felt them barreling through the back of his skull, steely and focused. He saw both of these traits in full force back at the docks.

Meena's slightly oval eyes and sharp, thin face betrayed little emotion. Jaylon easily outweighed her by a hundred pounds, but Meena's toned physique didn't convey a bit of weakness. Neither did her swimming.

Bluish-grey skin with small black spots covered most of Meena's body. As with Jaylon, the color darkened as it wrapped around her back. A white streak ran from her throat down just below where a naval should have been. He looked back at Jaylon and noticed neither of them had a belly button. Meena's tail began a few inches lower than Jaylon's and ended in a smaller but sleek, black tail fin.

Meena tapped her fingers on the upper half of her folded arms, and Benji caught a glimpse of the webbing between her fingers he had seen is his dream.

"We're glad you are here, Benji," said Jaylon.

"Me too," said Benji sheepishly. He looked back at Jaylon and saw the webbing on his hands, as well, stretching from the second knuckle on each finger down to the palm.

Meena and Jaylon both wore necklaces. Each necklace was uniquely decorated. However, there was a pattern to each of them. There was a shell on each with a sketch of something Benji couldn't quite see. Jaylon had four shells on his. Meena wore three on her necklace.

"You're ready to start swimming on your own, Benji," said Octavius.

Benji floated in the middle of the ocean staring at the other two sarcastically. His head still felt loopy from the kiss he received at the dock. He turned his head to the side and raised his eyebrows at Octavius with a 'say what?' look on his face. "Oh yeah. I forgot. I'm a mermaid."

"Man," said Jaylon. "You can be a mermaid if you want, though. We won't judge. Mermaid. Merman. Those are Topsider words anyway. You can use Aquarien. That's pretty broad."

Octavius nodded in agreement. "Simple for now."

"Well, just let me start swishing my fairy pink tail, and off we'll go," he said gesturing down below his waist.

Benji followed Jaylon and Meena's wide-eyed looks down to his legs. His legs were no more. His shorts ripped right down the middle and straddled his midsection like a rag. His left shoe split down the laces and spiraled down to the ocean floor.

What was once a pair of legs merged and formed a beautiful flowing pink tail. A tinge of silver spider-webbed down to the tip making him sparkle from every angle. He looked all ready for a mermaid wedding. The lacy translucent fin at the bottom stretched twice as wide as the others.

Where Meena and Jaylon's fins screamed speed, Benji's screamed take me to a ball and twirl me around under the chandelier.

Bubbles shot out of Meena's nose, mouth, and ears.

Complete shock covered Jaylon's face.

"What the… I don't want a pink tail! I want a black tail."

Immediately, his tail turned cobalt black.

"With a gold lightning bolt."

Poof!

A gold lightning bolt started at his right hip and wrapped around his tail. The point came to an end where his left ankle used to be. Benji smiled and puffed out his chest.

"Show off," said Jaylon.

"Uh… these are more than just fashion statements, you know?" said Meena, gesturing to her tail.

"Oops," Benji said. "Not a good choice?"

"Hardly!" said Meena as she floated in front of him shaking her head.

"If you're into getting chased by sharks, that will work. And now that you got that flashy tail, you're on your own, pinky," said Jaylon shaking his brow.

"That first one didn't count," said Benji.

"Did in my book," said Jaylon. Jaylon pinched his nose and closed his lips. His mouth inflated to match his bulbous chin. His face turned red as a beet and bubbles shot out of his ears, enveloping the three of them.

Benji cocked his head and stared at a miniature version of himself floating in a bubble with a fairy pink tail and the embarrassed color on his face to match. "How… what is this?"

"Evidence," smirked Jaylon.

Benji pinched his nose, closed his mouth, and blew as hard as he could. A stream of air shot out of his right ear and knocked Octavius upside his oblong head.

"Save your air. I wouldn't count on another breath from me," smirked Meena.

Benji stopped immediately. He studied Jaylon and Meena's tails then closed his eyes. He opened them one at a time and then looked down at a long silver tail. Two black spots the size and shape of tarantulas decorated the front and back. A sleek, black and silver tail fin wobbled at the end. He flexed it back and forth nodding as he did.

Not bad, he thought.

"Not bad," said Jaylon. "I like it. Covert and cool."

Benji's gaze traveled up his body. He shook his head and held each of his arms out when he saw they were different too. Pale grey stretched from his underarm to his wrist. A silvery sheen covered the backs, starting at the wrist and continuing onto and around his shoulders. He held his hands up in front of his face and wriggled his fingers. Webbing stretched between each finger as he flexed them back and forth.

"I've never seen that before," said Jaylon.

"Obviously. He's supposed to be one of the last," said Meena with a condescending scowl.

"You've never seen what?" said Benji.

"A Mystiquarien change," said Jaylon.

"Wait, I thought you said I'm Aquarien," said Benji as he careened his neck to the side to look at Octavius.

"Yes, we are Aquarien," said Octavius.

"But you're an octopus. I'm completely confused."

"Aquari is our word for the ocean. All the species who live here are Aquarien. Jaylon, and Meena are also Shequarien. That is the name for mer from Shequari, the Western ocean. Topsiders call it the Atlantic.

"You are Mystiquarien. Most believe your species disappeared from Aquari many years ago," said Octavius.

"Fled is more like it," said Meena.

"Your parents were the last known Mystiquarien family in Aquari. After their death and your disappearance, most believed the line had all but perished," said Octavius.

"Man! All of this exists in the oceans?" said Benji.

"Yep," said Jaylon.

"And more. That is just the beginning. There are related species in all the oceans of the world and other creatures you've never imagined," said Octavius.

"Even in the Arctic?" said Benji.

"There as well. They are much larger, but you are related. All creatures evolve to adapt to their surroundings or die trying," said Octavius.

"Dad!" Benji screamed.

"Easy, pup. No yelling," said Jaylon.

Benji panicked and swallowed a large gulp of water. His body started shaking, and his face turned blue from coughing. He kicked toward the surface, but his new gear made his movements clumsy and erratic.

"Breathe, Benji," said Octavius. "You can breathe here."

Benji ignored Octavius. He thrashed furiously toward the top. Meena caught up with him after a few feet. She grabbed each of his cheeks again and blew a gentle breath into his lungs. Benji slowed his pace, and the two of them broke the surface with her hands still on his face.

"What......?"

"Their breath gives you life underwater, Benji. Sanjowqua's powers are fading, so they don't last as long as they used to, but you won't need them much longer." Octavius looked at Meena. "Don't give him another."

"I'll take those while I can get them," said Benji with a sheepish grin.

Meena pushed Benji away. "Figure it out yourself next time."

Jaylon popped up beside them. "Don't get too attached Benji." Jaylon threw his arm around Meena. She pushed his arm away and dipped back below, splashing the three of them with her tail.

Benji looked up at the sky and took a couple of deep breaths before he relaxed and remembered what caused him to panic.

"My dad! I saw people falling in the water when the sharks were after us," said Benji.

As if on cue, three dolphins darted out of the darkness.

"What's going on? We could hear you a mile away," said Mai.

"Were there any casualties?" said Octavius.

"A lady in a yellow and pink sundress got nicked by one of the bulls. She'll live, but I'm not sure if she'll be dancing again," said Zeeke.

"There were a few more sharks back at the docks, but we took care of them," said Mai.

"Yeah, and we ran off the hammerhead trailing the big dummy, too," said Eeke with an air of bravado.

Benji recognized the voices. "Eeke, Zeeke, Mai?"

"That's us, Benji," said Mai.

The night before Benji had just seen their heads. They were much larger than he thought. Mai was about the same length as Jaylon was tall. Her voice was soothing. She stared at Benji with a mothering look in her eye. Benji grew accustomed to stares from a young age, but not with that kind of emotion behind them.

"You're coming with us? asked Benji.

"Yeah, but we'll be heading back after we run with you to the boat," said Zeeke.

"You're still going to watch over my dad?" said Benji.

"We keep tabs on our own, Benji," said Octavius.

"What does that mean?" asked Benji.

Octavius released Benji's shoulder and hovered amongst the circle of creatures. "Joe's father was a Mystiquarien. He left Aquari when he was a teenager. Joe's wife, Rita, was a Mystiquarien descendant as well, but much further out. Four generations ago, I believe, but once it's in your blood, it's hard to get away from the ocean."

"I don't understand," said Benji.

"Joe's dad was a bonafide merman a.k.a. Mystiquarien," said Jaylon.

Octavius spoke up. "Joe's father left Aquari for love. He couldn't get away from the sea because it's in his blood, so he became a fisherman. Joe doesn't have the same abilities as you, but…"

Benji paused. "Does that mean he could come with us, too?"

"Anyone who is invited may come. However, after an invitation is extended, the offer is only open until the next full moon," said Octavius.

"And when the next full moon passes?" pushed Benji.

"The invitation expires, and the person is never allowed another. Invitations are rare these days," said Octavius solemnly. "Many Aquarien have grown distrustful of the Topsiders."

"Has my dad ever been invited?" asked Benji

"No, he has not," said Octavius.

Benji's eyes sparkled, and his brain began churning out more questions. While he was getting answers, he thought it was best to keep at it.

"You told me the first night that Sanjowqua is in the Bermuda Triangle…"

"The Bermuda Triangle is Sanjowqua," said Octavius.

"Ok. Well, the ships and planes that have disappeared there. What happened to the people on them? I mean, were they invited to stay or did you just capture them because they were trespassing?" said Benji.

"Sanjowqua is guarded by Poseidon's trident. The power of the trident keeps many boats and planes away. Every once in a while one slips through. It's only then that we bring them in and extend an invitation," said Octavius.

"How come no one has ever been found again once they disappear into the Bermuda Triangle? I mean, why don't they go back?" asked Benji.

"You'll find out soon enough," said Jaylon with a wink.

"I hope that's a good thing," said Benji.

"We will leave that for you to decide," said Octavius.

"So, I only had until the next full moon to decide whether or not to come?" said Benji.

"No. In essence, you weren't invited. You don't need to be. You are a child of the sea and being a pure Mystiquarien, you are not bound by those restrictions," said Octavius.

Benji looked among the two Shequarien and the dolphins, then peered at Octavius. He didn't know a thing about any one of them, yet deep down he knew he belonged in their company. He smiled and suppressed a giggle spurred from the effects of the second kiss.

"I'm no expert on the Bermuda Triangle or Sanjowqua, but I do know it's pretty far. Swimming will take us days, won't it?" asked Benji.

"We have other modes of transportation. We have another hour's swim, though. Are you OK with swimming?" said Octavius.

The four of them had been mainly stationary in the water since Benji discovered he had a tail. Benji dipped down into the water. He dropped down twenty feet then pushed his arms to his sides and with a couple of swift thrusts busted through the surface. When his tail breached the water, he bent backward and flipped his tail up and over him, driving him back down into the ocean head first.

Zeeke looked at Meena and Jaylon with a broad smile as if to say 'told you so'.

"I think I'm OK," said Benji.

"Let's stick close to the surface. We'll have to go down once we reach the boat, but that's pretty far off," said Octavius.

"A boat?" said Benji.

"We made a few minor modifications to suit our needs," said Jaylon.

Octavius looked around at the assembled crew. "We need to keep moving. Mai, you and your brothers circle us. Meena, you lead the way, and Jaylon, you follow behind."

Octavius clamored around Benji's neck. The group broke apart and began moving again.

"Can we run full speed? said Eeke. "I've been dying to see him in action."

"He has to wade before he can swim, Eeke," said Mai.

"You saw him do that flip. He's way past wading, Mai," said Eeke as he stuck his tongue out at his sister.

They started slowly, picking up speed as Benji got comfortable. Benji caught Eeke glancing at him occasionally with a grin that half begged him to pick it up another notch. Then, the dolphin shot back into the open water keeping his eyes out for any more trouble.

Meena kept looking back over her shoulder to check on Benji's progress. Once satisfied she began performing maneuvers to see if he'd follow suit. The first time she broke through the water at full speed, Benji stuck right behind her. He cleared ten feet of water and let out a nervous "Woo."

Each time afterward, he flew higher and further until he nearly surpassed Meena when he splashed back down. Benji felt Octavius' grip tighten around his collarbones each time he began gathering speed to burst through the surface.

"You're getting the hang of it, pup," said Jaylon from behind him. "You were born for this, see?"

Benji couldn't do anything but grin. Meena could only imagine what it felt like to be freed into the water for the first time. She had spent her whole life there. Her competitive nature quickly took over, and she began twirling when she left the water.

Forty-five minutes later, Meena slowed her pace. Benji pushed forward up alongside her, but Octavius reminded him to hold his position, and he drifted back slightly.

Without notice, Meena dove down into the water with a few swipes of her tail and then shot back up toward the surface. She cleared the surface by ten feet then dove straight down. Benji misjudged her intentions and shot past where she descended.

"Follow Meena," reminded Octavius.

Benji looked back from an upside down position. His eyes locked on Meena then nearly bugged out of his skull as he saw where she headed.

"Is that a pirate ship?" asked Benji.

"They were all pirates to some degree or another in those days; each one taking from the other that which wasn't rightfully theirs," said Octavius.

The triple masts stood at a forty-five-degree angle to the bottom of the ocean. The ship looked like one of those swinging amusement rides that slings passengers back and forth turned sideways at the height of its swing; the bow of the boat stood ten feet higher than the stern.

There were no human passengers on this one, at least not any that Benji could see. It sat buried in sand up to the point where it would have sat in the water if it was still seaworthy. The clean lines of the vessel that propelled it over the oceans and pierced it through the waves were distorted by its newest inhabitants. Patches of barnacles and coral clung to the hull. The closer they got, Benji noticed colorful reef fish darting in and out of the portholes. A sea turtle popped up from the far side of the boat and scooted lazily above the deck looking for food.

"How is it still standing?" asked Benji with an impressed tone.

"A lot of the things you're accustomed to won't be that way from here on out, Benji," said Jaylon.

Benji scrunched his face together in disappointment. "This isn't Sanjowqua, is it?"

Everyone else chuckled.

"Looks like you're safe," said Mai. "We're headed back to Beech Mill."

"See you in a few weeks," said Zeeke.

Full of youthful energy, Eeke bobbed his head up and down in front of Benji. "I'll teach you some more moves when we get there."

Eagerly, Benji belted out, "Can't wait."

Mai looked at her brothers and with a nod turned her head and kicked off back toward Beech Mill. Her brothers raced over and under her, yapping as they disappeared into the darkness.

Umpahlaki Keemanasi

(setting sail)

THEY FLOATED IN the middle of the ocean just above the masts of a sunken pirate ship. Benji cocked his head to the side with a confused look and stared down at the wreck. "Is this, like… uh, your clubhouse?"

Meena laughed and swam down.

Jaylon came up beside Benji and nodded downward. "Follow me."

Benji followed him down zig-zagging between the masts.

"This will take us the rest of the way, Benji. The ship is quicker than swimming," said Octavius clenching to Benji's shoulder.

"More entertaining too," said Jaylon, spiraling around the center mast.

"This thing isn't quicker than the sand it's buried in," said Benji.

"Remember what I told you about appearances," said Octavius.

The closer they got to the deck, the more alive the ship became. Streaks of color blazed in and out of the doors, windows, and portholes.

"Does my vision get better?" asked Benji.

"What do you mean? said Octavius.

"It looks like I'm staring at everything through my teacher's glasses," said Benji.

"You're still missing a few things. That should correct itself soon," said Octavius.

The sight of a century old pirate ship and the underwater city it created mesmerized Benji to the point he didn't realize he needed more air until it was almost too late.

Meena floated a few feet away from him. Jaylon hung his head over the far side of the ship looking back and forth.

Benji looked at Meena. "I need another breath of air."

Meena looked at Octavius who shook his head.

"You're on your own," said Meena.

What? Benji shook his head in panic. His eyes darted toward the surface. They were a hundred feet below. Despite his new tail and the skills he practiced earlier, he felt sure he wouldn't make it. His chest tightened, and his head felt swollen.

Benji swung his tail under him with all his might. He moved five feet then stopped abruptly. A sudden jerk from below kept him from advancing. Benji thrust his waist back and forth. He reached his hands up and filled them with water pushing down with everything he had. His neck stretched frantically toward the surface; the veins bulged to the point of nearly jumping out of his skin. He looked down as he thrashed frantically, trying to free himself from whatever kept him anchored in place.

Benji's eyes popped in horror.

One of Meena's arms wrapped firmly around the center mast. The other arm extended up toward Benji. Half of Octavius' tentacles wrapped around Meena's arm, the other half flexed around Benji's tail fin.

Benji tried verbalizing his need for air. Nothing but a few weak bubbles escaped his mouth. He closed his eyes and thought, *SURFACE! AIR!*

"You don't need the surface air," said Octavius firmly.

"Can't breathe!" said Benji.

His thrashing slowed. His energy faded, and Benji turned blue.

His eyelids battled one another, and his eyes began rolling back in his head.

"Breathe, Benji!" said Octavius.

Jaylon leaned against the railing watching the drama unfold with both fists clenched.

Meena's lips pressed tight against each other, part from the strain of keeping Benji in place, part from nervousness. "Come... on...Benji!" she managed through grinding teeth.

Benji's head fell back, and his mouth gaped open.

Meena shook her head as the tension in her arm slackened.

Octavius released his grip on Benji's tail. "Breathe, Benji!"

"Wasted trip," said Meena shaking her head.

Benji's arms drifted lifelessly down alongside him. A final reflexive gasp for air pulled a pocket of water into Benji's mouth, and his eyelids fluttered. Short rapid bursts shook his chest. Another gulp of cool, salt water tingled the back of his throat. He coughed twice and instantly inhaled another mouthful of water. The water passed through his mouth, down his throat, and flowed out across the back of his neck noticeably warmer. Benji's eyelids shot open from the burst of oxygen through his body.

The veins in Jaylon's hands receded into his flesh as he relaxed his fists.

Benji coughed himself five feet back before he stopped and heard the clapping. He moved both his hands under his jaw alongside his neck and ran his fingers over a flap of skin on either side. Benji drew another cautious breath in and felt the water pass down his throat and out through the birthmarks his classmates had teased him about his entire life.

"Why?" said Benji with a bewildered look on his face.

"Because that is what you are capable of," said Octavius.

"What was that?" asked Benji.

Octavius hovered off to Meena's side. "Transformation."

"I can breathe," said Benji.

A bull shark off in the distance caught the corner of Benji's eye. "Shark!"

He scrambled backward before Octavius reached out and locked onto his arm.

"They're not all after you," said Octavius.

Benji settled down then bounced his attention from Octavius, to Meena, to Jaylon, then zeroed in on a red-tipped sea goddess nudibranch creeping its way along the railing behind Jaylon.

"Woah. I can see!"

Benji took a look toward the surface. The sun had long gone and the starry moonlit night twinkled above them without a trace of interference. Despite being under ten stories of water, Benji could still make out every detail around him. Only the shadows hid those who decided they were best left concealed. Bright colors betrayed those whose curiosity got the better of them.

He jerked his head left and right taking in everything. Two blue damsels chased each other around the center mast. A crowd of yellow damsels swelled and receded from the ship's wheel like an expanding and collapsing balloon. A red cardinalfish jutted out of one of the windows, shot back in, and reemerged with his head just sticking out of a broken pane in the captain's cabin. The mottled back of a sea turtle Benji spotted when he first saw the ship glided gracefully across the deck. His green and brown shell looked like a pirate map to an untold amount of riches. A purple and yellow royal gamma whirled over and under the opposite railing.

Benji swam to the port side of the ship and poked his head over. Several rusted and crusted canons stuck out from the gun ports. The mouth of a green moray eel gaped open from one of them.

Benji put his hands over his eyes to give himself a moment to adjust to the increased visual stimulation. When he did, he took half a breath through his nose. He stopped himself expecting to choke on the water up his nose, but it flowed down his throat and out the back of his neck, only this time he smelled. He smelled the little maloohwoo of the spotfin butterflyfish that paused in front of his face then swam down to dance around the nudibranch on the railing. Benji put his face on his shoulder and took a whiff. He had his own distinctive salty smell that he inhaled with a deep nourishing breath.

All of his senses awoke. He no longer viewed things through the eyes of a visitor. He belonged here, and all of his body told him so.

"A little warning would have been nice," said Benji.

"No more kisses for you, pup," boasted Jaylon as he winked at Benji.

"I am fishboy," said Benji with a nervous laugh.

Meena let out a snort of bubbles.

"If that's what you want to call yourself. To us, you are Aquarien. To us you are special," said Octavius.

"Back on land, special isn't always such a good thing," said Benji circling the others, his eyes busy on all the new discoveries.

"Jealousy inspires mockery, Benji," said Octavius.

Benji had both of his hands up under his jaw. He cracked his mouth wide enough for a straw and sucked in a stream of water. Then, he opened his mouth wide and took in a large gulp. He moved his mouth to each side then up and down making all kinds of funny shapes with his lips as he sucked in water.

"That's coming from my birthmarks?" he said as his fingers danced with the outgoing water.

"In a way they are birthmarks," said Octavius. "Gills would be a little more precise, though."

"Are there any more surprises? I'm not going to sprout another head or anything like that, am I?" asked Benji.

"There are plenty more surprises, but you don't have to worry about another head to contend with," said Octavius.

"Whew," muttered Benji.

"Yeah," said Jaylon with a smirk. "I think that one lump is more than enough."

A soft moan slowly emerged from afar. Benji felt the sound waves. They merged with him. They shook him. They carried him up and down in their frequency then left through the other side of his body.

"They're on their way," called Octavius perching himself on the wheel between two of the handles.

Meena and Jaylon turned their heads up staring silently into the deep blue ocean looking for the culprit.

"That's beautiful. What is it?" asked Benji.

"There's a pod of whales coming this way," said Meena from behind Benji.

She bent down and picked up a small conch shell, no bigger than an egg, lying outside the door of the captain's quarters and swam up in the masts with the shell extended toward the direction of the whales. Another wave of soothing wails bellowed through the ocean, and the shell began expanding with the volume of the approaching song until it was the roughly the size of Benji's head. Satisfied, Meena plugged the shell with a sea cucumber she plucked off the mast, swam back down, and placed it at the helm.

Octavius shimmied down to the bottom of the wheel, grabbed one of the handles, and gave it a quarter left turn. The ship creaked and lurched. A loud pop that sounded like a snapped two by four emerged from the bow; a crack on the sandy floor of the ship inched itself steadily wider at the bow and moved its way toward the stern.

Benji thought the masts were getting wider but soon realized the coral and barnacles that covered them were separating along with the crack below his feet. Everything covering the boat gently shifted to one side or the other; a boat-sized oyster shell of coral opened, revealing the treasure within.

Sand fluttered down and scattered like shattered glass on the polished, wooden surface of a sparkling new ship underneath.

The sound of an anchor chain sliding down quickly came to an abrupt halt as a thud from the ocean floor indicated the boat was steady. The ship stood proud and upright, floating several feet off the bottom now separate from its coral exoskeleton. A Shequarien figurehead jutted out of the prow. Her outstretched right hand clutched a spear.

Another song pierced the water. Benji looked up and saw a pod of humpback whales moving slowly together above him. Jaylon interrupted the beautiful song with the sound of a heavy plank sliding off the starboard side. The board dangled for a few feet until gravity took over and the extended end drifted slowly toward the sand.

Seconds later, a series of clicks and jabbering preceded several dozen crabs and lobsters scurrying up the ramp. As they crested the side of the boat and scuttled onto the deck, a few of them stopped and nodded toward Jaylon. A full-blown conversation erupted in which Jaylon updated them on his family and vice versa.

"Time to get to work, Jaylon," said the lead crab.

"Have at it. See you downstairs," said Jaylon.

"Crabs talk?" asked Benji.

"Everything in nature speaks. Not everything in nature listens," said Octavius nodding Topside.

The crustaceans dispersed throughout the boat, scaling up the masts and scurrying along the rails checking the ropes.

Three stingrays glided up and over the railing. The one in the rear came close to knocking a crab off as the little eight-legged creature grappled with a rope. The annoyed crab lifted one of its claws in the air clicking it at the oblivious ray in a rapid fashion. The rays settled down on the deck and began fanning their fins. The loose sand and debris that fell from the coral exoskeleton swooshed off the floor and blew off either side.

A band of seahorses trotted up the plank behind the crabs and lobsters merrily bobbing their heads.

"I was nervous about you coming here," said Octavius.

Benji twitched his head away from the animals emerging from the side of the ship and blinked his eyes as if he had just emerged from a deep sleep.

"Huh?" said Benji.

"We were all nervous," said Octavius.

"What were you nervous about?" asked Benji.

"I was worried you'd be spoiled from your time above. Worried you wouldn't find this place worthy of your presence," said Octavius.

"That sounds like something a fictional king would say," said Benji. His eyes held steady on the animals working together to prepare to ship.

"Your father was," said Octavius.

Benji jerked his head toward Octavius. "My father was a king?"

Octavius laughed. "No. He wasn't a king, but he was treated like one at times. Your father was one of the leaders of the Mystiquariens in Sanjowqua. I can see his humbleness in your gaze now, your astonishment for what surrounds us.

"Mai says that expression has been on your face since the day she saw you and she was part of the first team on your security detail which means that's a look of appreciation that's been there for a long time."

Benji didn't know what to say. He revered the ocean. Always had. Seeing things like this would take getting used to, but it only deepened his respect.

"That look can inspire opposite characteristics: appreciation or greed," said Octavius.

"I don't see what there is to be greedy about," said Benji scratching his head.

"So much of our world is disappearing. You haven't seen anything yet, Benji," explained Octavius.

"Where do we start? I guess I need to study to be like my father," said Benji.

"People don't study to be like your father. It's here," said Octavius poking a tentacle toward Benji's heart.

"I mean, do we start schooling when I get there? It's nearly summer break at my school. I hope you have the same schedule," said Benji.

"We have different views on schooling. You won't be doing much of what you are used to," said Octavius.

"I'm sold!" said Benji.

The movement of creatures through the door to the captain's quarters caught Benji's attention. Jaylon stood beside the entrance nodding and chatting to a whole slew of marine life filing past him. Benji thought he saw a six-inch girl with wings flutter up to Jaylon and exchange words. Benji blinked and shook his head in shock. When he opened his eyes again, the flying girl was gone.

"But there's obviously a lot for me to learn," said Benji.

"That's life," said Octavius, "in Aquari or Topside."

Benji had flown through his books at school. Facts and figures absorbed naturally into his brain; another quirk in his personality that made him an oddball Topside.

"How did you learn to tie knots on Joe's boat?" said Octavius.

"He showed...," a lightbulb went off in Benji's head.

"Knowledge alone is not power, Benji. Knowledge in motion rules the ocean," said Octavius.

"So you don't have books here?" said Benji.

"As far as physical books? No. They wouldn't last very long down here. Many a drunken sailor has tried parking his boat with us, and the books never make it very long.

"But there are other ways to pass along knowledge. The Mystiqs have been some of the most adept at doing so," said Octavius.

Octavius lifted a tentacle and pointed toward a cloud of krill moving off in the distance. The whales dove through it, refilling along their journey. Benji watched in awe as his new world performed in front of him.

"Follow me," said Meena as she reached out and swiped the conch shell off the deck by Benji's tail.

Octavius hovered back to the top of the ship's wheel. He plucked off a wooden pipe clasped to the backside of one of the spokes and dangled it under his bulbous head. Each inhale brought in a flurry of tiny sea creatures and ended with a satisfied hum.

Benji followed Meena toward the bow, his eyes zipping here and there admiring the action around him. Two crabs fenced with each other using their claws on the opposite railing. Benji stared at the crustaceans and bumped into Jaylon.

Jaylon fumbled with and almost lost his grip on the plank as he slid it back onto the boat. "No respect! Watch it, fishboy. Your maiden voyage is a pleasure cruise. Second time around you gotta work, and I'll be back there with Mr. O-so-better-than-everyone-else, steering the ship."

Jaylon nudged Benji ahead then yanked his tail as he passed.

Meena glided over the deck and stopped at the bowsprit holding the conch shell she had extended while the whales swam by earlier.

"What's that for?" said Benji.

"Protection. Whales get a lot more respect than Jaylon," said Meena, loud enough so he could hear.

"Obviously," said Jaylon.

Meena handed Benji the conch shell. It's beautiful ivory and tan swirls made it look as delicate as a flower.

"Unscrew the back," said Meena.

"What for?" said Benji.

"I already told you," said Meena.

Benji looked at her a bit confused then at the shell in his hand.

Righty tighty. Lefty loosey, thought Benji.

"Righty what?" said Meena.

"Helps me remember which way. I guess these are the same," said Benji.

Meena looked at him like he was from another planet. As far as she was concerned, he was.

The knob on the shell unscrewed, and he dropped it into Meena's outstretched hand.

"We may need that later," she said pulling a little pouch from behind her back. The pouch rested between her ribs suspended by a string. Her long black hair had concealed it behind her back. She dropped the knob from the shell inside then shifted the bag back around. "Now tie the shell around the bowsprit."

Benji looked down and noticed a rope around the bowsprit. He unwrapped it, revealing a shallow crevice the perfect size and shape for the conch shell.

"Leave the conch shell opening faced forward and upwards," said Meena.

Benji placed the shell in the crevice and tied it in place.

Meena gave him a look of approval then swam back toward the wheel, stopping to make a few last minute requests of the crabs at the anchor line who began slipping down the rope. Benji followed nodding toward the sea creatures he passed.

Jaylon stood behind Octavius; one eye closed, his hand on his bulbous chin, and his mouth furled up puffing on an imaginary pipe. "Ready to cast off Captain eight legs… I mean, sir."

Octavius held the ship's wheel ignoring the comment. Jaylon shrugged his shoulders then called out, "Lights!"

A seahorse, the size of Benji's hand, skipped across the deck and hopped up onto the railing. He took in a deep breath then tooted a departure tune that aroused every head on the boat. One minute everyone hustled around the ship making last-minute adjustments, the next they stood dead still staring at the parted coral exoskeleton.

Little glowing bubbles started popping out from the coral. The spheres were smaller than the one Uncle Bill had made a necklace with, about the size of a pen tip. Once a bubble made its appearance, a gasp or sigh slipped out into the collective group. Heads and beady eyes of all shapes and sizes danced around the interior of the ship looking for the next light ball to appear. Benji twitched as a moray eel's tail brushed against his fin and slithered up toward the center mast where a solitary blue bubble floated.

Soon, little glowing bubbles popped out of the coral in rapid succession. Thousands now drifted over the ship, each one like a tiny star gently floating down from the heavens.

Before he knew it, a glare of light came from below his field of vision, and Benji looked down at the deck. The entire surface glowed with millions of little bioluminescent bubbles hovering over and eventually clinging to every inch of the boat. The glowing spheres and all their energy made the ship look like it breathed as they wavered in the current. Benji looked back at Jaylon, Meena, and Octavius to make sure he wasn't dreaming. They were hypnotized by the beauty surrounding them as well.

Both Meena and Jaylon leaned against the outside wall of the captain's quarters. Most of Octavius' tentacles held him securely to the wheel. The one securing the pipe in his mouth strengthened its grip on the stem. Benji floated a few feet away looking back and forth, up and down at the entire glowing ship.

"Get back here, now!" screeched Meena.

Meena startled Benji. The second it took him to move cost him. As he rounded the helm and turned, the ship took off. His back was inches from the captain's quarters, but the sheer force at which they suddenly moved knocked a blast of water from the sides of his neck. The light show from the bioluminescence had stolen most of his breath; a hard smack in the rear took what was left.

Benji's skin stretched to the limit with a look of sheer terror plastered across his face. Water shot down his mouth and out his gills causing them to flap furiously from the force of water rushing through his mouth and out the sides of his neck. He felt like someone had hooked the skin behind his head and was pulling the line with an aircraft carrier. As he turned his head to the left to look at Jaylon and Meena, the left side of his face slammed into the wall, and he heard a few pops in his neck. He thought his eyebrows might slide off his face at any moment.

Jalyon's lips disappeared from his face and exposed the largest grin Benji had ever seen. Benji wanted to laugh but couldn't muster the strength. Jaylon's huge grin rivaled the size of the grill on Joe's pickup truck. Benji saw every one of Jaylon's teeth clear back to his molars. Benji was as scared as he had ever been, and Jaylon looked like he was being shocked by a lightning bolt and enjoying every second of it.

The only constants were the pulling of his skin and the long slow moan of the whale song.

We're going to run right through them, Benji thought.

"Don't worry, pup. Enjoy the ride," said Jaylon.

Does knowing this was coming make it fun? Benji thought. He hoped it did, but he doubted it.

"Yep," said Jaylon.

"This is crazy," said Benji.

"Yep. Ain't it cool?"

"Ask me again when it's done."

Benji saw a frown appear on Jaylon's face. Jaylon's hand reached down, and he grabbed the knob to the captain's quarter's door. The door flew open, and Jaylon gave a quick jerk of his head in that direction.

"Move?... I... can't... even... think," said Benji.

"You can. I can hear you," said Jaylon.

Benji moved his right shoulder with every ounce of strength he had. Momentum took over and sent him tumbling through the door before he had a second to think about it. Jaylon snatched Benji's tail and flew in after him. Meena came tumbling last, landing on top of both of them. Through the mass of body parts, Benji saw a large purple tentacle reach in, snatch the knob, and pull the door shut.

Meena peeled herself off the two of them, and Jaylon pushed off the floor underneath Benji. Jaylon strutted around the room full of energy, throwing his hands up and down and yelling with each breath.

"WOOOOO! WOOOOO!" shouted Jaylon.

"Jaylon! Calm down," said Meena.

"WOOOOOOO!!" yelled Jaylon.

"Jaylon!" said Meena.

"Sor... WOOOOOOOOO!"

Benji sat in the corner with his head spinning. He was sure his eyes had nearly been pushed through the back of his skull.

"WOOOOO!"

"JAYLON!" huffed Meena.

"My ba... WOOOO!"

"I didn't see that coming," said Benji.

"WOOOO! Last one. Promise."

Jaylon pumped his fist back and forth in front of his chest. Dinner-plate-sized eyes contorted his face making him look even funnier than usual.

"YES!!" chirped Jaylon. " OK. I'm done. Man, I love that!"

"Good thing I'm not wearing any underwear?" said Benji.

Jaylon stopped mid-fist pump. "Huh?"

"Never mind," said Benji.

Much of the room went unnoticed as he tumbled head over tail through the door. After everything had stopped spinning, Benji looked around and caught another surprise. The wood in the room sparkled. It was a light chestnut brown accentuated by bioluminescence that had settled throughout the interior.

Several maps and paintings of ships hung on the walls. One of the paintings had a picture of a sunken ship much like the one he found himself on at the moment. Mermaids carted unconscious sailors to the surface. Others transported chests and cases down to a cave where an array of gold and other jewels sparkled.

The largest globe Benji had ever seen sat in the center of the room. A thick trunk of coral protruded from the floor and quickly split into four branches creating both the support and a frame for the five-foot sphere. Another branch of coral wrapped around the belly of the globe forming a little railing in the middle that protruded eight inches around. The four branches of coral then looped over the top and met as one thick trunk again at the ceiling. On the underside of the supports between the coral and the globe itself, anemones waved their happy tentacles. Their little pink and purple dancing arms supported the globe and helped keep it from bumping against the coral frame. In the center, floated a gigantic three-dimensional map of the ocean floor. Benji had seen oceanic maps before, but never one like this, never one so detailed… and alive.

Benji swam around the structure looking at different spots marked in red. He reached out to touch it, and Meena smacked his wrist. He yanked his hand back close to his chest and pointed from as far back as possible toward some of the writing.

"What are those?" said Benji.

"Coordinates. Those are the symbols we use for numbers. A lot more logical than what you… they use," said Meena pointing up.

"The diagonal slash is one?"

"Yes."

"And two slashes is two?"

"Yes."

"The triangle is three?"

"You're smarter than you look."

"And eleven?"

"Ten, the circle, and one slash."

"And twenty-one?"

"Two slashes, the circle, then one slash."

Benji inched closer to the globe but made sure he kept his hands to himself. In the center of the coral frame, several pieces converged forming a circle. Inside the target, a miniature boat sped along the contoured surface of the globe. The anemone arms on the underside of the frame shimmied the globe as the boat progressed keeping it in the center of the bullseye.

"That us?" Benji asked.

"For the time being. Since we're all busy there, for now, let's go check out the scene below," said Jaylon as he waved his arm in a big circle and juked his head toward the back of the room.

Benji peeled his eyes away from the globe and watched Jaylon's ponytail disappear down a dimly lit staircase opposite where they fell in. A gold railing reflected some of the light coming from below.

Jaylon disappeared for a second then popped his head back up. "You guys coming or what? The fights've started."

When he reached the landing in the middle of the stairs, Benji realized there was a lot more to the boat than he thought. The wooden staircase broadcasted the noise from the room below.

Jaylon hovered on the outside edge of the bottom floor with his arms clasped behind his back bobbing his head to the music. As Benji made his way down, the shadow from the stairs above his head gave way to a well-lit room with tables that reached halfway toward the bow. Around a dozen tables, a dance floor, and the bar sat, danced, fought, and yelled every single sea creature Benji had ever heard of, except for a whale, and a few he had no idea even existed.

Every table was full of some various mashup of animals. A large round table in the center attracted the most attention. Fish, turtles, squid, octopuses, and several hiccuping seahorses crowded around the large wooden table. A dome-shaped cage covered the majority of the surface. Two crabs inside the cage parried back and forth, their claws snapping and clicking. One of them had a claw the size of Benji's hand. Gold coins littered the edge of the table, and everyone cheered wildly.

"Time for the fights," said Jaylon with electric eyes. "Come on."

Meena made her way to the bar at the opposite end of the room. Benji and Jaylon hovered on the outskirts of the center table jockeying for a spot to see the action. Every once in awhile Benji caught a swipe of the claw from either crustacean. Jaylon grabbed his arm and pulled him above the table.

"Best view of the action," said Jaylon, not taking his eyes off the fight.

"Come on Duke!" yelled a blue and yellow parrotfish below them.

"How come that one has an abnormally sized claw?" asked Benji.

"The other claw would be the same if he hadn't lost it in a match last year. The fight was fixed if you ask me," said Jaylon.

Three rusty looking groupers gave Jaylon an antagonizing look. The largest one snapped his mouth shut and almost chomped a blue streak cleaner wrasse in half as he eyed Jaylon with a distasteful look. His wide scowl accentuated by the down-sweeping jaw and pouty lower lip. "You ought to be careful how loose you are with those lips of yours, Jay," said the grouper.

"You're one to talk," said Jaylon shrugging his shoulders. "That's Don," he said, motioning to the large marbled-gray and brown grouper. "He runs the fights. I stopped wagering after that one. Never put that much in any way, but that fight left a bad taste in my mouth."

A roar erupted from the cage below. Benji saw Duke parading around the ring with his opponents claw clamped between his pincers.

Three blue crabs scurried around the outside edge of the table to distribute gold coins to the winners and immediately started taking bets from spectators ready for the next bout. The two fighting crabs hobbled out of the ring on opposite sides. Two electric eels entered the cage as the crabs exited.

"Let's head toward the front," said Jaylon. "These always make my hair stand on end."

As soon as they departed, a few loud zaps echoed from behind them, and Benji felt a buzzing sensation around his head. "I see what you mean."

Beyond the cage match, a table full of seahorses hovered above a checkerboard. Two of them from the same team argued and then butted heads. A third seahorse came over from the side of the board and wrapped his tail around one who had gotten jumped, tugging the loser off the board.

"If he hadn't gone left I would have been protected. He's been eating silly weed since we got on board," said the departing player.

The seahorse who apparently made a wrong move had red eyes and giggled as his sober teammate left the board. The rest of the team looked embarrassed.

The table behind the seahorses was full of miniature people, no more than six inches tall. A pair of translucent wings sectioned like a dragonfly's protruded from their backs. The wings were doubled up on each side; a larger one closer to the head and a slightly smaller one in the small of the back. The little people wore sequin, fish-scale garments. Thin strands of seaweed wrapped in and out of each of the scales forming a colorful chain mail suit of armor covering their chests below the arms down to the knees. Their perfectly proportioned arms and legs went bare.

The little people pipped and squeaked around an oval sand track carved into the table. The track was comprised of six lanes. A hermit crab sped inside each of the lanes, and one of the little-winged creatures sat on their backs chirping and spanking the shell with their lower wings.

"What are those little things?" asked Benji.

Everything on the entire table came to a screeching halt. Dozens of angry eyes glared in Benji's direction.

A big-bellied, miniature man came fluttering up and stopped an inch from Benji's nose. Short brown curls surrounded a bald spot on the top of his head which looked like a shiny white island. A vague aura of light surrounded his entire body. "What are those little things?" he said in a mocking voice with both hands on his hips. "Surely you're speaking of the crabs we're racing."

Benji stared at him cross-eyed and embarrassed.

"Huh? And what's this big obtrusive thing?" said the fat little man as he jabbed Benji in the nose several times with his pointer finger.

"Ow." Benji jerked his head back and pulled his middle finger against his thumb ready to flick the man all the way to the other end of the parlor.

A cute female came up from the track and fluttered right through the little man.

"Ahh," cried Benji, startling her.

Jaylon put his hand above Benji's elbow to stop him from raising his hand any further. "Payton, this is Benji."

Payton tilted her head left then right as she very carefully examined Benji. She looked deep into his eyes. She fluttered to either side of his head then swam around taking in everything about him. Once she was satisfied, she hovered next to the fat man.

"Benji, this is Payton," said Jaylon. "Her father was a… one of your father's trusted partners."

The fat one moved his head back and forth checking Benji out further. He slowly began shaking his head. His expression changed from anger to intrigue. "Uh huh."

"It's true, Jay?" asked Payton.

"Is what true?" Benji said sheepishly.

Jaylon piped up. "It's true, Payton. We've just returned. Had a heck of a time getting him here. He didn't mean anything. He's been Topside for the last thirteen years."

"That's my daughter, Mystiq," said the man. "I'd keep quiet about seeing me, by the way, unless you want the rest of them to think you're crazy."

Benji's eyes darted between Payton, Jaylon, and the half-there, half-not, fat man he wasn't supposed to acknowledge.

"Do you think Montal would approve?" said Jaylon.

"The eternal skeptic? Maybe," said Payton. "But if he's the son of Boone, then my father's approval would be a sure thing."

The rotund little man lifted his jaw at Benji. "I'll be seeing you soon, pup. You got a lot of work to do before I'll let my daughter by your side. Get yourself settled in Sanjawqua. I'll come for you when the time is right."

Payton hung around and stared Benji straight in the eyes for a few seconds. "Your father was a great man here. Hopefully, I can help you achieve the same."

Payton nodded her head at him and backed away. She turned awkwardly and fluttered off to rejoin the others. One of the little creatures on the sideline clapped two shells together, and the race resumed.

Afraid to mutter anything else, Benji ever so gently lifted his gaze and looked toward the front of the ship. Meena floated face to face with an eight-foot bull shark. Its jagged teeth jutted out like barbed wire. Meena and the shark both looked at Benji, and the shark shook its head.

Jaylon glanced over and noticed Benji frozen on the spot.

"Don't worry. That's Jaka," said Jaylon.

Jaylon and Benji hung close to the ceiling and passed over the rest of the tables. An open area separated the games from the bar. A beautiful young mermaid sat inside a giant clam shell on the starboard side of the boat. The bottom half of the shell was cushioned with woven kelp. Six-inch-thick leaves created a large checkered pattern. She was the first mermaid Benji had seen since he arrived, aside from Meena.

The mermaid's song was slow yet powerful. Benji stopped moving and stared at her with heavy eyelids. Her orange hair was longer than Meena's. Several strands of it nearly touched her tail curled in front of her. She closed her eyes while she sang and her head flowed from side to side with each verse. The mermaid had a pair of long, limber arms that swayed in front of her. Another two wrapped around her midsection.

"Beautiful voice, right?" said Jaylon.

"Yeah. Beautiful," said Benji in a slow, dreamy tone.

"She's from Natiqua. The Topsiders call it the Indian Ocean. Come on, lover boy." Jaylon snapped his fingers, and Benji reluctantly followed him.

As Benji moved toward the bar, Jaka turned her head and stared through the crowd. Her menacing snarl glared in the light, then she turned swiftly and headed through a large open door behind the bar.

A dozen green tubes hung from the ceiling along the bar. The tubes swayed gently from the tail swipes of Jaka's departure. Meena held one of them between her fingers and took a long draw from it then blew bubbles from her nose as she took another deep pull.

Jaylon grabbed one of the hanging straws beside Meena and shoved it in between his lips. His chest inflated deeply. He pulled his cheeks in forming a fish mouth. A steady stream of small bubbles dribbled out of his mouth up toward the ceiling.

"Everything OK? Any news?" asked Jaylon as he blew out several bubble rings that expanded until they bumped the ceiling and dispersed into smaller bubbles.

Meena shook her head. She nodded her head toward Benji and focused her eyes on Jaylon. Jaylon threw up his hands in a 'what-ya-gonna-do' expression as he shook his head to a jazzier tune the singing mermaid began belting out. Meena nodded back at him, then Jaylon became animated again as he leaned on the counter of the bar twirling his hand around.

Benji felt like he had suddenly disappeared. He stared at the two of them and looked down at his arms and the rest of his body. Everything still appeared to be the same color as before. He hadn't changed colors, disappeared, or done anything else with his body he wasn't aware of. He looked around the room. Nothing else had changed since they first swam down, except for the zapping sounds from the electric eel cage fight and uproars from the crowd every few seconds.

Benji turned back around toward Meena and Jaylon with a concerned look on his face. He floated off to the side and studied both of them and their movements.

Meena pulled her head back and stared at Benji. "What's wrong with you?"

"I lost the two of you for a minute," said Benji.

"What do you mean you lost us?" asked Jaylon.

"The last thing I heard was you asking Meena if there was any news, then everything went silent."

"We shut you out," said Meena.

"Habit, " said Jaylon.

Benji's curiosity spiked. "What does 'we shut you out' mean?"

"We can control who we send our thoughts to, Benji. Up there… you, they, whoever whispers." Jaylon made a mocking gesture covering his mouth with his hand. "That's silly. No need for it. If there's something you need to say to one or both of us, all you have to do is direct your thoughts toward us. No one else can hear them. Learning to do that, you'll also learn how to guard your thoughts, something that might have been helpful when you were thinking how beautiful Meena is. Might have also stopped that awkward incident at the water fairy table."

Benji blushed. An annoyed smile appeared on Meena's lips.

"Water fairies?" said Benji.

"Yep. They're sensitive about their height, but don't judge them by it. Tough little… I mean, they're tough," said Jaylon.

Flustered, Benji said, "Well, thanks for letting me know after the fact."

"Don't worry, you're gonna do some things wrong," said Jaylon.

"You've been in Aquari for how long?" said Meena.

"You're going to make some mistakes. We'd do the same if you took us out of Aquari and paraded us around Topside. That wasn't a mistake that would have killed you. It may have left you bruised, but those heal," said Jaylon.

Jaylon took another breath from the tube in his hand. Bubbles lolloped out from his nostrils.

"What are those?" asked Benji, pointing at the tube in Jaylon's hand.

"These?" Jaylon lifted his hand and stared at the tube as he thought for a second. "Pure bliss. One hundred percent oxygen."

"Where does it come from?" asked Benji.

"Same as yours," said Meena. "Plants."

"Picture, if you will, that you're out for a few errands. You need to pick up a few things here and there. You're going to make a day out it. Maybe visit some friends. And then… BOOM… you get ambushed by a team of sharks.

"This stuff," said Jaylon shaking the tube in his hand, "goes straight to the blood without any need for purifying. Imagine being able to wave your hand or snap your fingers and have your body completely nourished."

"Let me try," said Benji.

"You don't need it. You didn't do any work," said Meena.

"True," said Benji drooping his head.

Jaylon shook his head at Meena and elbowed Benji in the ribs. He reached above his head and pulled another tube down then nudged Benji.

"Don't take everything she says so seriously. She's not always such a grouch. You bring up some painful memories for her," said Jaylon.

"What kind of painful memories?" asked Benji.

Meena cleared her throat. "Jay, you're not leaving me out of anything are you?"

"Nah. I was just telling Benji how to use this. I said 'let me', not memory, Benji."

"Thanks, Jaylon," said Benji.

Benji felt something brush his arm, and he jerked around. One of Octavius' tentacles stretched out and grabbed hold of Benji's shoulder pulling the octopus towards them.

Wide-eyed and panicked, Benji blurted out, "Who's steering the ship?"

Octavius chuckled, "I am. Meena is. They are, Benji," he said as he looked back into the room of patrons.

"That's crazy," strained Benji. "We'll crash."

"That is not our intention," said Octavius solemnly.

"Intentions don't steer the ship," demanded Benji.

"You have a lot to learn, young Mystiq," instructed Octavius.

The glare from the bioluminescence outside the portholes faded. Light-blue morning water shone through the open window over Jaylon's shoulder. Jaylon turned his head to follow Benji's gaze.

"Honey! We're home," said Jaylon.

"We're there?" said Benji.

"Close," said Octavius. He lifted off Benji's shoulder and in a few quick bursts reached the stairs.

"Man, he's fast," said Benji.

Jaylon, Meena, and Benji followed quickly behind. Benji received a few nasty looks from the table full of water fairies when he passed. Montal eyed him the entire way back to the staircase. The last time Benji turned around, Montal shook his index and middle fingers in front of his own eyes and then pointed at Benji. Jaylon tapped Benji on the shoulder just before he ran into the wall.

As he ascended from the second tier of steps, Benji saw the captain's door wide open. Octavius floated against it with a tentacle on the knob. The last bit of purple faded from his tentacle as he camouflaged himself into the wood. Benji's eyes shifted slowly out the door. He could make out shapes of things he didn't think should be there. A vacant stare appeared on his face.

"Woah!" said Benji.

"Welcome to Sanjowqua, Benji," said Jaylon, Meena, and Octavius.

Kansifu Mohpango

(the fringe)

THE BIOLUMINESCENCE FINALLY petered out, overcome by the oncoming light of a new day. With each voyage, the ship's arrival and departure left its mark through the exoskeleton shell it fostered and left behind.

A gentle thud reverberated throughout the boat as it settled down on the sand and shifted slightly to the right.

Benji passed by Octavius, forgetting he was even there after the octopus blended into the door to give Benji an unobstructed first viewing. Benji had not slept the night before. The beauty of the surroundings obliterated a brewing yawn once he swam out the door.

The water in Sanjowqua was as pristine as any sunny day he had ever seen above water. If he didn't know any better, he could have sworn the fish swam in midair.

The sun had yet to peak its head above the eastern horizon, but its onward march was imminent from an oblong shadow cast down upon the white sand below.

"No way," said Benji as his head gravitated up toward the closest floating island on the starboard side.

An inverted mountain of white coral hung from the underside of the island and extended seventy-five feet to the ocean floor. Judging from the distance between the bottom of the coral and the sandy floor, there was at least five feet of nothing but water between the two; a gigantic hanging plant of an island quadruple the size of the ship below him.

Benji rubbed his eyes and looked again thinking he was looking at a mirage created by the light or the clear water. Anything reasonable or sensible did not seem to apply. Then, he looked down at his tail and decided rather assuredly that reasonable and sensible were now long gone.

Benji pushed himself up and over the bow with his fingertips. Curiosity propelled him through the water toward the gap between the island and the sand. The closer he approached, the more his mind raced.

That's not physically possible, Benji thought.

He settled down on the sand inches from the coral of the floating island. From a sheepish distance, he judged he could easily reach up and put his hands under the tip of the island and still touch the sand.

He snuck closer and stuck his hand underneath. He yanked it back quickly, expecting the island to come crashing down on his hand.

Nothing.

Next, with his arm extended straight, he ran his fingers through the open water looking for strings or… anything.

Nothing.

He lay flat on his back looking at the angles of the coral extending diagonally up toward the surface and kicked his tail furiously through the water out the other side.

More nothing.

Jaylon floated on the deck of the boat next to the plank he had extended off the side. He diverted the attention of several water fairies who hadn't noticed Benji. Meena halted over the bowsprit where the conch shell horn sat tied tight. All eyes curiously fixed on the strange actions of the newcomer.

Benji stretched his hands up to touch the coral and placed the end of his tail square on the ocean floor. He strained with closed eyes trying to move the white cone island. A few pieces of the coral broke off creating tiny puffs of white sand when they hit the bottom.

A sharp nick between the eyes brought him out of his obsession. He flipped his tail to the front and propelled himself backward a few feet.

"Atten-Shun!" shouted a little stern voice. ·

"Huh?" said Benji.

"Sleep swimming, huh?" said the pepper-filled voice.

"Excuse me?" said Benji

"Well, you wouldn't be crumbling my home if you were awake, would you?" said the voice.

"Uhhh. Of course not," said Benji.

Benji looked around but saw nothing.

"Keep your wits about you, son. You want to be careful out here around the Fringe islands."

"Islands?"

"Yes, I-S-L-A-N-D-S. Wha'cha on, pup?"

"Nothing. I'm just... How many are there?"

"Wha'cha mean? Been drinking rum with the Topsiders all night, have you?"

"Rum?"

"Wha'chew playing at?"

"I'm not playing anything."

Benji caught a flicker of red zip past his face. The little voice hemmed and hawed around either side of his head then stopped six inches from the bridge of his nose.

A faded-red squirrelfish bobbed and weaved between the center of each of Benji's eyes. He sat stationary long enough for Benji to get a glimpse of milky white eyes glazed over with age before the fish darted over in front of the other eye.

"Uh huh. Uh huh. Interesting," said the little red fish. "It's true."

"What's true?" said Benji.

"First of all, stop repeating everything I say."

"Sorry... I..."

"You're Yona Tukayu."

Benji looked at him with a blank face. "I'm Benji."

"Don't speak the old language, huh?"

"I've been gone a while."

"You *are* the missing Mystiq."

"That's what I've been told."

"Found you. Yes, sir. Celebrations in Cardy's honor tonight. Mark my words. Oh, yeah! 'Done it again, Cardy.' 'Another commendation for you, Colonel.' Yes, siree!"

The squirrelfish looked quite pleased with himself.

"We have to get you inside. It's going to be a big day for you and me, pup. What's it like up there, by the way?"

"I'm not sure where to begin."

"Hmmm. Well, I've heard enough stories from the Shequarien 'round here and seen enough of them bumbling back from the beaches after a night with them Topsiders that I got a pretty good idea. Bunch o' no-gooders if you ask me. Name's Cardy."

"I'm Benji. Nice to meet you, Cardy."

"Same here. Well, seeing as you're new, I'll cut you some slack, but keep your hands off my home, *and* the rest of the coral while you're at it. I ain't as tough as I used to be. Some of the others now... well, let's just say those fins of yours might be a little shorter if you had tried handling the coral elsewhere."

"Yes, sir." Benji looked off to his right. A series of floating islands extended and curved into the distance. "What did you call this place?"

"The Fringe. This is the oldest of the island chains in Sanjowqua. The older they get, the further they move out until they eventually dissolve to be reborn from Wuputa Wamkala."

"Who is Waputa Wamkala?"

"Not who, pup. Waputa Wamkala is the center of Sanjowqua. It's the giver of life. It's still a ways to go. Good days swim from here if you take the long way, but I know all the shortcuts like the back of my fin. Be there in an hour with a hero's welcome, you and me."

"Yo, Cardy. How's it, old man?" yelled Jaylon as he approached behind Benji.

"Who's that? Don't be old mannin' me. I still got some fight left in me, youngin'," said Cardy as he bounced from side to side peeking over Benji's shoulders.

"It's me, Jaylon."

"Don't be sneaking up on me, pup!"

"Card, we brought the boat. You should have heard that thing a mile away. I see your eyes are still holding strong though," said Jaylon smiling from ear to ear.

"Well. Well. Someone thinks they're funny. My eyes are good as new. Saw you coming from a mile away. Heard you even before that. Blasted whale tunes!"

"Yeah, yeah. Guess we need our best eyes and ears out here on the Fringe. And who better than Coronel Cardy?"

Cardy puffed up his jaws and wagged his tail fin. "Exactly right! Haven't seen you in a while. With your sense of direction and the amount you pay attention to the movements, I'm surprised you made it out from Waputa Wamkala. Doubt seriously you'll make it back in before you're my age."

Benji looked at the island behind Cardy and turned and saw the ship now twenty feet further away. In the time he had spent talking to Cardy, the island had indeed moved a considerable amount.

"That's what I got Meena for," said Jaylon.

Cardy looked over Jaylon's left shoulder then shuffled over to his right shoulder and back again.

"She's still onboard, Cardy."

Meena waved from the helm. Cardy looked ninety degrees off the bow of the ship.

"Ah, there she is. I'm just watching your back. In case......you know. You never know out here."

Jaylon looked at Benji with a 'sure you were' expression on his face. "New recruit, Cardy. Got to move him along."

Benji saw plans for a hero's welcome slowly dissipate from Cardy's face.

"Of course you are. I was in the middle of a serious interrogation before you came along. Teach this one some manners, huh?" Cardy said motioning toward Benji. "Caught him with his hands all over the coral. He'd have been court-martialled back in my days. Oh, how things are changin'."

"He's fresh in the water, Cardy. We spent half our time getting here dodging sharks."

"Donquarien scouts, no doubt."

"Not a one. They hooked him with a jambuku. He thought it was cute and fashioned a necklace with it."

"Ouch! You are green, pup. That's the oldest trick in the book," said Cardy shaking his head.

"Told you."

"Well, he's safe for the time being. If they had caught you…"

"I'd be a lot shorter right now. They came close with Benji, but Meena got us out of there with some quick thinking and smart moves."

"Wouldn't have expected either of those from you," said Cardy with a half-disgusted snort.

"Can't have it all," said Jaylon, flexing his biceps.

Cardy shot his clouded eyes up toward the surface and shook his head.

Meena swam up beside Jaylon. "Hi, Cardy."

"Hello, dear. We were just talking about you," said Cardy.

Jaylon looked at Cardy as if another fish had suddenly taken his place.

"Any news out here, Cardy?" said Meena.

"Most of the coral out here is dead, more or less disabling communications. Flying blind," said Cardy.

Jaylon snickered, and Cardy shot him a cloudy-eyed stare.

"I was able to pick up some surface level intel late last night from the few bits of coral still hanging on up there. Something about Gouguon. Too faint to make sense of it, though."

"He had his hand in the attack last night. I'd bet my tail on it," said Meena.

"That'd be a safe bet," said Cardy.

"We'd love to stay and chat, but we need to get him to the interior," said Meena.

"By all means. Hurry into the next circle. Coral's lively there. No chance of anything happening to you without a million eyes and ears as witness," said Cardy.

"Thanks, Card," said Jaylon and Meena.

Cardy grunted. "Don't be strangers. Get back 'round here to visit," he said, squinting his cloudy eyes at Benji.

"Sorry, Card. You know how forgetful us youngin's are," said Jaylon.

"Yeah, well in my day we respected our…"

Jaylon pulled Benji away from the island, and Cardy kept chattering up a storm.

Octavius swam up and grabbed onto Benji's shoulder startling him. Benji turned and noticed the ship had already lost its polished look. Thin shoots of green seaweed billowed from the bow like flags in the wind. Parts of the outer hull sported a rough texture from barnacles and coral sprouting off of it. A few of the water fairies bounced here and there around the boat. Multi-colored specks sparkled each time they hovered close to the deck.

A long stretch of white sand lay before Benji abruptly stopping at a large, dark wall that ran from the ocean floor to the surface a few hundred yards away.

Benji glanced back at Cardy's island. It was another twenty feet away from the last time he gauged it. A solitary red flash smeared streaks in the water looking for a bone to pick with the next intruder.

Meena and Jaylon flanked Benji, and Octavius motioned forward.

"Peculiar little guy," said Benji.

Jaylon gave a half chuckle. "Cardy? Yeah. He's good for a laugh and a little info from the Fringe sometimes. As you can see, he still keeps active and alert in his old age. All he's good for now is gossip, but with it being so barren out here there's not much to gossip about. Every once in awhile you get something good out of him, though. If you're ever bored and want to hear about 'the good ole days,' come back for a visit."

"It's lonely out on the Fringe. Death is more certain now," said Meena.

"So is rebirth," said Octavius. "Energy can be harnessed, directed, and even controlled, but it can not be destroyed. Even the act of destruction propagates it."

Benji nodded silently. "Cardy said the islands move."

"Yeah. They're always on the move. Eventually, they dissolve and are reborn inside the circle. Knowledge in motion. That's the Sanjowqua way," said Jaylon.

A spot on the sandy floor in front of them shifted. A flounder skirted off into the distance and disappeared again fifty feet away.

"What do you make of Gouguon's name popping up, Octavius?" asked Meena.

"He's still in Muyu Munda. Maybe he won a game of charades with the other inmates," said Jaylon.

"It's doubtful Aquari is chattering over a game of charades," said Octavius scornfully.

The dark wall Benji had seen from a distance began to show detail. It wasn't long before Benji realized it wasn't just a wall. A living, breathing tower of coral stood in their path. As they approached, he noticed a fifty-foot gap. Another island behind the clearing gave the appearance of it being solid from a distance.

They passed through and turned right. Benji's shoulders shuddered from a piece of fan coral brushing against his tail. The reef came alive. Bubbles shot up from the bottom to the top of the coral wall in successive gurgles like a stack of dominoes trickling after one another. The clicks and pops multiplied each couple of feet. Anemone tentacles waved, and tube worms fanned out from their capsules.

Jaylon looked back and saw the fan coral reaching toward Benji. "They're excited you're here. They're jabbering a million bubbles a minute."

Meena looked back, too. "Anyone who didn't know we're coming will surely know now. Remember what Cardy told you about the coral. Be more careful next time."

Benji eyed the two of them and then looked back at the reef wall they left behind. "What's going on?"

"The coral is talking. Once that happens, everyone knows what's going on pretty soon after. The coral is the communications system of the entire ocean. Anything happening in or around it is instantly known to all of us. We're all connected, Benji," said Octavius.

"Some more than others," Meena said nodding toward Benji.

"But I don't hear anything," said Benji.

"Your time will come. Your system is blocking a lot of things from your perception. Your senses are grabbing and holding onto everything they are familiar with and reapplying those things wherever they can. Keep an open mind, and your body will soon follow the lead.

"You asked at the boat why we wanted you now. The true answer to that question has more than one answer. Gouguon is one concern," said Octavius.

"He's a concern to everyone," said Meena.

"True, but he's a direct threat to Benji. Also, waiting any later decreased your chances of being able to assimilate down here and realize your true powers.

"Your father could manipulate water and other objects and even himself," said Octavius.

"I don't even understand how that last part would work," said Benji.

"Your mother exhibited her powers in helping others heal physical and mental problems that had either manifested through thought or action," said Octavius.

"That's deep," said Benji.

"Basically, she helped people. She freed them from the effects of their negative thinking and helped them heal. She also helped people with physical injuries in the case of a fishing accident, fight, or run in with a boat, or…"

"What am I supposed to be good at?" asked Benji.

"There are expectations from others in Aquari, Benji. Not from us. Our intention is to bring you here, so you begin to discover that for yourself.

"Some Mystiq pups inherit their father's skills. Some take on their mother's. Some neither. Some a little bit of both. Either way, you will discover yours in due time," said Octavius.

Two walls to their right and left met the next island in front of them boxing them into a horseshoe five hundred yards wide. Meena's directions had them headed straight to an apparent dead end.

"You sure you're going the right way?" asked Jaylon.

Meena shot back, "Would you rather lead?"

"Oh no. I can barely get out half the time. Getting back in is twice as difficult," said Jaylon.

"What's so difficult?" asked Benji.

"Like Cardy said, the islands move. Some of the islands have perpendicular appendages that form a maze when they line up with another island in front or behind them, kind of like the one we're headed toward.

"You need to know the positions and patterns of the islands as well as the time and date. Depending on all of that, you can get inside with no problem. Otherwise, it would take you... well, let's just say I got lost once," admitted Jaylon.

"Why not just learn?" said Benji.

"Why not just learn?" said Jaylon in a mocking voice. "That's what Meena and Octavius are here for. Plus, numbers aren't my strong suit."

"Wouldn't it be like reading a map?" asked Benji.

"Sure. Why didn't I think of it like that? That would be so much easier. A map with four hundred and ninety-six islands, in nine concentric circles, with each circle moving in the opposite direction to the previous one. Thanks, Benji," said Jaylon as he smacked himself in the forehead. "I've seen the light."

"There are two hundred and forty-eight islands in the outer ring?" said Benji astonished.

"Show off," said Jaylon.

"Precisely, Benji. Sanjowqua is an archipelago. Waputa Wamkala is in the middle. There are two islands on the next ring, four on the next, eight, sixteen, thirty-one, sixty-two, one twenty-four, then two forty-eight," said Octavius impressed.

"A new ring emerges every eight years. The year before, Waputa Wamkala reverses its rotation creating the frictional energy to yield a new ring that will continue the harmony once it rises the following year. The year of Waputa Wamkala's reversed rotation causes quite a stir in Sanjowqua," said Jaylon.

"I can imagine it would mess with your sense of direction," said Benji.

"Finally, someone's got my back!" said Jaylon.

Meena stuck her tongue out at Jaylon.

Benji glanced at Meena with a shocked look plastered across his face. It was the first time he had seen her be playful.

"Leaving makes me nervous. And this time we got a little more than we bargained for," said Meena catching the look on Benji's face.

"Sorry," said Benji.

"Don't be. Would have been boring otherwise," said Jaylon.

As they approached, a hole opened up as the islands drifted apart, and the coral in front of them began bubbling. This time it started on the opposite side, obscuring the crisscrossing shapes moving toward Benji.

"Meena, stop where you are," called Octavius.

"Well, well, well. Look who it is. He's finally back, and in safe hands I see," said Gouguon with a wide-brimmed smile emerging from the mist of bubbles.

Gouguon's large square head slid around the corner followed by broad shoulders twice as wide as Jaylon's. His razor-sharp black hair looked more like a tight fitting helmet angled at the contours of his head. He had thin black eyes and a sharp bridge of a nose with nostrils that flared with each breath. His tail started just under his chest. A sharp gray fin emerged from the middle of his back. Light, black, vertical stripes ran from the side of his chest all the way down to his tail fin. His tail swept slowly from side to side with strength and purpose. A pair of black-tip reef sharks slipped through the water on either side of him.

He's huge, thought Benji.

"Yes, yes. Well, evolution has been more generous to some of us," said Gouguon with an air of self-appointed dignity. "Much more generous than some our own kind."

"You chose your fate, Gouguon," nodded Octavius.

"Bygones. I shouldn't have mentioned it. Now, is this the Mystiq I've heard so much about? Where's his jambuku?"

"You..." said Octavius.

"Rumor has it. I presumed it was sent as a precaution to keep him safe. Don't think you are the only ones who knew about his location, O' wise one," said Gouguon.

Octavius applied gentle pressure to Benji's shoulder. *Benji, guard your thoughts and clear your mind.*

Benji took a breath and closed his eyes to mere slits in his face. He recited to himself: *Clear my mind. Clear my mind. My mind is clear. Mind is clear.*

Benji opened his eyes. Gouguon floated in front of him. Benji stared at his head and thought, *Man, he's got a big head.*

Gouguon grimaced and ran his hand through his mane.

Benji shook his head. *Oops! Mind not clear. Clear my mind. Clear my mind.*

Meena blurted out, "If the Donquarien had known for sure, you would have acted sooner."

"Don't be silly, Meena. We are all concerned about the pup's well-being. Not only for himself but for all of Sanjowqua," said Gouguon.

"You don't care anything for Sanjowqua!" spouted Meena.

"Au contraire. Our cultural hub? The birthplace of the Earth's pride and joy? The mother and father of the devolved species of Topsiders who now destroy our homeland? Not care? Meena, dear, I think you have me mistaken for someone else," said Gouguon.

"Your interest doesn't lie in Sanjowqua," said Meena.

Gouguon glared at her. "My interest, young pup, lies in the continuation of Aquarien glory which, if you haven't noticed, is clearly on the downswing."

"What are you doing out, Gouguon?" said Octavius.

"Stretching my fins," he said with a cocky smirk.

"You're not due out for another year," snapped Jaylon.

"The brawn of the bunch counts. How admirable," said Gouguon.

Jaylon clinched his fists. Gouguon eyed Jaylon's hands briefly and shook his head as a clear warning.

"My time has been deemed served. Do you not agree? Thirteen years for tracking down a deserter and his cohorts? Is that just?" said Gouguon.

"You served thirteen years for the deaths of countless Aquarien!" said Meena, her teeth grinding against each other.

"Seven is not countless, and I was protecting the glory of Aquari. Now the Mystiq prong is gone, and well, just take a look at the Fringe, and I think you'll agree my efforts were warranted," said Gouguon.

"A group of your peers thought otherwise," said Octavius.

"I never accepted those charges," said Gouguon. "It was in the best interest of Aquari that some form of closure happen quickly. I took it upon myself to absorb the loss of my peers so all of Aquari could grieve and move on with their precious lives."

Meena huffed and crossed her arms. "That is the biggest load of whale…"

"Meena!" cautioned Octavius. "Surely you didn't come here as a welcoming party, Gouguon."

"Surely, you are right. Merely consequential. However, it's nice to see old friends," said Gouguon as he nodded at Octavius. "It feels almost like a family reunion. Albeit, a much smaller one."

"Benji. It is Benji, correct?" said Gouguon.

Benji nodded.

"Your presence in Aquari changes things… for the better, of course. The Mystiq line is not lost. This is good news," said Gouguon.

Jaylon and Meena eyed each other.

"You've no doubt been briefed on what happened to your parents," said Gouguon.

"I was told they were hunted down and murdered," said Benji.

"Yes. Very unfortunate. It's important you choose wisely which side you align yourself with going forward. There are some divisions in Aquari concerning our… treatment of the Topsiders. As I said, your safety is everyone's main concern right now, and we don't want any rash decisions to destroy the future of the Mystiq line," said Gouguon.

"What are you getting at Gouguon? We're on our way in," said Meena.

"You've obviously had your time to fill his head with your theories. He'd be swimming by my side staring at you with the same distaste in his brow if the tables had been turned," said Gouguon.

"No chance," said Meena.

Gouguon didn't pay her any attention. "The Topsiders encroach on our habitat daily. Their disregard for our home is not to be tolerated. You all know it, but for some reason, you encourage a peaceful solution, you encourage our kind to roll over and dismiss the fact that their pollution is our problem."

"It is our problem," said Jaylon.

"Duly noted. But should it be?" quipped Gouguon.

"Peaceful solutions are being considered," said Octavius calmly.

"Consideration has cost us too much already. The Mystiqs are all but dead, meaning the representation we have with the Topsiders is gone. You'll send this pup? He'll end up in an aquarium," said Gouguon.

"And who's fault is that?" said Meena.

"I see my words fall on deaf ears. Now, I believe we both have homecomings to attend." Gouguon nodded his head. The two reef sharks flanked him, and they swam off toward the Fringe.

Benji watched as they glided through the open water. He felt strange. The Donquarien he had been told murdered his mother and father faded into the distance. Very little emotion stirred inside of him. Whatever happened to him as a child led him to Beech Mill and Joe Fisher was his dad, as far as Benji was concerned.

Meena and Jaylon stared at Octavius in disbelief.

Jaylon's mouth hung half open. "How did he get out?"

Octavius glanced at them and extended a tentacle forward. "We'll find out soon enough."

Kenyabi Kolikra Makawindi

(homecoming)

A MILE OF white sand separated the second set of islands from the next. Despite the clarity of the water, the following chain of islands appeared as a shadow in the background.

Benji slowed his progression and looked back over his shoulder. The backside of the second set of islands was more prosperous than the ones out on the Fringe. Multi-colored streaks darted in and out of the greenish-brown rocks. Clusters of fan coral swayed, large bony hands waving goodbye in the current.

As Benji back turned around, he noticed Meena, Octavius, and Jaylon further ahead and swiped his tail hard to catch up.

"…and that's what you have to look forward to when we get back. Hopefully, you're not shy, Benji," said Jaylon as he turned around and saw Benji scuttling up behind the three of them.

"Uh, yeah. Well, a little. I'll be fine, though. I've made it this far, right?" said Benji.

A school of yellow jacks came swirling toward them like a flickering, silver tornado. The whirlwind of fish kicked up loose sand from the bottom then shot toward the gap in the islands Benji left behind. A pod of dolphins followed the bait ball, crisscrossing over and under each other in hot pursuit.

"That's the Mystiq," said one of them.

"Well, he's not going anywhere, is he? Tighten up! I'm starving," said another dolphin.

Sand eels popped their heads from their holes. One of the eels spotted the Shequarien headed his way and zipped into his hole. Dozens of others quickly followed behind.

A clumsy sea turtle bobbed up and down near the surface. When Jaylon got a few yards behind him, the loggerhead pushed both of his flippers toward his shell and shot down into their path.

"Speed delivery. Coming through," hollered Jaylon.

"Little help," choked the turtle.

The shellback careened his head up and to either side. Meena swam up behind him and grabbed both sides of his shell.

"Whoa!" hollered the turtle in surprise.

"Gotcha," said Meena. She slid from behind the turtle and popped up over his back.

"Meena?"

"Hey, Chelli. What'd you get yourself into this time?"

"I dozed off and woke up with this new necklace. Cardy couldn't do anything with it."

"Well, that won't do. Close your eyes," said Meena as she slid the plastic six-pack ring off his neck.

Benji looked at the trash in disgust and embarrassment while Meena reached around her back and stuffed the plastic into her pouch.

"Where you headed, Chelli?" said Meena.

"Big party tonight! Cardy said he found the Mystiq and sent him along with Jaylon and... you!"

Chelli flapped his right flipper hard and swung about face in front of Benji.

"Where is it?" demanded the turtle.

"Nice to meet you, too," said Jaylon with a sarcastic smile.

Chelli cut Jaylon a sharp stare.

"You didn't find it, did you?" said the weathered turtle, shaking his head at Octavius. "Bit of a wasted trip for this young one wasn't it, Octavius?"

Benji looked at Meena and Jaylon for a hint of what the turtle was talking about.

"Retrieving the Mystiq unharmed was the priority," said Octavius.

"And now Gouguon's out," said Chelli.

"We've seen. How…?" said Meena.

"Mumkaza called for an impromptu parole review. With Octavius absent, the vote swayed in his favor," said Chelli.

"What's his name?" said Chelli, gesturing toward Benji.

"I'm Benji."

"Talking are we? Well, at least you've got that far. You got big fins to fill, pup. I knew your parents. They were never too busy to help out an old shellback. Same as these two," said Chelli, nodding toward Jaylon and Meena.

"How long did you know them?" asked Benji

Chelli grunted. "Knew their parents, too. Been around a while. Good Aquarien they were, but plenty of time for details later. Now it's time to celebrate, or start praying now I've seen what we're dealing with."

"Let's get you inside," said Jaylon as he grabbed Chelli.

The turtle tucked his flippers in as they soared through the water toward the next set of islands.

"How'd you make it out in front of us, Chelli?" said Meena.

"Tubes. There are still a few even you don't know about, my dear," said Chelli with a wink.

Black tip reef sharks hovered along the perimeter of the next set of islands. Big, blue lobsters with three-foot antennae scaled the rocks of the reef. They scurried into crevices once their antennae picked up the vibrations in the water of the approaching party.

The third set of islands sloped more gently into the water, unlike the vertical wall of the second set of islands and the diagonal, deteriorating slopes of the Fringe.

On the approach, Jaylon moved in front. Benji followed his lead. Meena and Octavius brought up the rear.

"Watch it… Watch it… HEY!!!" Chelli pushed both flippers down and shot up from under Jaylon seconds before Jaylon nearly smacked him into a rock jutting out from the bottom.

"I got it from here, thank you very little," said Chelli shaking his head at Jaylon. "I've made it a hundred and fifty years on my own. If I ever want to break that streak, I'll make sure I let you know!"

Chelli's tail was a few feet from Benji's face. Benji poked his head up over the turtle's shell and saw Jaylon's tail fin disappear with a silver flash inside a dark cave carved in the reef wall. Benji slowed and watched Chelli wobble in and zip away with the same head-spinning velocity.

That turtle's a lot faster than he looks, thought Benji.

"Tubes," said Meena with a chuckle.

"Huh?" said Benji.

"Slip inside and keep your arms and hands close to your body," said Meena.

"And?" said Benji.

"Enjoy the ride," said Meena.

Benji stuck his hand on the outer rim of the cave and poked his head inside. A massive suction pulled at his hair. He looked up and saw his bangs laid out horizontally in the water. He felt a sharp pinch on the index finger clinging to the coral wall. An angry warning followed, "Hands off!"

Benji jerked his head out of the cave. He yanked his hands off the coral and peered up at a blue lobster. She had her pincers folded in front of her shaking her eyes back and forth.

"You're going to end up minus a digit before the day is over," said Meena from behind him.

"And yours don't grow back," said Octavius as he waved several tentacles in the water.

A huge gush of water lifted Benji up, curled his back, and dropped his chin to his chest barreling him into the cave. The last thing he saw was Meena fanning her tail towards him and slapping a hand against one of Octavius' tentacles.

Benji knew he yelled, but he moved so fast he disappeared down the tube before he saw a single bubble wobble out of his mouth.

He banked left then right, up then down. The last thing Meena said,

"Enjoy the ride," echoed in his head. He tried keeping his hands by his side as she instructed, but hearing it and doing it were two completely different things. Benji spun, dipped, bucked, and slid at twice the speed of thought.

He hit a sharp bank to the left, and his entire body slammed into the tube. Water's persistence made the walls smooth as glass. The next collision threw him back into the right side and then sent him head over tail until a dip clocked him in the chin and popped his arms out. He used his hands to steady himself and suddenly realized he was going tail first face down. He tucked his hands close to his body and rolled over into what he thought was an upright position.

A straight section of the tube tricked him into believing he could slow the speed with his hands to flip over and proceed face forward again. He slowed himself enough to begin to lean forward when he heard, "Woo Hoo," followed by a "WOO!!"

Meena and Octavius swiped him from below and shot past him mumbling something about first-timers.

A dim glow poked out from the end. Benji squinted his eyes, took a deep breath, and threw his hands over his head. The last turn twisted him onto his belly, and he shot through the opposite end of the tube with his arms and hands bringing up the rear.

A webbed hand on either side of the exit snatched his arms. His momentum slowed from several fin kicks in the direction he exited. Wavy ripples of white sand stared him in the face until his arms were yanked back toward the tube and he twirled upright.

Benji blew out an exhausted breath, his lips vibrating together. Bubbles swirled around his head and mosied their way up to the surface. He shook his head, and a few stray bubbles disentangled from his hair and joined their friends.

"That was pretty sloppy," said Meena. "What'd I tell you about…"

"About my hands? Right before you shoved me in?" said Benji.

"You'll have plenty more chances to practice your form," said Jaylon.

"I'll take the long way the next time," said Benji.

Movement over Jaylon's shoulder caught Benji's attention. Jaylon's bulbous chin and crooked smile fell out of focus.

A five-foot wall of coral spanned out in both directions behind Jaylon. The entire scene breathed; bubbles from coral danced lazily upward. Hundreds of floating island bungalows hovered near the surface. Shadows swam under the bungalows behind one side of Jaylon's head and emerged in the sunlight as twinkling tails and flowing hair on the other.

Benji's hips undulated several times pushing him a full length above his companions. The wall of coral formed a circle half hidden by a massive island temple jutting down from the surface. Eight more embankments lay below the first circle of coral. A large stepped terrace of at least a hundred feet of sand separated each of them.

A hundred feet down, the center of the inverted temple stabbed the sand, a giant coral dagger a hundred feet wide. Two eight-foot seahorses guarded a large opening at the bottom.

Between the final wall and the temple, large mounds of coral dotted the white sand foundation. Ten-foot stands of glowing pink brain coral, purple and orange acan, green artichoke coral, blue bird's nest coral, and yellow and brown sun coral formed statues of mermaids and other sea creatures.

In front of the main temple, off to the left and right, two smaller shoots of the island hung halfway to the bottom. Benji drifted off to the left, carried by a small current circling throughout the enclosure. Two identical hanging islands hung further back behind each of the ones in front forming four towers surrounding the main temple. The entire formation looked like a hand with monstrous craggy fingers stretching toward the bottom.

Looking up, he stared at hundreds of floating bungalows. A coral sphere hung ten to fifteen feet into the water from each of them. Tails waved from several of the doorway-sized holes in the homes.

Shequarien boys and girls breached the surface, some of them on their own power, others clutched dolphin fins as they whizzed through the water. Many of their faces had ear to ear grins plastered across them.

In open space in front of him, Benji caught sight of two Shequariens racing toward the surface. One of them held the fin of a dolphin gliding diagonally from the bottom. The other one raced vertically with both her arms extended; her jet black hair formed a cape down her back. Just before reaching the surface, the Sherquarien on the dolphin clasped the hand of the girl coming straight off the bottom. At the last second, the Shequarien on the dolphin swung his arm, and the girl went flying clear out of the water. Seconds later, the flying mermaid came splashing back down. She sliced a bubbly wedge in the water upon her re-entry. Whitewater cascaded down her body.

I gotta try that, thought Benji as he shook his head in amazement.

A group of Shequarien fishermen came struggling through a gap in the first ring of Sanjowqua. A large sagging net of squirming fish dangled between two large poles. Three supported the front half of each pole and three on the backside. One of them glanced over, then broke off from the back of the pole. The shift in weight caused the others to grunt. Several fish slipped out of the net. Chelli had wobbled up behind the net and snatched one of the fleeting fish as soon as it tasted freedom.

"Missed a good hunt, Jaylon," said the fisherman.

"So did you, except we were the bait," said Jaylon.

"Looks like we were both successful," said the fisherman with a cocky smile. "This him?"

"Yep. Fins and all," nodded Jaylon.

"Already figured out how to suit up, huh?" said the fisherman.

"Did it without even realizing it," said Jaylon shaking his head.

"First one was pink," jabbed Meena.

Benji blushed.

"Welcome to Sanjawqua, Benji. Name's Tan. Hope you like tuna," he said gesturing toward the sagging net making its way through the interior of Sanjowqua.

Benji's stomach rumbled for the first time since his departure from Beech Mill; its echo carried in the water.

"Someone's ready to eat now," said Jaylon grinning at Benji.

"What's on the menu?" said Benji.

"Those," said Tan, pointing back at the net, "and some of the freshest fruits and vegetables ever tasted. You'll have a fantastic meal, guaranteed."

A few more struggling grunts came from the party toting the sagging net behind Tan.

"Alright! Alright! I'm coming you light-weights." Tan turned back and nodded. "We'll see what you think in a few hours, Benji."

Chelli was still nipping at the net and had pried a second fish out by the time Tan reached his vacated end of the pole.

"Easy old man," said Tan. "Save some for dinner."

"You pups eat too late, and I'm hungry now, so fin off," said Chelli.

Benji watched as they disappeared with the net behind the central tower.

"What's the occasion?" asked Benji.

"You! Don't get a big head, though. We roll out the red coral for all new Aquarien. You *are* the first in... well, I can't remember," said Jaylon.

"Eight years," shot Meena.

"Yeah. Well, however long it's been, everyone's excited about a welcoming party," said Jaylon.

"Meena!"

A shout echoed through Benji's head followed by a black and silver blur that zoomed in from the distance and slammed into Meena sending her tumbling a few feet. All Benji could see at first was a huge tangle of black hair and mangled arms. Benji looked at Jaylon for a clue when a small hand appeared from behind Jaylon's back and tapped his right shoulder. A shy face popped up behind the other. Jaylon looked right and then left.

"Hey, pup!" Jaylon wedged a little blonde head between his forearm and his bicep and massaged it with his knuckles.

"Ow, Jay!"

"You snuck up on *me*," said Jaylon.

"Benji, this is my brother, Yuri. That blur you just witnessed..."

A cloud of black hair obscured Benji's vision, and two black eyes popped up in front of his causing him to back up and run into the coral behind him.

"Stay off!" shouted an electric eel.

An electric current shot through Benji's back and up his head, sending his hair straight out in every conceivable direction.

"...is Meena's sister, Lin," finished Jaylon.

Lin gritted her teeth. Lips parted and face tight, she covered her mouth with one hand, "Oops."

Benji's eyes flickered as he wobbled in the water, and Lin grabbed one of his arms, pulling him off the coral. She yanked it back quickly after being buzzed from the current still running through him.

Lin studied Benji's face, then backed up to get a better look. "So, what do you think?"

Benji lost his tongue and scampered for words. "I liked that maneuver you just pulled out there."

"Not that, but thanks. What do you think about being back?" said Lin.

"I don't ever remember being here, but for the first time... I... I...,"

"Give him some breathing room, Lin," said Jaylon. "Imagine what it'd be like to be thrown Topside without any warning."

Lin looked him up and down. "I thought he already met with Octavius."

"And then we had to rescue him from a party of Donquarien sharks," said Jaylon.

Lin backed off still studying Benji then looked over at Yuri. Yuri had come from behind his brother's back and floated in front of Jaylon. The top of Yuri's head just reached Jaylon's chin. Lin bobbed her head a few times then grabbed Benji's arm above the wrist and took off down the stepped terraces toward the bottom.

"Come on, Yuri," demanded Lin.

Benji flailed in the water behind her, and Yuri swam up next to him headed down to where the central tower met the sand.

"Did you see Gouguon? You must have. I heard he went out the way you and my brother came in. He's big isn't he?" said Yuri.

"Yuri!" snapped Lin.

Yuri shrugged his shoulders at Benji.

Lin led Benji down to the bottom terrace between a coral statue of a Shequarien man with a spear and another with a net formed by brown fan coral. Lin swam out in front of Benji a few feet, looked out toward the east and tilted her head up toward the surface cupping her hands around her mouth.

Yuri raised his brow up and down with excitement and grinned ear to ear. "Darmik is one of the fastest."

Benji looked lost then turned his head toward Lin and the sound of a long wail followed by two short clicks and another short wail that echoed from her hands.

A dolphin breached the surface in the direction Lin wailed then dove back into the water. The same Shequarien who tossed Lin through the surface moments before hitched onto Darmik's dorsal fin, and they both soared to the bottom fifty yards away.

Lin turned toward Benji with a wicked smile on her face and grabbed both his hands, raising them above his head. "Keep them above your head. Swim as fast as you can. You won't outswim Darmik. Try and time it so you meet him ten feet from the surface. Follow his pace, and you'll meet up. As soon as you grab hold, sweep your other hand by your side, and get ready to soar."

Benji shook his head and took a deep breath as he tried to remember everything she rattled off.

"Best do what she says, or she'll be pestering you all night. Mess up, and she'll be teasing you all night. Either way, she's going to be on your case all night," said Yuri.

Lin pulled Benji's arms forward, moved out of the way, and gave him a nudge in the back. Benji drifted forward and caught sight of the large dolphin coming off the bottom diagonally toward the surface.

Benji took a breath and swiped his tail. Sand stirred and shot up in a cloud covering Lin and Yuri. The first couple of whips of his tail were slow and full motion. The more speed he picked up, the faster his tail moved, and his strokes became more powerful until he was sprinting toward the surface.

The dolphin's eyes got bigger when he realized Benji was outpacing him. Not to be outdone, Darmik picked up speed and darted through the water.

Yuri and Lin moved up a few feet to escape the cloud of sand Benji stirred up.

"He's fast," said Yuri with an open mouth. A bluestreak cleaner wrasse slipped inside and tickled his cheek. Yuri giggled, and Lin elbowed him in the ribs.

Benji swiped as hard as he could with his hands extended upward.

Darmik's face strained as he tried to outpace Benji. Lines formed around the dolphin's mouth and clenched his jaws. When he realized he wasn't going fast enough, Darmik gave a swift buck, and the Shequarien holding onto him flew off tumbling behind. With the extra baggage gone, Darmik matched Benji's speed within a few strides and moved slightly ahead of him in time to rendezvous at the top.

They met five feet from the surface. Benji's fingertips brushed the underside of the dolphin, and his hand slid around his tail. Darmik flipped over and threw his tail toward the surface at the same time Benji dropped his other arm to his side, giving him an extra burst of speed. He broke through the water with his eyes closed and his nose pointed toward the sky. Benji felt his tail leave the water and a sheet of water wash off his body.

When he opened his eyes, he was sailing through the air. The last swipe of his hand had been a little off center, and he twisted around like a corkscrew with a three hundred and sixty-degree view of the world above Sanjowqua. The light blue water went on as far as he could see to the east and west. The water got darker off to the south. At the apex of his cata-pult, Sanjowqua sat sunken thirty feet below him.

He stalled in the air and noticed the coconut trees on the beach of the main island ten feet below him. He had cleared them with ease. Behind the coconut trees, through palm trees and dense tropical bushes stood a volcano in the middle of Waputa Wamkala. A thin wisp of smoke slipped out of the mouth and disappeared into the afternoon sky.

Benji's eyes took in more than he thought was capable for the brief time he flew out of the water. When gravity finally took hold, he threw his hands above his head and bent at the waist. He thrust his tail up in the air and plunged back down.

Darmik's approving nods to him were the last thing he saw before he splashed back in. His re-entry caused a clatter of noise around him. Darmik flipped his tail over his head and slipped down into the water beside Benji.

"Whoa," said Benji.

"Whoa is right," said Darmik. "You got speed, pup."

"Thanks," said Benji.

"Lin's a tough one. You just passed her test with flying colors. I won't tell her how high you went. Best you don't either, unless you're looking to show her up on the first day," said Darmik with a nod.

Yuri swam up with his eyes wide. "You must have cleared the treetops!"

Benji shrugged his shoulders. "It all happened so fast. I'm not sure how high I was. I had a nice view though."

"I don't know if Lin's ever been that high and…"

Lin tugged Yuri's tail, and the chattering Shequarien dropped a few feet. Benji watched Yuri sink and then caught Lin's eyes. Her face was tight with a tinge of jealousy; her eyes wide from astonishment or fury. Benji couldn't tell.

A low wail echoed from the ocean floor. Benji's eyes followed the sound to the opening of the main temple doors below.

Lin held her gaze on Benji for a few seconds then glanced down as well.

The statuesque pair of seahorses guarding the door came alive. Their long snouts shook in the water from each echoing blast they tooted out.

Benji looked down and saw Meena and Jaylon hovering on the second terrace surrounded by two coral statues. One depicted a Shequarien female from the waist up slashing through the surface of the water, her head thrown back, hair splayed above her, and arms stretched out to her sides. The other was a Shequarien male in the same posture. Thirty feet separated the two statues. Meena and Jaylon floated between them. Meena had her arms folded in front of her, and Jaylon bobbed his head from side to side. From what Benji already knew about him, he thought Jaylon was probably humming a tune and jiving along.

Tails started flickering in the doorways of the floating island bungalows. The tails withdrew inside followed by heads of swirling hair that poked out in return. Shiny streaks of silver, green, purple, and blue came swishing from the surface, from the bottom, and from holes in the temple. Some of the Shequarien raced in small groups; others mosied toward the center at their own accord.

The seahorses shot out another series of short blasts and moved to the side. A large shadow crept from inside the double doors, a powerful darkness contrasted on the white sand. Octavius scuttled through the doors then spread his tentacles wide making him look much larger than he was.

The octopus brought his tentacles back underneath him, propelling him up a few feet in the water.

A hush fell over the crowd of Sanjowqua. Benji's wide eyes betrayed his amazement.

Octavius looked up at Benji and slowly scanned the crowd of eyes.

"Yesterday we had the pleasure of welcoming back one of our own to Aquari. Today we welcome him home to Sanjowqua."

The entire semi-circle of Shequariens floated silently facing Octavius. All eyes fell on Benji. Yuri and Lin inadvertently drifted away from him. One by one, the onlookers balled a fist and smacked it with the open palm of the other hand creating a gentle roar of claps.

Over the roar of the clapping, they chanted, "Olindawa Mystiq. Olindawa makbole Aquarien." *Welcome Mystiq. Welcome brother Aquarien.* "Olindawa Mystiq. Olindawa makbole Aquarien."

"Benji, come down," said Octavius waving a tentacle toward him.

Benji looked down and then at Lin and Yuri. Lin thrust her chin forward to say, *hurry up.* Benji's hands trembled. He bent over and began the journey toward the bottom. Octavius swept his tentacles back and forth propelling him upwards to meet Benji halfway.

A mumble of voices swam inside Benji's head like a swarm of bumblebees. Sentences crawled over each other, so he could only make out a word or two before another voice interrupted it and drowned the others out:

"…short…," buzz.

"…he's cute…," bizzz.

"…fast…," buzz buzz.

"…almost beat Darmik…," bizzy.

"…father's presence…," bizz.

"…skinny…," bzzzzzz.

"…Topsider…," bzzzzz buzz.

Octavius' voice overrode all the other sounds buzzing around in Benji's mind. "Keep your attention on my thoughts. It's a lot to handle."

"Yeah, it is. Thanks," said Benji, ready to shake his head furiously and claw at his ears to get the noise out of his head.

Octavius floated at head height with Benji, one tentacle extended out to rest on his shoulder, another raised to shush the crowd.

"The Mystiq line is alive and well. Peace between the four oceans and the Topsiders lies ahead. I trust that all of you will give Benji a good Sanjowqua welcome and help teach him our ways, as well as be open to learning from him the ways of the Topsiders. He is one of ours, and his youth has been sacrificed to help us all understand one another."

The clapping died down, and the muttering picked up again. *Bzzzzz. Buzz. Bizzy. Buzzzz.*

A second set of blasts from the seahorses stationed beside the door rattled Benji's nerves, followed by another shadow that slowly began to emerge from the doorway. This one was much larger than the oblong blob Octavius had cast. The darkness crept out of the temple and wove its eery way out over the sand where Meena and Jaylon floated between the two statues. The tail end of the shadow tapered until it met with the looming figure of a Shequarien female carrying a staff as tall as she was. She used the gnarled and knobby staff to pull herself through the water. Each time she settled it down little tufts of sand exploded around the base.

Another hush fell over the crowd, and she raised both arms in the water, the staff extended out toward the onlookers.

"This is a special night for all of us. Aquari welcomes *two* brothers back," she said.

"Who's that?" asked Benji.

"Mumkaza," said Octavius.

The crowd jittered restlessly.

"Both have returned from confinement related to the Topsiders. Benji's knowledge of the world above will help us make clear decisions on how to move forward. Gouguon's presence in Donquari will help us strengthen the Aquarien family across the oceans," said Mumkaza.

Octavius glanced down at Jaylon and Meena shaking his head.

"Let us surface and show our hospitality," said Mumkaza as she raised her arms and gestured upward.

The seahorses behind her sounded their tubular noses, and the crowd elevated with each blast until they all breached the surface.

Meena and Jaylon came up beside Benji looking bewildered. Yuri popped up beside his brother, his head disappearing as quickly as it surfaced. Lin popped up beside the ripple of water Yuri left behind.

"That was an interesting little intro," said Meena.

"Yeah, what was that about bringing Gouguon back?" said Jaylon.

"Mumkaza obviously thinks Benji's return puts too much emphasis on a relationship with the Topsiders. Releasing Gouguon sends a clear signal to the rest of Sanjowqua and me that the interests of Aquari come first." Octavius turned to Benji. "You must show her that your time Topside does not influence your actions against Aquari. You four stay here with Benji. I'm going for a swim."

Benji stuck his head in the water watching Octavius grow smaller as he headed down to meet Mumkaza.

"Who is she?" asked Benji.

"Mumkaza's head of the security council of Sanjowqua," said Meena.

Benji didn't have any other time to process stray thoughts. A crowd of mermaids and mermen made their way through the maze of floating islands toward him. Benji greeted them with the handshake Melvin had taught him. He smiled and nodded vigorously at each before Jaylon or Meena moved them along.

As the line of well-wishers thinned out, a hefty smell of charcoal meandered up Benji's nostrils. The aroma pulled his head toward a floating barbeque pit fashioned together with oil drum pontoons. In the center, floated a six-foot-wide giant clam shell stuffed with flickering nuggets of burning wood. Some of the fish from Tan's hunting expedition hung on a makeshift rotisserie. Other pieces had been filleted and pinned to wooden boards and stacked side by side along the edge of the clamshell to smoke. The scent of fresh rosemary and lemon drifted lazily throughout the enclosure of the first ring of islands.

A merman swam by with a tray full of fresh mangoes, oranges, star fruit, bananas, pineapples, and papayas. Jaylon pulled off a handful of fruit and tossed a piece of pineapple up into the air as he cocked his head back. Meena snatched it away before it entered his mouth and popped it in her own. Jaylon bit his lip and threw the rest of the fruit at her. Meena caught one piece in her mouth and one in the eye. The two of them raced away horsing around with each other in the water.

Another tray came by carried by a mermaid with orange hair. She stopped in front of Benji and gave him a flirty smile. "Hi."

Her skin was slightly bluer than most of the other Shequarien whose shades trended gray. A white dot on each cheek made her look as though she might have strings attached to her arms.

Benji bowed his head nervously. "Uh, hi."

"Coconut?" she said.

"Yes, please," said Yuri as he swiped three off the tray. "Thanks, Peca."

"Thanks," said Benji looking at the cute mermaid.

"See you later," she said swimming off with a twinkle in her eye.

"I hope you're better with your Mystiq powers than you are with your conversation skills," said Lin.

"Me, too," said Benji.

"What do you mean?" said Lin.

Benji looked at her confused.

"You're the Mystiq. You're supposed to be able to heal, manipulate and move things. I mean, I don't know what else your kind is supposed to be able to do. What *can* you do?" said Lin.

"I'm not sure," said Benji.

Yuri had his coconut turned up spilling the sweet milk mostly in his mouth, partly on his chin. With Benji's words, Yuri sprayed out what he had managed to get in his mouth.

Lin turned and stared Yuri down as she wiped the spray off her shoulder.

Wide-eyed and confused, Yuri stared at Benji completely oblivious to the gift he left on Lin's shoulder. "What? You don't know what you can do? Gouguon's out, and he's going to be going full steam for the Mystiq prong, wherever that is, and you don't know what you can do?"

"Octavius told me it wasn't a big deal," said Benji.

"Was that before or after he lost his mind?" asked Yuri.

Lin floated in the water staring at him with a stone cold look on her face. She lifted her coconut up to her mouth and sipped slowly from the bamboo straw hanging lazily out of the top.

Benji looked at the two of them not quite sure what to say. Without another thought, he put his coconut down. The round shell bobbed on the surface twice then turned over. Yuri and Lin's eyes followed his every move. Benji lifted both his hands, closed his eyes, and took a deep breath.

He snapped his fingers, and a dollop of water jumped out of the ocean in front of his chest. Lin and Yuri followed the blob up twelve inches and then back down, their eyes transfixed on the spot where the ocean swallowed the drop upon its return. Neither of them said a word. Benji watched the excitement they held of his arrival drain out of their face along with all the color.

Lin raised her eyebrows, and her head slowly followed. She made eye contact with Benji and opened her mouth. Whatever words she had prepared failed to materialize on her tongue. She just stared at him bewildered.

"Benji! Benji! Benji!" cried an overly anxious voice.

He turned his head and met the eyes of Mumkaza. Two Shequarien on either side of her supported a basket chair that she lounged in. She extended one hand toward him. Most of the mermaids Benji had seen so far had long flowing hair. Mumkaza had a head full of purplish-black hair but wore it two inches long on all sides. Her dark mane of bristly hair held the same shape wet or dry. Her eyes sat close together over a wide nose propped over her large pouty lips.

"Welcome home, young man," said Mumkaza.

"Thank you," said Benji still hanging his head from the effects of disappointing Lin and Yuri.

"I hear you had an eventful swim home," said Mumkaza.

"I won't be forgetting it anytime soon," said Benji.

"I should expect not, the first time here is an eye-opening experience for any Topsider," said Mumkaza

"But I'm not..."

"I'm sure you're not. You must be awfully tired, dear boy."

"I'm..."

"Yes, yes. Well, make sure you get enough to eat. I see your life as a Topsider left you malnourished. There's plenty for everyone. Come along," she said motioning her head to the two Shequarien balancing her in the water.

Yuri looked at Lin. "Did you notice how she addressed him?"

"Boy? Young man? Topsider? Pretty obvious. Any more good impressions you want to make before the night's over?" Lin said, looking over at Benji, but he wasn't there.

Benji slipped down under the hundreds of fins swirling around near the surface then doubled back and swam over the floating sand off the beach of Waputa Wamkala. He found a rock in three feet of water and lay back against it looking on in awe at the festivities going on around him.

A little crab scurried toward him. Benji snapped his fingers underwater and scared the little critter away. The flurry of sand the crab left in his wake quickly settled and a whirlpool above Benji's fingers caught his attention. He snapped his fingers again, and a current of water gushed over his thigh. He snapped his fingers again. This time he held his left hand up and reflected the water back into the current of water swirling above his tail. Benji used his hands to massage the current in and out. The closer he brought his hands together, the faster the little whirlpool spun. He played with different angles of his hands and different speeds. He pushed his hands in quickly then pulled them back out again until the current of water fused and warped, creating a bubble the size of a basketball.

An exasperation from the crowd jolted his attention away from his creation as a Shequarien broke through the surface and flew through the air.

Benji pulled his hands away quickly, and the bubble disappeared leaving a spinning circle of water above his tail.

He surveyed the scene, his eyes coming to rest on Jaylon and Meena having an animated conversation with Yuri and Lin. Jaylon rapped his younger brother on the top of the head twice with his knuckles and pulled him in for a one-armed hug.

Once his bubble disappeared and his attention stopped wandering, Benji's eyelids began flirting with each other.

"There you are. Long day?" said Yuri swimming up beside him.

"Long two days. I was just trying to see what the back of my eyelids look like."

"Looks like you had them in your sights," said Yuri. He pulled a padded lump wrapped in banana leaves from around his back and laid it behind Benji. "Lean back and enjoy the show."

"So, now what do you think?" said Lin as she came up on the other side.

"I'm overwhelmed. Everything's so beautiful," said Benji.

"More than Topside?" said Yuri.

"It's different. I've always loved the water, but I've never seen it from this perspective. Once my vision adapted, I was blown away by everything down there. And then this," Benji said, looking around, "…is paradise."

"So what's it like Topside?" asked Yuri.

"Nothing like this. I mean, it's pretty boring in comparison," said Benji.

"Oh, come on. Cities? Robots? Airplanes? TVs and computers?" said Yuri.

"A lot of that is overrated. Most of the people I go to school with would disagree with that, but that's my opinion. A lot of it is supposed to make life easier, but that's the funny part. I don't think it makes things easier. So far, I like the simplicity here the most," said Benji.

"We love our home, Benji. And we're losing it," said Lin.

"You didn't come back with the prong? Do you know where it is?" said Yuri.

"What's the prong?" said Benji.

"Your parents disappeared with it," said Lin.

"I was only a baby. What is it?" said Benji.

"The Mystiq prong is part of Poseidon's trident that guards Aquari. There are five prongs to the trident. One prong of the trident was given to the inhabitants of each of the four major oceans. We have one. Donquari has one. Nanquari has one, and Beiquari has one. The Mystiqs were also given a prong to protect their domain. A long time ago, the Mystiqs chose Sanjowqua as their home. The Mystiq prong along with the one in Shequari expanded the protective power and created the massive area that Sanjowqua now covers. You're one of the last known Mystiqs, and the prong can only be controlled by one of your kind," said Lin.

"Yeah. Gouguon wanted to get to you first, so he could use you to control the prong. He wants to punish the Topsiders for their destruction of Aquari," said Yuri.

"What does it look like?" said Benji.

"The Mystiq prong is diamond. It's about half as long as a marlin's bill." Lin grabbed Benji's wrist and extended his arm. "About as long as your forearm."

"I'm pretty sure I've never seen anything like that," said Benji.

A shooting star blazed across the sky.

"Make a wish," said Lin.

Benji closed his eyes. "If this is a dream, I don't want to wake up."

Nombaki ndi Modzulu Muwini

(fishing with the fisherman's son)

THE PALE BLUE sky and incoming light of a new day slowly drowned out the twinkling stars. Warm ripples of water lapped over Benji's tail like a comforting blanket.

Half asleep, Benji swatted at his nose. The tickling stopped then settled on his forehead. He swiped again and missed. At the same time, something tightened around his fin. He jerked up sending water and sand cascading in an arch above him as he swiped at his left foot or where his left foot was before he had a tail. His fin made a "splat" as it smacked back down. He shielded his eyes from the morning's first light and caught Lin staring at him from under his palm. The grin on her face spelled trouble. Bliss, mischievous bliss, spilled out from her clenched teeth and wove its way all over her face like mutant ivy claiming everything in its reach.

The next thing Benji heard was "Go!" The last thing he saw was Yuri off to the side, eyes as big as jellyfish, clutching a stick with a leaf tied to the end. Yuri's lips moved forming some pattern of words closely resembling 'Holy maholy…,' but that's all Benji gathered before his head grazed the sand, skipped twice on the surface, then plunged down into the interior of Sanjowqua. He tossed and turned, flailed his arms, and scratched at the water, doing anything he could think of to try and put something in his hands to slow himself down.

Water shot up his nose and out the slits on the side of his neck. Frantic bubbles raced up his torso and clouded his vision. Swatting them only made them multiply.

Benji thrashed and jerked, fought and tumbled. His hips barreled over and around, and once he got righted, he got wronged again almost immediately.

He threw both hands out and pushed them to his sides as quickly as he could. At the same time, he swiped his tail. Suddenly his backward progression slowed.

As soon as he swiped again, the pull slowed further and he and whatever was on the other side hovered at a standstill in the middle of Sanjowqua. Both sides strained. The tension in the rope started cutting into Benji's tail, but once he had the other end struggling, he knew he could overpower it. Straining with all his might, he ducked his chin to his chest and peered under his body. The rope ran from his tail about fifteen yards back and then split off in two directions. Each end went another ten feet before a loop anchored it around two large bottlenose dolphins furiously pulsating their tails back and forth matching Benji's strong, powerful kicks.

Every eye out in the open followed the back and forth action. A few strong swipes and Benji seemed to be tiring them out. Then, the two dolphins opposite him would kick frantically and move Benji a few feet.

Yuri and Lin appeared from behind one of the floating bungalows giggling.

A quiet chatter began to rumble through the crowd of onlookers.

"...strong...," buzz.

"...changing colors...," bizz.

"...on our side...," bzzz.

"Haven't seen that in ages," bizz.

"...beautiful...," buzz.

Benji's top and bottom teeth ground on each other. A grain of sand between the two rows would have created a beautiful pearl in seconds. He balled both fists and put his entire body into the next couple of swipes, leaning hard and lurching with his shoulders, pulling with everything in him. The two dolphins slipped backward. Veins ran from Benji's forehead, down his neck, and twirled around his forearms.

Benji heaved forward again. One of the dolphins slipped, then the other lost his advantage within seconds. Benji aimed to return the favor and headed full speed out of the center of Sanjowqua.

"That's enough!"

Benji rocketed past Lin and Yuri as the tension in the rope went slack. He shot off like a pellet from a slingshot.

An angry voice bellowed in his head. "Through showing off Benji?" said Meena.

Benji wheeled around completely exhausted. The sudden release of tension between him and the two dolphins relieved him of his energy. He pulled his head back; his eyes grew big and bewildered. "You're kidding, right?"

"Do I look amused?" Meena floated in front of him with her arms crossed. She clutched a small jagged knife. Both eyes measured Benji, coming to rest at his tail. She stared at the gash, shaking her head. "Follow me. We need to have that cut fixed. You're going out with me this morning. Blood in the water, especially with Gouguon out, is not a good idea. He'll smell you a couple of miles away."

Benji followed Meena through the collection of floating bungalows. Meena reached out and grabbed Lin as they passed hers and Yuri's hiding place. Lin nabbed Yuri, and they both bobbled up and down behind Meena. Meena drug them for a few feet then let go once enough Shequarien saw, and she was satisfied the two of them received their fair share of embarrassment.

"Just because I let go, doesn't mean you're off the hook. Let's go!" said Meena

"Sorry, Meena," said Yuri.

"Did I just get yanked through the middle of Sanjowqua?" said Meena looking at Benji.

Benji shrugged his shoulders.

Meena looked back at Lin and Yuri. "Get your fishing gear. We're headed out after Benji gets mended. Meet us at the south side tube."

The two of them quietly took off in the opposite direction with their shoulders slumped.

Benji followed Meena to a bungalow with a blue light shining from the bottom. A small circle had been carved into the rock and bioluminescence fluttered around inside it, shining a halo of light down into the water. Despite the sun being out, the glowing emblem was still quite visible on the shaded underside of the floating hut.

Meena stuck her head in the doorway. "Hey!"

A banded coral shrimp looked up at her from the entrance way.

"Anybody here?" hollered Meena again.

The shrimp snapped his claws together, and Meena glanced down at him.

"Hey there," she said.

"What's the problema, señora?" said the little candy cane-striped shrimp.

Meena jerked her thumb in Benji's direction. "Rope burn. A little more than a burn actually......"

"Sí, I can smell the bluh in the water. Get in here, before you start a fee'ing frenzy, esé." The shrimp waved his claws for both of them to hurry in. "Doc we have a blee'er. We nee' so' no-blee' from the sea cucumber, pronto."

A white-cheek surgeonfish scuttled into the room from the back. "And have you finished your doctorate training, Sandival?"

"It's a cut, señor. It's no amputation." The shrimp looked up at Benji and then down at his tail as he passed. "On secon' thought, maybe he will nee' an amputation, señor."

Benji jerked his head back at the shrimp and caught a wink.

"Have a seat, pup," said Doc.

Benji sat down on a rock table in the middle of the room. The surgeonfish swam up to his head and poked around in each ear while several cleaner wrasse appeared from under the table and started pecking at Benji's tail.

"Señor, it's his tail. That's down this way, sí?" said the shrimp.

"Sandival, I'm more than aware of where the tail on these creatures is located," said Doc.

Meena cleared her throat and startled the perky little doctor, then he bounded back and forth down to Benji's tail, spiraling at the end.

"Yes. Yes. Sandival, I'm going to need some no-bleed from a sea cucumber," said Doc.

Sandival scurried around the corner talking under his breath and returned just as quickly lugging a giant sea cucumber draped over his claws.

Sandival shifted around Benji's tail pointing the sea cucumber at the wound while the surgeonfish bounced on the slug's midsection to shoot out the gooey mucous used to cover the wound.

"Here and there and, that'll do it," said Doc. "Don't touch this stuff. It'll get all over everything. Leave it be for the next two days then grab some sand and rub it off on the third day. You'll be good as new."

A flash of light caught Benji's attention. He jerked his head toward the doorway, and it was gone.

"What's the problem?" said Doc.

"I thought I saw something," said Benji.

"That wound of yours isn't from an urchin. You shouldn't be seeing things."

"Maybe it was the sun reflecting off the water."

The surgeonfish swam up and stared into Benji's eyes. Benji pulled his head back, and the little fish followed him.

"Hmmm… Ummmm… Hmmmmm…" motored Doc.

"What is it?" asked Benji.

"I knew a Mystiq once with eyes just like yours. Used to come in here and help with patients from time to time."

"Who was she?" said Meena.

"Her name was Kila," said Doc.

"That was his mother," said Meena.

"You knew my mother?"

"I suppose I did. That would explain it. You're pretty big for your age," said the surgeonfish.

"What do you mean?" said Benji.

"Mystiqs start with the auras and other light sensitivity when they're ten or even earlier. You look……"

"I'm thirteen."

"I wasn't aware she had been gone that long. Time flies. You're a late bloomer, pup."

"I've been away."

"Doesn't matter where you've been. Someone didn't convince you that you were a shark did they?"

"No, I thought I was a Topsider."

"Is that where you've been? Well, that may have had some effect. Not knowing what you're capable of can cause some limitations. And then being out of your natural habitat would have suppressed it further. Have you had any signs of your lineage?"

"I'm not too sure what I should be expecting. Octavius told me my father could move things and my mother was a healer."

"Anything out of the ordinary might be a good place to start."

"Well, a few days ago I was Topside. I spent the last thirteen years there. Pretty much the last forty-eight to seventy-two hours has been out of the ordinary."

"But nothing before that?"

"I began hearing voices a few years ago. Animal voices."

"Yes, well, that Topsider mentality is pretentious enough to suppress your ability to hear us for that long. That's understandable. Anything else? Any other visions or sensitivity with light, or energy?"

"I realized, recently, I can manipulate water."

"How so?"

"Well, up there I could make it jump. I'm not sure down here. I've only played with it a little."

The surgeonfish wiggled his tail fin and scooted back from Benji. He waited for a few seconds then said, "Well, what are you waiting for? Let's see."

Benji thought about his disappointing performance in front of Lin and Yuri.

"Put those away," demanded Doc.

Benji looked down at his hands.

"Not those! Your expectations. Put your expectations away. Play a little. That's how great discoveries are made."

"It's nothing much, really."

"Go on," said the surgeonfish eagerly. "You're not going to break anything in here."

Sandival lifted his eyes toward Doc.

"Well, if he does we can clean it up."

"Sí, señor. *We* can clean it up," said Sandival, shaking his head and backing up toward the wall.

Benji shrugged his shoulders. He held up both his hands in front of him, palms facing each other. He raised his eyebrows at Meena then looked at Doc. They both gave him an insistent nod. Benji snapped the middle finger and thumb of his right hand. A jet of water appeared and shot toward his left hand. He used his palm to bounce it back the other way, then snapped his fingers again. Another stream of water shot out toward his left hand. After the third snap, he had a pizza-sized current of water circling in front of his midsection. A funnel slowly emerged from the side of the circle facing Doc and pulled the surgeonfish toward it.

"Woah there," said Doc as he backed up to escape the pull of the water.

"That's interesting," said Meena.

Benji moved his hands in and out massaging the circle of water as it turned faster and faster. He had his eyes focused intently on the speeding current and started bobbing his head with the rhythm of the revolutions. He glanced up and saw Meena, Doc, and Sandival all staring at the circular current of water, completely mesmerized.

Benji looked back down at his little creation spinning furiously. Each time he moved his hands inward, the speed picked up. It slowed down the further out he pulled them. Benji pushed his hands in toward each other quickly and expanded them just as rapidly. A hole in the water opened up, and everyone's eyes widened with the circle. A thin layer of water circled the bubble very slowly. Benji took his hands away and watched it hover in front of him.

Sandival scurried across the floor, scaled the table, and pranced out Benji's right arm. He stuck one of his antennae up toward the bubble, and it bounced off. Benji extended his hand a little closer. Sandival crawled out further and reached up with both his claws. The current swept the little shrimp up and around.

"No! No! Hel..me! Hel..me!" cried the little candy cane-striped nurse.

Around and around he went. Benji lifted both his hands toward the outside of the bubble, and when he did, the little shrimp got sucked into the middle. Sandival settled into the bottom of the bubble with wobbly legs and fell over. He put his claws up around his head and started crying, "No water, amigos. Dying! I'm dying! Dios mío!! Hel..me! Hel..me!"

Benji guided his hands up around the bubble again and began pumping them in and out faster and faster. With each revolution, he expanded his hands further and further. He finally reached the end of his arm span with the last opening of his arms. The bubble yanked Meena and Doc's heads inside. They both jerked their heads back out and stared at Benji with shocked faces. Benji pushed his hands together and clapped. The bubble collapsed, and water rushed in to fill the void. Sandival went flying around in the whirlpool, bumping into the sea cucumber and a few vials of different colored coral that had been yanked off the shelf behind Meena and Doc. Sandival hooted and hollered all the way through the main room and continued while the current swept him into the back.

Doc shook himself from head to tail and looked around at the room. "A messy room is a sign of genius. There's been some smart work done in this space today. Now, was there anything else, you two?"

"I'd like to hear about my mother," said Benji.

"Ah, yes. Kila. A wonderful healer. I was never sure if her power came from being a Mystiq or just plain caring more than anyone I had ever met. She brightened any room she entered. We fed off of her energy. Radiated it, she did."

"What kinds of healing did she do?" asked Benji.

"Well, there were no limits to what she could do. None that I ever saw. She closed wounds, gashes, mended broken bones…"

"Doc, I have a sickness in my family," mumbled a green and brown grouper in the doorway.

"Which one is it this time," said Doc.

"All of them," said the mother grouper. She opened her mouth, and dozens of little grouper fries swam inside her mouth all wailing and moaning.

Meena grabbed Benji. "Doc, we'll catch up soon. I don't do fries too well."

"Keep me posted on that rope burn and your other progress, too," said Doc nodding toward Benji's hands. "You might want to practice that bubble maker some more. Maybe out in the open next time," he said as Meena yanked Benji out the door. "Sandival! We have a mess to clean up, and we have patients."

"Sí, señor. *We*," mumbled Sandival.

Meena swam through a maze of floating bungalows before she arrived at her own. She grabbed a couple of metal pipes, threw her pouch over her shoulders and moved it behind her back. Benji fluttered in, and Meena pushed him out with the things she had in her hands. "Out!"

Benji backed out as quickly as he could to stay out of her way.

"You have a few tricks you can teach the son of a fisherman?" said Benji.

"You might be surprised. Up there," she said nodding her head, "they call it fishing, so they don't upset themselves if they come back empty-handed. You better not come back empty-handed, especially after a day with me. Make me look bad, and it's the last thing you'll ever do. I don't care what the rest of them say about protecting you," said Meena.

"Don't worry. I won't disappoint," said Benji.

"I know you won't, or you won't be coming back," said Meena.

Benji gave her a nervous glance to see if she showed the slightest amount of jest. She didn't.

"Where are we headed?" said Benji.

"Beyond the Fringe. Early morning is the best time, and we're off to a late start, but you needed the rest, or else you would have been a wreck today."

"Is that what you call my morning training session with those two dolphins?"

"No. I was talking about you sleeping late."

"What's so different about fishing down here."

"First of all, we can see what we're after. I've never been hunting for fish Topside, but I have to imagine it's mostly guesswork, or it used to be before they had all that fancy equipment. We don't need all that equipment. We have it built in ready for deployment at any time," said Meena, jabbing a finger in the middle of Benji's forehead. "Best place to go is the southern part of Sanjowqua. The fish migrate out to the cooler water late in the morning."

"How do you find your way around here? There are nine rings of islands to Sanjowqua. What's the best way to navigate?" asked Benji.

"There are moving replicas of the entire Sanjowqua archipelago on the bottom terrace on the north and south sides of the temple. The best way is to consult the replica before leaving. You can manipulate the islands forward to project where they will be when you're ready to come back in. Then you need to remember the route. It's not as difficult as Jaylon made it out to be. He's not one for planning or details, so he gets lost."

"What about the Topsiders up on the islands? The ones who came here or got lost going through here?"

"What about them?"

"How many of them are there? Why haven't they tried to leave?"

"From what I know, there are a few Topsiders on the outer rings, six through nine. They're not allowed any closer unless they get invited in. One did a few years ago. Other than that, you should go find out for yourself."

"Yeah. I can just swim up there and walk out of the water with no clothes on."

"You're not wearing any now are you?"

"Well, that's different. Everything's tucked in nice and neat now."

"It's no different up there. Grab a coconut on your way up the beach or something."

"You don't like me too much, do you?"

"You coming here brings up some bad memories. I was hoping I could put them past me, but it's a challenge."

"What did I do?"

"Things have been difficult down here for years now. Once the Mystiqs started disappearing, all of Aquari got nervous. Gouguon stoked a lot of fear in each of the oceans. The Topsiders made it pretty easy for him, though.

"The Topsiders seem so relentless. Each year it's exponentially worse. There used to be mer in all the oceans in such variety and numbers it would make your head spin, but today the numbers are pitiful. Entire species have disappeared.

"As each species disappears, their life force fades, and as their life force fades, the oceans grow weaker. That has a compounding effect on all of us. It's hard to stop something with that kind of momentum once it gets started. It took a long time to get to the point that things slid in that direction, but many factors came into play.

"Pollution is the biggest problem. It seems to be the root of everything else and definitely attributes to the anger that Aquarien, like Gouguon, show toward the Topsiders. I am not saying that he is going about it the right way, but there is definitely some sense in the way he feels about the Topsiders.

"There has to be some middle ground between Gouguon's view and the rest of us," said Meena.

"What about your parents?" said Benji.

"They died the same time as yours."

"I'm sorry."

Meena bowed and shook her head slightly.

"It's not your..."

She didn't want to say it. She had held on to the fact that it was Benji's fault for a long time. She didn't want to admit to him that he had no part in it. Holding onto it and the bitterness it produced had become a part of her. She had grown accustomed to that weight. The thought of losing it made her uncomfortable.

"Look. Here's our first tube. This one takes us all the way out to the Fringe. It's a longer ride than yesterday, but it's a lot shorter than swimming, Just keep..."

"My hands off the coral," said Benji.

"You're starting to learn," said Meena.

"I think that electric eel seared it in me," said Benji.

Benji caught sight of something blazing toward them over Meena's right shoulder. He grabbed her arm and moved her to the side. Meena pushed his hand away and followed his eyes behind her.

"Sorry we're late," said Lin blazing through the water nearly out of breath.

She stopped at the last minute arching her back and sliding to a stop in front of Benji. Yuri pulled up too late and ran into the back of Lin. Benji scooted out of the way, and Lin and Yuri shot into the entrance of the tube in a tangled web of hands and hair.

"Yuri! Get your hands off me!" yelled Lin as they disappeared.

Benji snickered then slid in behind them. This time he was prepared and shot straight in. The first bank came in no time flat, his body rolled with it and every turn that came up after that. Within minutes he was shooting out of the other end of the tunnel. Benji drifted out of the line of fire expecting Meena to follow him shortly and looked out into the distance.

Almost immediately, the floor sloped downward, and deep, dark, navy water stared back at him. There were half a dozen rocks the size of refrigerators strewn across the floor along with a few car tires in the distance. Lin sat on one of the rocks with her arms wrapped around the middle of her tail rocking back and forth. Her black hair waved at Benji a thousand times over. That was the only part of her that showed any interest in him at the moment.

Yuri sat on a rock ten feet to Lin's right. He tried to apologize several times, but she cut him off with a "Whatever, Yuri!" as soon as the first syllable started rumbling off his tongue.

Benji turned his head and looked back at the Fringe island they had shot out from. The coral was bleached and brittle. Benji counted a half dozen fish swimming in and out of the perforated underside of the island. The fish out here were skinnier and had far less color than the fish around Waputa Wamkala. Their movements deceived any cheerfulness left in the faded, pastel colors of their scales.

The sound of whales singing in the distance snapped Benji back into the environment. The thought of the boat ride to Sanjowqua crept into his head, and he winced thinking about the initial screaming shock he got when the ship rocketed forward, and his shoulders nearly left his head floating in the water.

Meena shot out of the tunnel and nearly clipped the side of him. Her hands were clasped together held out in front of her head. She threw her arms out to the side as she emerged and slowed her progress forward with a quick swipe of the tail. She hovered beside Benji and gestured out toward the darkness.

Lin and Yuri both popped off the rocks waiting for Meena's command.

"Get your gear ready, you two. I'm going to hit them from the front. You guys hit the rear."

"Got it," said Yuri.

"Lin?" said Meena.

"Yeah. Yeah," said Lin.

"There isn't much out here," said Benji.

"Big fish require big water. Jaylon and the guys went in the shallower water today. The bigger fish are meatier. Less bones to mess with," said Meena.

"What's the fish du jour?" said Benji.

"Thon," said Meena.

"Who?" said Benji.

"That's tuna in French, wise guy," said Lin.

Benji looked sheepishly at Lin and then turned back to Meena. "How'd you know that?"

"We follow the boats sometimes. Untangle some of the animals they aren't supposed to catch, or the ones they would throw back anyway. Boats are…"

"…giant speakers. Eeke told me the first night I met him and the other dolphins," said Benji.

"What'd you think of them?" asked Yuri.

"They seemed pretty nervous when we spoke at the boat. They helped us get away from the shark's, too. Other than that, I haven't really talked to them much."

"They are the best three gold spotters around. If they hadn't been on guard this whole time, I think they'd probably own the ocean by now," said Yuri.

"Half of Topside, too," said Lin.

"Once the guard on Joe's boat drops, they'll be back. I've heard them several times speak about wanting to swim with you. Eeke, especially," said Meena.

"He's the younger one, right?" said Benji.

"Yeah. He's the troublemaker," said Yuri.

"But a good troublemaker," said Lin.

Meena put her index finger to her mouth. She sat on the bottom of the ocean and took the pouch from behind her back. She reached inside and pulled out a wad of plastic. It looked like a mesh of six-pack holders. She began unraveling it, and Benji noticed she had gathered dozens of them and tied them together to make a net. She took the two metal poles she had laid on the floor and slid them through hooks fashioned on either side of the net then set it all down next to her.

She looked out into the ocean, cupped both her hands around her mouth, and began making a loud clicking noise with her tongue against the roof of her mouth. She started off slow then gradually increased the frequency.

Meanwhile, Benji mimicked her with his tongue in his mouth without making the sound.

He accidentally let a click slip out. Meena reached out and gave him a punch in the shoulder accompanied by an ice cold stare. Benji stopped immediately, avoiding her stare by looking out into the ocean.

They waited for a few minutes, alternating between silence and Meena's rapid clicking. After her last round, Benji looked at her and shrugged his shoulders.

Gonna be a long day hunting, unless she's got a secret spot, thought Benji as he looked into the dark water that swallowed the barren landscape.

"You ain't seen nothing yet, Fisherboy," said Meena.

I need to be more mindful of my thoughts.

"No. You need to practice a little less judgment," snapped Meena.

Meena took two fingers and pointed them at her eyes and then out toward the deep darkness of the ocean. Far off in the distance, Benji saw a pin-drop-sized splash. A single silver streak shot through water, moving toward them at breakneck speed. A second later, he saw another splash and then another, as the fish tickled the surface with their fins. The next thing Benji knew, a silver tsunami that shimmered like lightning made its way toward them.

Meena grabbed the two poles lying on the ground next to her and pointed her two fingers at her eyes again and then at herself, indicating Benji watch her.

The first fish swished through the water above them followed by half a dozen more.

Meena sprung off the bottom of the ocean and shot upward. Within seconds, she was ten feet from the surface, poles in each hand. The netting from the plastic six-pack holders dangled under her right armpit. She quickly opened both arms wide and swallowed a three-foot tuna with the net. She skimmed the surface with her shoulder blades and used the school's momentum to head back down. She twisted both handles around until the tuna couldn't move anymore and sped back, making the whole thing look like a game.

The roar of the fish above was thunderous. The fish in her grasp squirmed, but the net was so tight the tuna only tired itself out.

"Your turn," nodded Meena at Yuri and Lin. Once she had their attention, she gestured for them to wait for her next signal. They both nodded back at her.

"I thought we weren't supposed to talk," said Benji.

"Even our thoughts carry energy, but they'll be drowned by the pandemonium above us right now," said Meena.

Meena slid the two poles out of the net with the tuna and tucked the fish under the rock she and Benji hid behind.

She pulled her pouch from behind her and took out another bunch of plastic six-pack holders and slid the poles through on either side.

"Did you see what I did?" said Meena.

"Yeah, I got that," said Benji.

"There are two places you want to hit them. When we first call them, the front is easy pickings. Once the main part of the school is overhead…"

The school of fish was midway past them. As soon as Meena handed Benji the two poles, he took off.

"Benji. No!" Meena swiped her arm up barely missing his tail.

Benji exploded toward the mass of rushing fish with intention plastered across his face. He had the poles in each hand. The netting flapped against the right side of his torso. He dodged one fish that nearly took his head off and spread the net to capture another in the same path. A flash of light materialized in the bottom corner of his eye. Benji jerked his head down and then back up. During his lapse of concentration, a second fish crashed into the one he had his eye on, and he soon had them both wrapped in the net. They were both the same size as the one Meena caught minutes earlier. Benji swiped his tail to the side and let their momentum carry him forward.

So far, so good.

When he went to twist the poles together, sealing the tuna in the net, he got clobbered in the stomach by an oncoming fish. Another one hit him in the chest immediately after. They both swatted him in the face and around his body as they tried to get away.

The first two hits bowled him over into the fetal position with his back facing the crowd. Another fish smacked him in the side, and two more swiped his tail sending him tumbling over and over.

The pole in his left hand slipped away from him, and the fish plunged toward the floor with more room to swim. He lost his grip with his right hand, but the netting twisted around his wrist, pulling him down with two fleeing fish. They plunged down twenty feet and shot back up. The immediate change of direction shook the fish loose from the net and left Benji barely conscious floating in the middle of the ocean, the net dangling off his arm.

Meena arrived first. "You idiot! Benji! Are you OK?! Benji!"

Meena grabbed his face and blew a breath of air into his mouth. When the coast was clear, she put one of his arms around her neck and swam up.

Once they reached the surface, she slid her tail underneath him to keep him floating.

Yuri and Lin popped up on either side looking for injuries. Several bruises had already formed on his chest and his ribcage.

Meena laid into him. "That was stupid! I can't believe you just…"

Benji began coughing and spewed water out of his mouth. His arms flailed and smacked the surface on either side of him. Meena lifted her tail a few inches, and his head fell back as he took a deep breath.

"I was…"

"You were an idiot! That's what you were!" said Meena.

"Made a fool of myself, did I?" said Benji through clenched teeth.

Talking sent pain through his chest and under his ribs like it was searching for internal organs to terrorize.

"Yeah, you did. And it almost got you killed. I don't know what you think about being a Mystiq, but you're not immortal," said Meena.

"Came pretty close to proving it," said Lin.

Meena had both hands on his head and threw her head back looking up into the sky with a loud exasperation.

"Sorry," said Benji.

Meena didn't say anything. She took another deep breath. "Are you ok?"

"A little sore," said Benji.

"Can you swim?" asked Meena.

"I'll manage," said Benji.

Without notice, she kicked him off her tail. Benji flew five feet in the air and landed square on his back with a loud smack.

"Ow!" grimaced Benji.

Yuri and Lin both pursed their lips and gasped.

"That'll wake him up," said Yuri.

"Serves you right!" said Meena.

Meena threw her hands over her head, kicked her tail, and dove back toward the bottom. Benji sulked behind and nearly ran into her. Meena floated in the middle of the ocean staring at the rock where the two of them had hidden from the school of tuna. A feeding frenzy of sharks was in the process of ripping apart the tuna Meena had left anchored under the rock.

"I messed up big time, didn't I? said Benji.

Meena glared at him and swam back toward the Fringe.

Jaylon sat on the edge of his and Meena's bungalow fiddling with a spear. He pushed it to the side with a smile when he saw them swimming up. He wiped the smile off his face when he saw Meena's glare. Lin and Yuri sauntered up behind her. Benji brought up the rear.

"Rough day?" asked Jaylon.

Meena kept going. She removed her pouch and tossed the pipes aside when she swam into their bungalow. As soon as the last wisp of her tail disappeared, both Lin and Yuri lit up.

"Oh, we had a few, but Mr. Mystiq got belted in the middle of the pack," said Lin.

"By the time we rescued him, sharks had already torn into the fish Meena caught," said Yuri.

"It took three of you to rescue him?" said Jaylon.

Lin and Yuri looked at each other.

"Yuri tell you about his first day out, Benji? asked Jaylon.

"You said you wouldn't say anything, Jay," moaned Yuri.

"I didn't expect you to rag on someone else either. The only people who don't mess up on their first outing are the ones who don't do anything," he said as he turned his head to Lin. "What, you got stage fright, again?"

"But mine was…"

"Just as bad, minus the bruises?" quipped Jaylon. "Don't let them give you too much of a hard time Benji. I've seen worse."

Benji began to smile and then grimaced. His face and his ribs hurt from the gesture.

"Where'd you end up?" asked Jaylon.

"When Meena got back, I took off straight for the middle of the pack and…."

"And all you got was a few bruises?" said Jaylon.

"I heard something crack," said Yuri.

Jaylon swam alongside Benji and had a look at his side.

"Might be a broken rib. Tough luck if it is. Nothing you can for that. That's a grin and bear it wound. Looks like all of them are.

"You hit the middle of the school and come away looking like you do, and I'd say you need to teach the rest of us how you made it out alive," said Jaylon.

"I don't think I'll be doing that again. I can't remember much of what happened after the first fish blindsided me," said Benji.

"I got a friend who says, 'If I can't remember, it didn't happen.' Most of his memory problems are due to the rum, but I think this might be a good instance to put his quote into practice. Just remember *why* it happened. Got me?" Jaylon nudged Benji in the side.

"AH!!" whimpered Benji.

"Oops. Well lucky for the rest of you ole Jay and crew caught enough fish to feed all of Sanjowqua today and tomorrow," said Jaylon as he patted Benji on the shoulder.

"OW!"

"Well princess, you'll just have to suck it up for a few days. You can do that over here. You'll be wanting to follow me." Jaylon looked at Lin and Yuri. "You two are free to go clean the nets, or you can come along and check out Benji's new digs."

"He's got his own place? That's not fair." Lin whined.

"We fixed up one of the older bungalows on the south side for you. It's nothing to write home about, but I think it's a good place to start," said Jaylon.

They glided down over the terraces and the courtyard surrounding the entrance to the temple. Benji noticed the replica of Sanjowqua Meena had told him about. He winced as he turned over on his back and kept swimming. Looking back at the stepped terraces of Sanjowqua from this angle made him feel like a quarterback looking up at an empty stadium. He closed his eyes and imagined the crowd's roar echoing throughout the enclosure.

The temple of Waputa Wamkala sliced upward through the water. Every inch of it clobbered in glorious colors: yellow, purple, blue, red, green, pink, white, black, and all the ones in between. It floated in the water as a palette of dancing color that swayed with the current and swelled with the comings and goings of the fish that called it home.

On the south side, Benji flipped back over and stared ahead. The water was darker over here.

He hadn't noticed on his way over, but the sun had nearly set. He looked back at the north side and saw bioluminescence glowing from several of the doorways behind them.

"Home, sweet home," said Jaylon motioning toward an empty bungalow.

Lin and Yuri slipped inside.

Benji grabbed Jaylon's forearm before he headed in. "Speaking of home, do you know anything about my dad?

"Joe?"

Benji almost spoke before he thought, but quickly remembered the dual life he had, but until a few days ago didn't know existed.

"Yeah."

"I might. What do you need to know?"

"Is he ok? Does he have protection like before? Does he know what happened to me? I mean, Octavius met my dad. He explained everything to him."

"Octavius left with another crew this morning. Part of the reason was to let Joe know you're ok."

"And the other part?"

"To oversee the new crew looking after Joe. Gouguon getting out early set off all of Octavius's warning bells. He wants to be extra careful."

A large circular platform took up the majority of the space in the bungalow. It stood about three feet off the bottom covered in a thick blanket of corkscrew anemones with Yuri sprawled out on top. Several blue-iridescent Penderson cleaner shrimp and sun anemone shrimp emerged and pecked at his tail. Behind the head of the bed, the wall receded into a semi-circle alcove with a shelf. A giant anemone hung from the ceiling; a gray and purple chandelier playing host to four black and white damsels who danced around the swaying arms.

Lin swam around the room twice then headed back out the door. "Not bad," she said shooting back off toward her own home.

Yuri watched Lin take off then followed quickly behind her.

"I think a lot of people are just as nervous about me being here as I am," said Benji watching the two of them swim back to the north side of Waputa Wamkala.

Half a dozen heads popped out of adjacent bungalows to check out their new neighbor. Benji recognized Peca, the coconut girl from his homecoming party waving at him with a flirty smile. He gave her a bashful flick of the fingers accompanied by a blush.

"Red's a good color on you," said Jaylon.

Benji shook his head trying to hide a smile.

"Give it time, Benji.

"I got to help with the nets and gear for the morning. Get yourself settled in here, and then get lost for a little while. I'll send one of those puffer lips to fetch you before dinner."

"Puffer lips?"

"Yeah, that's what we call it when you pout, 'cause you stick your lips out like a puffer fish when it blows itself up."

"Thanks, Jaylon."

Nichidan Chimbi

(operation whale)

BENJI SAT ON the white sandy beach looking out over the water. From the shore, he could see the bottom thirty yards away. The water resembled a calm lake in the mountains, not off an island hundreds of miles into the Atlantic Ocean.

Benji heard his name being called out beyond the floating reef of Waputa Wamkala. He looked up and saw his dad and Miss Wendy bobbing up and down; Joe's Fisher and Son hat on backward, Miss Wendy's hair tied in a ponytail high on her head. They waved their arms signaling Benji to join them. Benji tried to move, but the lapping water had buried his feet in the sand. Each time he flexed his muscles his feet sank deeper.

Behind his dad and Miss Wendy, a triangular fin emerged, cutting effortlessly through the surface. He cupped both of his hands over his mouth and yelled at them to get out. They only waved more. Benji's legs thrashed together in the sand digging him deeper in place as he struggled. He called out again, but they showed no indication that they heard him. Each time they waved their hands, another fin popped up behind them. And each time Benji jerked his legs forward, he sunk deeper into the sand. A dozen sharks now surrounded Joe and Miss Wendy. Sand covered Benji all the way to his hips. He slammed his palms down on the sand and pushed up with both of his arms to no avail.

A gush of water poured down his throat. He rolled over on his side coughing. A minnow flew out of his mouth, and the little fry flicked furiously in the sand until a lap of water pulled him back into the ocean. Benji wiped the salt out of his eyes and pushed himself up.

No Joe.

No Miss Wendy.

No sharks, either.

Octavius floated in the water just beyond Benji's tail fin. Benji overlooked the purple head on his first scan for his dad.

"You fell asleep on the sand again last night," said Octavius.

"Yeah. I like looking up at the stars. It's a beautiful place to be, out here in Sanjowqua."

"You might make a few more friends if you slept in the bungalow the Shequarien prepared for you."

"I've woken up every night with a ceiling full of anemone tentacles in my mouth. Not the most pleasant way to be woken up. The second night I got a tongue lashing, literally, from a sexy shrimp whom I inhaled along with half a dozen tentacles."

"The sexy shrimp are beautiful little creatures."

"Yeah, especially when they're nipping at your tonsils in the middle of the night."

"Can't say I blame her."

"Glad I'm entertaining everyone so much. Maybe I should trade in my tail for a clown outfit."

"You *can* change it, you know?"

"You're full of them today. You want to do standup comedy with me tonight in front of the rest of Sanjowqua? I'll keep setting you up, and you can keep knocking me down. Seems to be everyone's favorite game around here. Which, come to think of it, why am I here anyway?"

"First of all, you are home."

"I had a home. With my dad and…"

"…beloved friends, a sharp direction in life."

"Yeah, well, my dad made up for all of the other things."

"Your dad is still your dad. You have to follow your own path, Benji."

"Mine or yours," said Benji, fingers digging into the sand, his lips puckered in frustration.

"Yours, Benji," said Octavius with a soft voice.

"Nothing's like I expected."

"Just because things are difficult doesn't mean you're not doing the right thing," said Octavius. He perched on the end of Benji's tail. "Sometimes the path with the most obstacles leads us to the biggest prize."

"I'm on the lottery trail then," said Benji pumping his right arm beside him. "SWEET!"

"You do sarcasm well."

"Thanks. That's from my uncle."

"Tell me about him."

"My uncle?"

"All of them. Indulge me."

"I don't get to see my uncle much. He travels a lot. Uncle Bill lives for today. Tomorrow isn't even in his vocabulary, I don't think. He's a funny, light-hearted guy who takes it upon himself to remind those around him that life's not as difficult as most people make it."

"The world needs more creatures like him, above and below the ocean.

"How about Joe?" said Octavius.

"Dad and I spent a lot of time together, especially on the weekends. He fishes for work, but he'd always be ready to get back on the water the minute I asked. Surfing, fishing, kiteboarding. He taught me all of them. We never did scuba. I was curious about that. He wanted to keep that part of his job separate. It's a different world down there. There's so much to appreciate. He thought if he appreciated it too much, he'd throw in the fishing gear and get a desk job. That would kill him for sure."

"He told you that?" said Octavius.

"No. He'd never admit something like that to me. That would make him too vulnerable. I could read it off of him."

"Did your 'reading' him ever make him uncomfortable?"

"He never knew I was doing it. It hasn't been that long since I've been able to anyway. I didn't start hearing animals until about two years ago. My dad, about a year ago. With the animals, we more or less had conversations. With my dad, I picked up what he was thinking some-times, some of the big things that worried him. The 'loud' things."

"And what does a Topsider father worry about?"

"Whether I'm happy, making enough money, whether dating would make me uncomfortable, if anyone is bothering me at school, why I don't have more friends."

"Sounds like a typical dad to me."

"Yes, and no. At my age, a lot of kids kind of grow out of that rela-tionship with their father. My dad and I got closer."

Benji fumbled with his hands. "Jaylon said you went to tell him I was ok. Is that right?"

"I did."

"And?"

"He said he had known. He wasn't sure how, but he knew you were alright. I assured him you are and you're beginning to adjust here."

"Will I see him again?"

"That's completely up to you, Benji. There's nothing holding you back.

"I want you to start training your mind so you can blossom into the Mystiq that's inside of you waiting to grow. I've wanted you to acclimate here first, which is why you've been fishing with Meena, managed equip-ment with Yuri and Lin, and tended to the reefs with Chelli."

"Thanks. Meena thinks I am a moron. Yuri and Lin are still under the impression that I'm going through my initiation phase, and Chelli thinks he would have been better served by you bringing him back a hamburger and french fries rather than me."

Octavius chuckled. "Chelli feels that way about everyone. When you're his age, you can say whatever you want, too.

"You've got one more chore that you have been specifically requested for. Knock that out of the way, and I think it will be time for you to begin," said Octavius.

"Who is going to train me?"

"I will help show you the way, but you'll be more or less retrain-ing yourself. A large part of this will be done in the temple. Our, so to speak, 'library' has one of the last remaining compilations of bubbles on

Mystiq powers to awaken your latent talents. A large portion of them went missing around the days of your family's disappearance, but it's a good place to start."

"What are these sleeping talents of mine supposed to be again?"

"You woke up healed the day after getting smashed by a school of tuna. If you can do that for yourself, you can do it for others, too. I'd say your mother's healing powers are in there waiting to be developed. I also heard a story about a certain doctor's bungalow you made into a post-hurricane zone with a water manipulation trick you pulled."

"He told me to try it out. I had no idea what I was doing."

"Don't worry. Sandival was the only one miffed by the situation, but he's always a little hot under the shell from working with Doc, so all is well."

Octavius paused. "Feel better?"

"Actually, I do. Thanks."

"You can return the favor by following me. I have someone else who needs a little help."

"Deal."

Octavius turned his tentacles to one side and spun them around like a helicopter blade propelling himself over the surface into deeper water. Benji shook his head as he still tried to grasp the oddities of his new world and swam out to meet him.

"We're headed to the cleaning station today. It's on the south side of the fifth ring of the islands. There's a tube near your place that will put us out there," said Octavius.

Octavius latched onto Benji's shoulder, and they both disappeared under the water.

"Head toward the south side of Waputa Wamkala. There's a replica of the archipelago over there I'll show you how to use. I instructed everyone to keep you away from it while you get your bearings around the interior first. I also didn't want you wandering too far with Gouguon out."

They rounded the south bend, and Octavius pointed a tentacle out in front of Benji's eyes.

"Got it," said Benji as he dodged a barracuda and darted down toward the miniature model of Sanjowqua.

The replica looked like the cross-section of a large oak tree spread eight feet in diameter. It stood on a large stone five feet off the sand. Waputa Wamkala sat in the middle of the configuration followed by the growing number of islands making up each of the concentric rings circling it. The first ring moved slowly clockwise. The second ring moved a little faster counter-clockwise and so forth and so on. A tenth ring of the replica had the Aquari symbols for one through twenty-four etched into it. This ring stayed stationary. The eleventh and final ring held one black and orange marbled stone about the size of a softball. The polished stone glistened in the sunlight poking down through the clear water. Several blue and yellow damsels skirted away as Benji swam down and gently placed his hand on the stone.

"Move the map by shifting the stone. The numbers are the times of the day. It's lined up with nine now, so it's…"

"Nine o'clock," said Benji with a cocky grin.

"You get it," said Octavius.

"What time do you want to come back?" said Benji.

"See what it looks like at eleven," said Octavius.

Benji laid out and kicked a stroke propelling him around the table a few notches. Each of the concentric circles turned in opposite directions. Benji swam slowly staring at the layers of islands twisting around Waputa Wamkala. He arrived at eleven and let go of the orange rock. As he did, dozens of multi-colored fan worms popped out in various spots on the map. Some of them fanned out in circles. Others spiraled up out of their tubes looking like brightly colored Christmas trees.

Octavius spun slowly above the map. "See those?" Each of his tentacles pointed to a separate fan worm. Dozens more escaped his multi-appendaged reach.

Benji nodded as he scanned the map.

"Those are all the spots where you can catch tubes. The colors match the entry and exit points. Colors mixed with white indicate an entry point. Pure colors correspond to the exit points," said Octavius.

"So, that orange and white fan worm points to the entry point, and the solid orange one over there is where it comes out?" asked Benji pointing to fan worms on the first and fifth rings.

"Correct. Move the time another two hours," said Octavius.

Benji glanced over the map once more then grabbed the stone. As soon as he touched the orange and black ball, the brightly colored fan worms sucked back into their tubes. He laid out, kicked, and watched them reappear as soon as he stopped.

A few of the entry and exit points stayed the same. A few lined up with different spots, their colors changing to match each other, and a few emerged from places he hadn't seen the last go round.

"Alright, here's where we are, and that's where we're headed. There's only one tube from here. It pops out here until eleven," said Octavius pointing at a green fan worm. "Returning, you got that blue and white one that brings you just over there just past your bungalow," said Octavius pointing over Benji's shoulder.

"Got it," said Benji.

"Good. Let's go meet the Blue," said Octavius.

"Sounds like a secret agent code name," said Benji.

"I assure you. It's quite literal," nodded Octavius.

* * * *

"That's the one you want to talk to right there," said Octavius as they approached a tall, lanky Shequarien with black and yellow striped hair. "The big docking stations are on the outside close to the sixth set of islands. You'll be going out there today."

Octavius squeezed Benji's shoulder then lifted off. "I need to get back to the interior to meet a few visitors from the other oceans."

"Is that common?" asked Benji.

"Nothing concerning Gouguon is ever common. I'll go with you over to the temple tomorrow to start your training. Good luck," said Octavius as he cruised into a returning tube.

The foreman spun around and saw Benji floating there in the middle of the water. "Hey, what are you doing there with nothing going on. Get to your station."

"I just got here. I'm Benji."

"Ah! You're the new pup, huh? Name's Volo."

The jolly foreman slapped Benji on the shoulder.

"Nice to have you over here, Benji. Tan thinks you may be able to help with an extraction."

"That sounds painful," winced Benji.

"I can think of a few other ways I'd prefer to spend my morning, but when you got Topsiders trying to kill, maim, or catch everything in the ocean, you're gonna have a few extractions to deal with from time to time."

"I'll do what I can," said Benji.

"Good. Follow me," said Volo.

Volo and Benji took off through the cleaning station. Dozens of floating bungalows bobbed lazily in the depths between the fifth and sixth ring of islands. Mingled in between the first set of bungalows, Shequarien men and women worked on the animals giving dolphins, turtles, and sea cows brush downs and polishings.

Benji heard laughter coming from one of the bungalows above his head and when he looked up saw a sea turtle on his back, his flippers smacking the water one by one as several mermaids scrubbed his belly.

"Hold still, Chelli!" giggled one of the mermaids.

"I met Chelli the first day I arrived. I also went out to clean a reef with him one morning. That turtle looks a lot younger," said Benji.

"Oh, yeah. That's one of his sons. He didn't want any of them to feel left out or less privileged than the others by giving the first son his name, so he named all his sons after him," said Volo.

"How many does he have?" asked Benji.

Volo snorted then rubbed his chin. " Uh, three thousand? Give or take a couple hundred." He shrugged his shoulders, and Benji laughed. "Yeah. Chelli 'the original' has been around for a while.

"Hey, Jaylon told us you slowed down, actually, threw the Riviera brothers in reverse in the middle of Sanjawqua. One of those beasts would have ripped my tail off, for sure."

"I had no idea what was happening. One minute, I was fast asleep. The next, I got yanked into the water backward," said Benji.

"Whatever happened was enough to leave an impression on Tan. He comes off as real fun-loving and easy-going, both of which he is, but he's seen a lot, so he's not that easy to impress," said Volo.

"Going out fishing every day will notch some stories on your belt," said Benji.

Volo stared down his long, thin nose at Benji. "Fishing won't put the kind of stories on your mind like being part of the guard."

"I thought he was a fisherman. I saw him my first day here on the way back from a hunt," said Benji.

"Slow day around these parts and the boss ain't one to sit still," said Volo.

"Who does he guard?" asked Benji.

"He doesn't anymore. He used to guard the higher-ups here. They folded not long after Gouguon got sent away. Not sure if they'll be recruited again. The security council has their own detail now," said Volo.

"Did he help my father?" asked Benji.

"He did. He was with another party the day your father and mother...... the day you went Topside. Blamed himself for the longest time. I still think he does," said Volo.

"What happened?" asked Benji.

"He thought Gouguon would go for a sneak attack. Maybe send some trailing Donquarien to spook the group and force the party to split up. He didn't realize how bold Gouguon had become. None of us did. Gouguon went straight at your parents out in the open ocean. There are always eyes in the ocean, no matter where you are. Remember that. Anyway, Gouguon's hatred of the Topsiders had overtaken most of his senses by then, and he was on a mission to destroy your father.

"Your father said we were much better off letting the Topsiders know we're down here. He said their ignorance was mostly to blame for their carelessness.

"I'm getting off track. You asked about Tan. He was one of the top guards. Some people thought he set your father up and gave him to Gouguon by not being there," said Volo.

"What do you think?" asked Benji.

Volo patted Benji's shoulder. "I think anyone who questions his honor ought to have the harpoon you're about to help extract put through them."

Benji looked up in awe. A bigeye scad coasting through the water ran clear into his mouth, flitted around, and shot back out as fast as he had gone in. Benji coughed several times and shook his head. He was inclined to keep his mouth shut after the fish dinged his uvula, but once he saw the extraction victim floating in front of him, Benji's jaw dropped immediately. "Oh... My... God... She's huge."

A large female blue whale hovered above them. A slow moan echoed throughout the cleaning station. Benji felt her pain which sent a quiver up his spine.

"She's got a set of lungs on her, right?" said Volo.

Benji's mind was blank. He had never seen a creature so large. He did a research report on blue whales in the third grade, but seeing the animal close up was nothing like he had written about.

Volo loosened his grip on Benji's shoulder and watched him float up toward the whale. She undulated gently, more to the rocking of the surface waves than from her own accord. She could sense that the harpoon was coming out, and Benji felt some relief in her after a long trip here. He floated alongside her, coming up from beneath, between her left pectoral fin and her massive body. Her fin alone was twice Benji's size.

Benji placed his hand on her side. As soon as he did, he felt a tremendous amount of pain. His first reaction was that the pain was due to the rather large harpoon in her tail. Her fin closed in on him and held him close to her body. She squeezed tight, and Benji pushed back a little so his eyes wouldn't pop out of his head.

"What's wrong, girl?" asked Benji.

As soon as he asked, images began flickering in his head.

The sun cast a glorious halo over the water framing the magnificent couple below. The whale slid through the water, all her motions fueled by the love and joy she felt for being alive and being blessed with a healthy young calf. The two of them had been singing together all morning. Mother and daughter making silly songs about the sun, the krill they ate, and the seagulls cackling above them.

The Blue had given birth in the early spring. Her calf had been as healthy as any she could have asked for. The last three months she saw her baby double in size. The proud mother enjoyed watching her offspring breaching and swimming over and under her belly, but most of all she loved the mother-daughter duets.

The boat came out of nowhere. Her calf's scream hit her like lightning. By the time she turned around, a blurry trail of blood was the only thing left of her calf. She knew it was no use, but that thought had as much sway over her as a jellyfish. She surfaced, took a deep breath, lifted her tail, and dropped her head. She dove down two hundred feet before she felt ready to head back up. When she did reverse course, she put everything she had into her stride. Her baby was gone. Nothing she did would bring her back now. She realized this wasn't smart, but she also didn't care.

Just before impact, she tilted her head slightly to catch the boat's keel with as much of her as she could. The boat inched up out of the water. Three man-sized splashes from above followed her attack. One of the men attempted to hold onto her tail. She swatted him under immediately. As soon as she lifted her tail again, a harpoon sailed through just above the fin. If it had hit her fluke, it might have gone straight through making her getaway a little easier. She hadn't planned that far ahead. It had been more instinctual, more reactive than anything. She knew there was nothing she could do after her baby was taken from her. Rage boiled in her veins. She was the personification of sorrow and grief, anger and loss. They took her calf. Someone had to answer for it. Vengeance soared through the water and attacked that boat cloaked in the skin of a mother whale.

There was no slack in the rope attached to the harpoon. As soon as the winch cranked into action, the Blue's resistance shuttered the boat. Another man fell into the water. She felt him graze her right side and rolled on top of him. Her body roll sent creaks and screams from the ship as the rope whined against metal. She blew out a massive spray of water that cascaded over the hull briefly forming a beautiful rainbow above all the chaos. When the water rained down on the deck, she was finishing a deep inhale and immediately began to spin. Each turn yanked the boat closer and closer to her. She slowly realized before it was almost too late that she was tangling herself up and tying herself closer to her captors. She spun herself so close to the ship, a good portion of her body was now exposed. She had one more turn left in her. She twisted with every bit of energy she had left and every bit of anger. The men above held onto the rail and began to cheer, assuming the "big, dumb animal did herself in."

When the last bit of her energy was inching its way through her strained muscles, the rope snapped. She spun against the boat and rolled under it. Her body went limp, and she floated motionless for a few seconds before she started to flex her tail muscles. Her contractions loosened the rope's grip, and she paddled off into the deep. She coasted down toward the bottom and set a slow pace, hoping to catch the trailing rope on a rock crevice she might use to untangle it from her tail.

The Blue had no such luck.

She reached a point after a few dives to the bottom where the rope had become loose enough that it didn't bother her. In time, it untangled itself and picked up some of its own stragglers in the process. A few days of drifting out in the open ocean added some stringy green algae, a few barnacles and a host of remoras. A pod of dolphins swam beside her and tried to see if they could help, but she ignored them. She pushed herself through the water out of habit and nothing more.

Benji felt his eyes welling up, and he pulled his hand away. He swam up between her fin and her long torso then skirted up her side. He stopped beside her eye. Her deep dark eye sucked him in immediately and caused him to choke up again, but he pulled back and stared at his reflection hoping the imprint he was about to leave would do her some good.

"I lost my parents right after I was born. Gouguon killed them. He wants to kill all the people Topside. Some of which are the ones who killed your calf."

The big Blue sighed.

"Another man, a Topsider took me in and raised me as his son. I didn't know I was from down here until a few days ago."

She blew out a stream of air and water and took a shallow breath in along with another sigh.

"They aren't all like the people in that boat."

She sighed again and jerked her body. Her tail brushed a separation wall sending pieces of rock crumbling down to the sand. A handful of Shequariens laid their hand on her to try and calm her down.

"Hey! What are you doing, Benji?" Tan grabbed Benji by the shoulder and spun him around.

"Octavius said you wanted me down here. Here I am."

"I want to keep her calm. Don't start making her upset."

"Uh, I think it's a little late for that."

"How do you know?"

"She told me. Didn't she tell you what happened?"

"We've been trying to talk to her all morning. All she's done is moan."

"She lost her calf before she got here."

"Sick?"

"Same way she got that piercing."

Tan hung his head for a minute. Then, he looked down the tail with the harpoon and swam up beside her placing his hand on her side. "You don't deserve that pain. I don't want you to forget. I just want to help you heal."

She moaned again and nudged Tan gently.

"We got the rope off, although once I thought about how I wanted this done, we should have left it attached," said Tan

"Octavius said you want me to help."

"Yeah, that's the part I want you to help with."

"You sent for me to help you attach a rope?"

"I sent for you to get that harpoon out. Best way is a quick, clean removal. I figure we give you a rope and enough slack to get you up to speed and then 'pop,' out it comes."

"Why me?"

"I saw you the first day you got here almost blow Darmik out of the water, then I heard you reversed the Riviera twins the next morning."

"Why not Darmik? Surely, he's got some experience with this kind of thing. Or what about Jaylon?"

"Darmik is out on patrol, and Jaylon is one of the most squeamish people I know."

"Jaylon? Really?"

"He's tough as they come, but if he saw this he'd lose his lunch and breakfast, and half his insides, I'm sure of it."

"I didn't see that one."

"Neither does anybody else, and I'd keep it that way unless you want to make him upset."

"No. I think we'll leave that alone. So, when do you want this done."

"Now."

Benji looked down the side of the Blue. A pair of Shequarien tied a rope around the head of the harpoon which faced down at an angle.

"Looks like I'm going down that way," said Benji pointing over a wall that dropped off another hundred feet toward the sixth ring of islands.

"That a problem?" asked Tan.

"This is my first extraction, so I'm leaning on you guys to show me the way."

"Don't worry, pup. We'll give you plenty of slack in the rope. You ought to be able to reach a nice clean extraction speed after a hundred feet. Stay above that shelf right there by ten or fifteen feet, so you don't risk getting the rope tangled up before you yank the harpoon out."

"I've never done anything remotely like this, so I'm trusting you guys," said Benji, then he lit up momentarily. "Oh, I did use a doorknob and some dental floss to rip a tooth out once."

"Same principle. Only you're the doorknob, and if you get this wrong, you'll be the one getting yanked out," said Tan.

"You ready?" said Volo.

Benji rubbed his hand on the Blue's side. "We'll have this out in a minute, girl."

She let out a mellow wail and dropped her head.

Benji followed Tan back to the tail. Three mermen floated under the whale's fluke. They had attached the rope to the head of the harpoon and were ready to get Benji in a harness.

"So you're the one that burned water?" said a tall Shequarien holding a vest for Benji to slide into.

"Burn water. I like that," said Benji with a chuckle.

"Heard you're pretty quick. Lift your arms up for me. Don't look that quick to me, pup," said a fat one coming around in front of Benji to tighten the makeshift vest they attached to the rope.

Benji changed his tail to a black background with a gold lightning bolt, and the three assistants laughed.

"Alright, let's see what you got, Speedy. I wouldn't worry, so this is a moot point, but you got one shot at this," said Volo.

"Alright, you can put your arms down now," said the fat one in front of him.

Benji felt a few tugs on his back, then the Shequarien patted him on the shoulder and spun him around. "All set, pup."

"Thanks," said Benji.

Benji looked back toward the whale's head. She turned back a fraction and let out an encouraging tune. He nodded his head and looked back at his pit crew.

"You got a hundred feet, pup. We're going to float back here with the rope. Follow a diagonal line down," said Volo pointing down toward the shelf. "If you don't get it all the way out... well, it was nice meeting you."

Benji mustered a nervous smile.

Volo double-checked the excess rope coiled up in the fat one's arms.

Benji looked up through the water at the clear blue sky. Two puffy clouds hung above his head. They were about as indistinguishable as any clouds he had ever seen: two puffy white clouds. He nodded his head and looked down at his target point above the shelf wall.

"Ready on three... two..."

Benji closed his eyes.

"...one! Move it, pup!" yelled Volo.

It took him five good swipes of the tail before he was really moving. By that point, he was a quarter of the way down. If it was possible to burn water, Benji thought he might be pretty close by the time he flew past Tan at the halfway mark. He pictured the water behind him burning, sending monstrous flames toward the surface with dark plumes of heavy smoke to give those two little puffy clouds some company.

The shelf lay near the end of his run. Ten feet from the shelf, the flash of light appeared again. Benji blinked his eyes and looked down and away from it. The spark of light illuminated two heads and a very sharp looking spear he headed toward.

Benji pulled up a few feet, shooting him out into the ocean at a smaller angle than they had discussed. He dared not look back for fear of losing any of his speed. He saw a spear. He definitely saw a spear. It had twinkled with the burst of light.

He pulled up a little more and strained every muscle in his body. The moment he crossed the edge of the shelf, he felt a pull that stuttered him for a few feet and then the line went slack again.

The Blue let out a short wail of pain that was quickly followed by a more soothing sound of relief. Seconds behind that followed a wave of yells, high fives, and chest bumps from the crew.

Benji slowed up and threw out his right arm spinning him around. He swam back, pausing before he crossed the edge of the shelf. He looked down as far as he could see. Nothing but bony coral and a few large parrot fish weaving in and out of it. There had been two heads there. And a spear. He shook his head and swam back toward the excitement.

His pit crew patted him on the back when he got back to the whale. The Blue rewarded him with a beautiful, relieved tune.

One of the guys undid Benji's harness and the fat one coiled the rope.

"Looks like you got a little too close to that shelf, Benji," said Volo inspecting a frayed part of the rope.

"Yeah, I pulled up, but I didn't get as close as it may have looked. I cleared it by a good twenty feet," said Benji.

"You sure about that?" said the fat Shequarien, holding the mangled rope between his two hands.

"They didn't…" stammered Benji.

"Who didn't what?" asked Tan.

"I cleared that shelf by twenty feet. You guys fed me the line without much slack. Right?" said Benji.

"You betcha we did. You were running with it, pup," said Volo.

"Yeah. I'm glad we wrapped up beforehand," said one of the others as he held up his hands covered in some twine they had used to protect their hands from the speeding rope.

"I pulled up twice down there. There was a flash of light that messed with my eyes. I pulled up a little when I saw that. That alone was more than enough to clear the shelf twice. Right before I went over, I saw two heads and a spear. Someone was down there, and someone took a swipe at that rope. I pulled up when I saw them, too."

"More than a swipe. I'm surprised it held for the extraction," said the fat Shequarien, shaking his head at the torn rope in his hands.

"You sure you saw two heads down there?" said Tan.

"I saw two heads and a spear," said Benji.

"Get a good look?" said Volo.

"No. I was focused on the line. I didn't think anyone would…"

Tan pointed at two of the crew. "You two get down there and see if you see…"

"Whoever it was is gone. I looked on my way back up," said Benji.

Tan stopped and stared at Benji, then turned back toward the crew.

"What are you waiting for? Move it." He held his arms out as far as they'd go. "Start out wide and work your way back in toward where Benji went over. Any Aquarien, and I mean *any* whosoever, I want brought up here. Question any fish near the incident point."

"Got it, boss," said the three in unison.

"Good. Now go!" hollered Tan

The pit crew shot out toward the shelf. Benji felt relieved but sure they weren't going to find anything. A couple of minutes had passed and whoever it was didn't hang out long enough for Benji to see them when he looped back toward the Blue.

"What now?" asked Benji.

"We wait and see what they find. We'll have to be a little more careful with you in the future," said Tan.

"I mean with the whale," said Benji.

"Benji, that was pretty serious. Being down here isn't a game. Some big changes are happening, and they're all happening pretty quickly. I'm not trying to scare you, but you need to be aware, OK?" said Tan.

"Got it. I'll keep my eyes open. I did a pretty good job earlier. I mean, I did spot them in time."

"Yeah, you did good, with the Blue and with yourself," said Tan.

Tan turned around and rubbed his hand on the edge of the whale's fluke. "I want to keep her here and fatten her up a little. Keep her in a protective environment where she can relax. She needs to be out in the open ocean as quick as she wants to go, so we'll monitor how she feels and let her go as soon as she's ready. My guess is she'll be gone in a few days. We do treat them right, so she's in no terrible rush to leave. Her plates are clean, we've relocated some barnacles to the shelf below, and she's had a good massage. She's in good hands," he said with a wink.

"Hey, what are you guys doing slacking?" said Jaylon coming up from the direction of the shelf with a spear in his hand.

"Well, you're just in time. You missed all the action," said Tan.

"I heard. Your boys down there accosted me before I came up. What's this about someone trying to sabotage your surgery?" said Jaylon.

"Benji said he saw two heads down there with a spear that swiped at the rope we used to pop out the harpoon. What were you doing down there?" said Tan.

"I rode the current 'round the edge. I was on the east side when I heard Benji was over here. We had a good haul this morning, and I wanted to patrol the Fringe on my way over. With Gouguon out, a lot of people are worried he's going to attack Sanjowqua," said Jaylon.

Tan turned, put his hand on the big whale, and gave her a good rub. Jaylon shook his head and looked back down the way he had come up. "Here are the clamheads that hassled me."

"Following orders, Jay," said the fat one.

"Yeah, yeah. No worries, guys," said Jaylon.

"Anything?" said Tan.

"Not a thing, boss. We did run into a grouper who said he saw a pair of pups down there but didn't pay them any attention. Said they were all camo'd out. About ten minutes ago. Would make it right around the same time Benji sailed over the edge. We checked the area where he went over the shelf, too. Nothing there."

"We'll just have to be extra careful with our near extinct Mystiq then won't we." Jaylon put his arm around Benji's head and rubbed his knuckles on his head.

"Ow, Jay. If that's how you're more careful, I'll take my chances with whoever is out there."

"Come on. Octavius told me to bring you back after you were finished playing doctor. You can lead the way. He said you played with the replica on the way out here," said Jaylon.

"Thanks for your help, Benji. She'll be here another couple of days if you want to stop back by," said Tan.

"Yeah, I'll be back," said Benji.

Benji swam up beside the Blue with his hand on her side. She responded to his touch and moved gently.

"Don't get her all riled up, Benji," called Tan.

He swam up to and over her pectoral fin and stopped at her eye. He almost missed it because she had it closed.

"Safe travels, girl, if I don't see you beforehand. I got a strange feeling I won't," said Benji.

Her eye stayed shut. "Be careful, Benji. Listen to that feeling. The more you trust it, the sharper it becomes. I'll be fine. I had a run-in with a pack of Orcas a few years ago that would make this look like a scratch."

Benji turned to go.

"You have your mother's eyes, you know?" said the Blue.

"No, I didn't. Thanks for telling me. Did you know her?"

"A little. In passing. She was difficult not to notice. She was a beautiful creature, inside and out. She and your father tried to change things, and they paid dearly," said the Blue.

"I wish I had known them," said Benji.

"One day you will. The further along your path you go, the closer you'll be to them," said the Blue.

"I'm not too sure what I'm supposed to be doing here, though," said Benji.

"Listen. You'll get your answers soon enough. Be patient and listen. The ocean always talks to those who are willing to listen to it," said the Blue.

Benji patted her side and turned back toward Jaylon.

"Let's see how well you remember the map from this morning," said Jaylon as they swam toward the return tube.

01

Madawana Ninjoo

(water fairy)

EEKE, ZEEKE, AND Mai shot through the tube in one jumbled mess of fins and tails; each of them battered, bruised, scraped, slashed, and bleeding. Mai suffered the worst of the injuries. A third of her dorsal fin lay somewhere between Beech Mill and the sand she now thrashed on. Jagged marks indicated teeth were involved. Big teeth.

Meena, Lin, and Yuri were tending to some of the coral around Waputa Wamkala. A honeycomb cowfish brushed Yuri's back with its feathery little fin. Yuri looked over his shoulder.

Benji and Jaylon shot through the water toward a spot on the first terrace with sand billowing up everywhere.

"That doesn't look good," said Yuri.

Zeeke's mangled head poked out through the cloud of sand, and Yuri gasped.

Lin turned and immediately threw her hands over her mouth.

Meena caught the wave of anxiety and pushed off the coral before she had fully surveyed the scene.

Benji arrived first. He knelt beside Mai, cradling her head on his tail. "Blow out."

Mai shook her head in a jitter. A handful of bubbles piddled out of her air hole.

Benji took a deep breath and blew, inflating her lungs. He felt a soft hum vibrate through her midsection. The tension in her body released and the weight of her head sank hard onto him.

Zeeke watched his sister's body relax. "No, Mai. No!"

"Zeeke. It's OK. I feel her. She's not going anywhere," said Benji.

Zeeke nuzzled his head under his sister's belly and closed his eyes.

Meena came from behind Zeeke and lifted him at a slight angle. "Breathe out for me, Zeeke."

He did, and Meena gave him a fresh breath.

Jaylon slid beside Benji and slowly pulled Mai toward him. "I got her, Benji. Go take care of Eeke. He's OK, physically, but we need to keep him calm."

Jaylon looked up and saw Yuri and Lin with blank stares plastered on their faces.

"Yuri! Lin! Snap out of it. Go get Sandival and Doc. Now!" said Jaylon.

Benji scooted next to Eeke and pulled the dolphin's head onto his lap stroking his side behind the pectoral fin.

"You're OK, Eeke. Everything's OK now," said Benji.

Eeke shook his head slowly and closed his eyes. "Benji, I need some air."

Benji bent over, and Eeke let out a short stream of bubbles. Benji placed his mouth over the blowhole before Eeke stopped and when he didn't feel any more pressure coming out, he filled Eeke's lungs with a big blast of fresh air. The dolphin shuddered as if a chill had come over him and then he started mumbling.

"Gouguon… the prong…

"Joe… Miss Wendy…

"Boat… destroyed…

"Too many…

"Dead… Sorry… Benji… Sorry…"

Eeke's words crept into Benji's head and wound their way through his body, clamping down on his muscles, and seeping into his bones. The more he heard, the more each word hurt, and the more Benji rocked with Eeke in his lap.

Benji progressed quickly from rocking to shaking. Eeke lay in his lap mumbling. A light touch on Benji's shoulder nearly shot him out of his skin. Octavius pulled himself from behind Benji and settled over Eeke's head.

"Give me some room, Benji. It's OK, Eeke," said Octavius.

Meena finished giving Zeeke a fresh breath of air. Zeeke's head flopped over on his sister's belly. His fluttering eye caught a glimpse of Benji.

"Benji, we're sorry. We didn't see them coming. We were overwhelmed," said Zeeke as he coughed and nodded his head at his big sister. "We held them off as long as we could." He coughed again.

"It's gonna be OK, sis. You got this. Eeke's got some goodies for you when you're all patched up. Got some hidden treasures to make that fin good as new. Jazz it up. You'll be the most blinged out dolphin in Sanjowqua," said Zeeke.

Benji almost cracked hearing Eeke's mumbled, jumbled words, but he told himself it was nothing but muddled confusion. The bits and pieces of Zeeke's speech set Benji's head spinning even faster.

Benji opened and closed his fists in rapid succession. Open. Close. Open. Close.

Shock talk, he thought. *That's all it is.*

Benji heard it once on the docks with Joe. One of the fishermen was in the wrong place at the wrong time and had a five hundred pound crate dropped on his leg. A few minutes after the yelling died down, the shock talk took over. Joe held the man's hand while the ambulance came. The conversation went from the floor of the warehouse to a big top circus tent when the man was ten years old, and an elephant sat on a trainer.

"That was all part of the act. The trainer walked away from the incident without a scratch or limp, boss," the man told Joe with tears in his eyes. "I suspect I'll be at work tomorrow morning, no problem. Right boss?"

"Of course, you will," said Joe nodding his head and squeezing the man's hand.

Benji had wished for an old, graffiti-sprayed clunker filled with clowns to appear and cart the man away to work their circus magic on his leg. He knew for a fact the man wouldn't be back at work tomorrow, much less any time that season, and seriously doubted if he'd be at work with Joe ever again. A desk job seemed to be the only thing that leg would accommodate in the future.

Shock talk. Crazy talk, thought Benji.

Octavius sat perched behind Eeke's blowhole growing and shrinking with each breath. He started out purple, and as he began reading Eeke's thoughts, his color changed spastically, from purple to red, to blue, to green. Next, Octavius' skin pulsated in different patterns making him look like the sandy floor, the reef, an algae covered rock.

Eeke's eyes rolled back in his head.

"What are you doing to him?" asked Benji.

"Eeke needs air, Benji," said Octavius, ignoring his question.

Benji raced over and cradled the dolphin's head, giving him another deep breath, then Octavius shooed him away. As he floated off, Benji surveyed the dolphins' injuries. Out of the three of them, Eeke looked to have fared the best. He had a few scratches on his tail and a long one down his back, but that was it. Zeeke's body carried a few more scratches and a couple of nicks on his fins. Mai's entire body was scratched, and her dorsal fin was a nub of its former self.

Benji got up to see if the others needed any help. He hovered beside Jaylon and Mai.

"She'll be fine. She's the toughest one. That's why she's got the most scratches. Took a few too many for the team this time, though. But, ole Doc has a few tricks that will get her in tip-top shape in no time," said Jaylon.

"What's Octavius doing with Eeke?" pleaded Benji.

Jaylon looked over at Octavius and Eeke. His eyes locked on Octavius and his face went blank.

"Jaylon?"

"Sorry. That thing he does with his skin is hypnotic. Sucks you in without you even noticing."

"So what's he doing?"

"He's pulling everything he can from Eeke. He's the least hurt, so he gets the brain drain."

Benji looked horrified.

"It's not really a brain drain or whatever you think it is that looks as horrible as the look on your face. He's going over the events with Eeke, as Eeke saw them unfold. He'll play them back a few times making sure he doesn't miss anything."

"He's not messing with his brain?"

Jaylon cracked a grin. "You think Octavius would do that?"

"I guess not."

"Of course not. We need to get to the bottom of whatever happened as soon as possible. Best to get it from them while it's still fresh. Time has a way of distorting events or at least the way we perceive them."

"I'm worried about my dad."

"I heard Eeke."

Benji looked even more frightened.

"Sorry, pup. Whatever happened, we'll know more shortly, and when we do, we'll deal with it then. There's nothing you can do right now, and speculating doesn't do any good. Give Mai another shot of air would you?" nudged Jaylon.

Benji went to take a breath, and his chest seized up. Jaylon grabbed his shoulder. "Here and now. That's what you can control. Here and now. Got it?"

Yuri and Lin scooted down from above, both with satchels over-flowing with Doc's medical supplies, including seaweed, sea slugs, and a special tonic Doc had mixed from octopus and starfish blood that helped the body regenerate tissue. Sandival popped out of the satchel Yuri carried with two tubes of the healing juice. Doc darted under Yuri and winked at Benji.

"Good as new in no time," promised Doc.

"Si, señor! No problema!" said Sandival shaking the tubes like maracas at a birthday party.

Benji rubbed Mai's side and glanced back at Eeke.

Octavius lifted himself off the dolphin's back shaking his head. He opened and closed his tentacles several times and propelled himself up several feet to survey the entire scene. Octavius shook his head in disgust, closed his eyes briefly, and when he opened them again, he stared Benji in the eyes. "I'm sorry, Benji. Joe's…"

"Don't say it," said Benji, floating up and away from the scene.

Octavius stared at Benji with a blank face, his tentacles spread out beneath him. "There was nothing they could do."

Benji shook his head. He threw his hands against his temples and shook. He looked around him at the dolphins laid out on the sand. Doc and Sandival patched up Mai and Zeeke. Lin now sat on the floor stroking Eeke who floated beside Zeeke gently nudging him with his nose.

"Not true!" said Benji.

Octavius swam over and tried to put a tentacle on Benji's shoulder. "No!"

Benji shot straight up, breaking the surface in seconds. His departure made light look slow. Benji looked in every direction, found a break in the islands, and dove back down into the water disappearing in a flash.

He broke the first barrier islands and sailed through the next. The third approached, and he picked up even more speed. The islands got further apart the more he distanced himself from Waputa Wamkala. Despite the increasing distance between each subsequent chain of islands, Benji moved past each one faster than the last. Anything caught in his wake got turned over and under several times. His goal was to put as much distance between his thoughts and actions as possible. The only way that seemed to work at the moment was going fast. Lightning fast.

Burn water, he thought.

Speeding up slowed everything else around him.

He broke the fifth chain of islands and surfaced. He kept his head out of the water and skimmed on top like a torpedo. Nothing but blue sky and blue ocean lay before him. Before he knew it, he had broken the outer rim of the Fringe and was out in the open ocean. The protective walls of Sanjowqua were long gone and before he knew it, so was any hope of finding it again.

Benji slowed to a crawl and eventually stopped. He closed his eyes and wanted nothing more than to sink and keep sinking. The air in his lungs was the only thing keeping his head above water. The weight of everything else tugged at him like a sinking school bus tied to his fin.

Benji put his forehead in his hands and aimlessly sputtered his lips in the water. "This isn't happening. None of this is happening. How does everything get turned upside down so fast? I'm literally in another world. I'm an alien on my own planet. This can't be happening!"

His eyes welled up. He clenched his jaw tight and squeezed his eyes shut. "Dad. Where are you? Who am I? Where am I? WHAT AM I??!!!"

Benji jerked back and forth, not sure which way to look, much less which way to go. He was as lost in the moment as he was in life.

Benji wiped the tears from his eyes.

The sun glared off the water. He cupped his hand over his brow and squinted his eyes. "That's not the sun."

A little glowing ball of light bounced up and down off the surface fifty yards ahead. As soon as he noticed the light, it crept closer. Benji stretched his neck and squinted his eyes.

It moved closer.

Benji stretched his neck from side to side to get a look at the ball of light, and it zipped across the water straight toward him.

A swift thump landed right between his eyes. Both of Benji's arms flew out beside him, and he skidded on the surface a few feet.

"What are you doing way out here. This is no place for you right now. Didn't Sanjowqua get the news?" quipped a little, deep voice.

Benji looked around him, over his head, and poked his head in the water. A thump in the back of his head pushed him down a few inches. He popped back up shaking his head.

"Better to stay in Sanjowqua. Gouguon's got the Mystiq prong. Now that he's got it, there's going to be some changes. I'd expect them to change fast, too. He's had plenty of time to figure out his plans," said Montal.

The water fairy popped up from under Benji's arm and hovered above the water before dipping back down.

"You're the light," said Benji.

"Whoa, pup. I'm just a water fairy. Don't go worshipping me now," said Montal.

"I mean you're the light I've been seeing. You've been following me," said Benji.

"Guilty," said Montal.

"Why are you following me? Each time I've seen you, I've been in trouble."

"Keeping a promise to an old friend. You've managed fine so far."

"I just came from Sanjowqua. Eeeke, Zeeke, and Mai were attacked. My dad is…" Benji wiped his eyes with the palm of his hand.

"That's just the tip of the iceberg, pup."

Benji shook his head. "OK, so where did Gouguon find the prong?"

"Right under everyone's nose. He's the only one to have thought to look Topside. I guess others thought it. They thought it was with you. Little did everyone know, it wasn't really out of reach at all. Only a few feet by my best guess, but that was far enough to keep it off the radar."

"Where?"

"Joe had it on his boat."

"All I ever saw was that old turtle shell, and I never paid that any attention until a few weeks ago when… the jambuku. Gouguon used the jambuku to find it. He didn't want me. He wanted the prong."

"It was hidden in the turtle shell. I think by most accounts your father did a little too good of a job hiding it. If it was a shark, you'd be dead right now."

Benji hung his head.

"Not the best timing. My apologies." Montal stalled for a moment. "Look, we all lose people, pup. Things are always moving. Always in motion. Always changing. People are here today and gone tomorrow. Appreciate where you are now and what you have at the moment."

"That's easy to for you to say."

"I've lost before, too. On both sides. It's different when you're a parent."

"Sorry," said Benji. "I feel like the weight of the world is on my shoulders and now…" he sniffled. "People expect me to…"

"Don't try to live up to other's expectations. Do what you feel is right and follow that. You'll get the hang of it."

"I don't know where to begin with what I am supposed to do, know, or master. I'm this Mystiq thing, but as far as I can tell, the only mystical things I can do is have crazy dreams and do a few magic tricks with my tail."

"That crack in the water you created behind you on the way out here was a pretty impressive trick," said Montal.

"And I'm fast, too. How does that trump a merman who has some magical thing that can form islands and bring massive destruction Topside? He can probably level me with a single swipe from that part of the fork," said Benji.

Montal laughed. "That's a big fork."

Benji shrugged his shoulders. "It's Poseidon's, right? He's a big god."

Montal nodded. "Come on, pup. I got something to show you."

"You got a magic spoon we can use?" said Benji.

"I got a few utensils that might help," said Montal with a chuckle.

Before he took off, Montal looked back over his shoulder. "Based on your little display earlier, I'm gonna assume you won't have any problems keeping up. Give a holler if I lose you."

With that, Montal sauntered forward lazily for a few feet then shot through the water like a blazing tennis ball. He left a tunnel in the water a hundred feet behind him.

Benji's jaw dropped. He popped his chin with the back of his hand, and his teeth clattered together. Then, he threw his hands by his side and took off after Montal.

The water fairy glowed at the end of the tunnel he formed as he zoomed through the ocean.

My light at the end of the tunnel, thought Benji, shaking his head.

Montal weaved back and forth looking like he whistled while he beamed through the water while Benji stayed in the middle of the tunnel that corkscrewed around him.

All of a sudden, Montal's tunnel moved downward. He shot through an archway and then maneuvered through a canyon. The jagged walls toward the top were covered in coral and teeming with life. Closer to the bottom, where the two of them cruised, there was nothing but a cold sandy bottom. A few crabs and shrimp shouted and clicked their little claws when the two of them shot overhead. Montal's stream was tight and buzzed the animals with nothing more than a little annoyance. Benji's stream flipped them over and reset a few of them on their backs.

Benji shot up ten feet after almost taking a large rock in the face then shot back down when an overhang jutting out from the side almost gave him another part in his hair. Montal zipped ahead with ease like he knew this route better than the back of his hand.

Immediately, after the near parting overhang, another arch appeared. Montal shot up quickly like he was going to go over it and, at the last moment, jerked back down. Benji thought he'd save the drama and go over the arch.

He went up and over following Montal's stream until the point where it broke and went back down. Benji shot over the lip of the archway and quickly realized he'd made a mistake.

"And here he comes… and here he comes… and… Oops. Not an archway. That's a cave."

Benji wheeled himself back around and dipped below the lip of the cave. He looked for Montal's stream of water but found nothing more than a few straggling bubbles wagging their way up to the surface.

"Those could be oyster burps or mahloowos for all I know."

Montal grabbed Benji's tail and yanked him down. "I thought I told you…"

"The one time I zig instead of zag, you lose me," said Benji.

"Remember that," said Montal.

"Huh?" said Benji.

"That was my Octavius impression. A few words with some supposedly deep meaning. Not much further. Come on," said Montal.

A small circle of light emanated off Montal. He bobbed like a little swaying lantern on a stick. The cave they headed into was fifty feet from floor to ceiling and Montal chose to swim right down the center, making it almost impossible for Benji to see anything other than the little, glowing water fairy.

"Any way you can shine a little brighter?" asked Benji "Or swim a little closer to the walls?"

"Can I get you anything to eat or drink while you're back there, an extra blanket, fluff your pillow, princess?" said Montal.

Benji took that as a no and kept up his pace behind his escort. They drifted on and on for a good thirty minutes. Montal didn't say a word the rest of the way. If they made any turns or went up or down they were so slight Benji couldn't tell.

Montal began making a clicking noise. It sounded like random noise to cut out the monotony of going up or down or left or right through the deep, dark, cavernous tunnel.

After a few minutes, Montal's noises became a little more pronounced and began to pick up a rhythm Benji could distinguish.

"Been a while since I've done this. Keep your fingers crossed," said Montal.

"How long is a while?"

"I stopped coming down here three years ago. I didn't think you were coming back."

"Why not?"

"Ten years is a long time to wait."

"How do you know about this place?"

"It was your father's. He built it for you. He and your mother were two of the last Mystiqs that Gouguon hadn't run off. Your father built this place for you to learn the way if anything ever happened to him."

"What way?"

"The Mystiq way."

Benji's interest spiked. Montal kept clicking. Benji noticed they were near the bottom when Montal grabbed two shells and began banging them together in unison with his clicking.

"My uncle could teach you a few things about rhythm."

Montal looked at him with an odd stare. "You sure about that?"

"Of course. He plays in a band. In fact, his guitar is the last thing I heard before I almost got bitten in half by a great white shark."

"Ah, that one."

"What?" said Benji.

Montal ignored Benji and began humming a low pitched noise in conjunction with his shell banging and clicks. The combination of the three sounded like an ancient tribal song to bring rain or praise the sun for a bountiful harvest.

In the darkness, a new light appeared. At first, the little white light was faint, a pinprick in the distance. Montal's persistence awakened the light and coaxed it into opening further. The tiny sliver of light soon became five dots. Montal raised his voice and went deeper into his tribal groove. The dots moved away from each other, and more lights followed them until the entire pattern blossomed and the shape became fully recognizable. They were petals on a blooming flower. As the points of light gently unfolded, five triangular petals of white light appeared, hovering above the floor of the cave, no bigger than the palm of Benji's hand.

As all of this happened, Montal kept on with his clicking and banging and humming. Another tiny beam of light came shining through the darkness beside the one that had already unfolded. This one was neon green. Then another: opaque pink. And another: electric blue. Each one that unfolded revealed tentacle-like leaves that seemed to grow and shrink as the sparkling microscopic shards of light purred up and down them.

Before Benji knew it, the entire floor of the cave swayed as the glowing flowers bobbed in the gentle current. The cold, hard darkness that enveloped them upon their arrival receded and gave way to the warmth of life, light, and the cushiony plushness of all the underwater flowers covering the floor, walls, and ceiling. Some were blue, some red, some were green and yellow, others were bright white with specks of purple and pink running through them, fluorescent veins of happiness and intrigue that captivated Benji to no end.

Montal hovered behind Benji watching him slowly move his head around the massive cave, taking it all in with the wonder of a child.

"Do the surprises ever stop down here?" asked Benji.

"Nope," said Montal.

Benji stretched his neck up and down, left and right. He turned upside down, right side up, left side down, and all around gazing, staring, and admiring.

"The ocean's a big place. Much more so than all that land the Topsiders treat like garbage. More space means more surprises. I suppose it would take you hundreds of years to see all that Topside has to offer. It would take you thousands more to see all that Aquari has hidden amongst its vast nooks and crannies. I see things I've never seen before every single day," said Montal.

"Like this?" said Benji spreading his arms wide.

"This place is special, but there are more places like this, and based on what I just said, I would wager that a lot more of this exists in the oceans, seas, rivers, and lakes all over the world," said Montal.

"This is amazing. What kind of trick do you have hidden in here that's going to help us with Gouguon?" said Benji.

"This isn't the place I wanted to show you. This is the, uh, welcome area."

Montal swam into the sea of colorfully lit sea flowers poking out from the wall. He started up the side and stopped about six feet up looking for something behind all the floating, glowing petals.

"Need any help?" asked Benji.

"Yeah, but you can't do anything for me right now. You don't know what you're looking for," said Montal.

"Give me a description, and I'll see what I can do."

"You're looking for a handprint on the wall. A hand about the same size as yours. First, look for a cluster of sea flowers in the shape of infinity. That will lead us to the handprint."

"Infinity?"

"The symbol. Looks like the Topsider's figure eight... sideways."

"Gotcha."

"It's been a while, so there's a good chance they've overgrown your mother's intentions."

"My mother designed this?"

"Yeah. Some talent, huh?"

"Wow."

"You gotta coax them. Be gentle with them. Love them. That's why the cachazi are better with that sort of thing. Mothering instincts, you know?"

"Cachazi?"

"The females."

Benji backed up until he was almost touching the opposite wall. He felt the sea flowers reaching out toward him. Their energy carried a small charge that tickled his spine.

The glare overpowered Benji's ability to sort out many details. He closed his eyes to a sliver and began surveying the opposite wall. Swaying flower light and Montal's grumbling beneath the moving patch helped Benji locate the water fairy.

Benji scanned the wall above Montal and stopped suddenly. "I think I see it."

Montal popped out of a tangle of sea flowers, shot back a few feet, and followed Benji's gaze.

"Yep. I didn't think it was that far up. Shows how long it's been since I've been here. It's a lot smaller than I remember."

Montal dove back into the spot Benji found.

Benji swam over looking for Montal under the shaking petals.

"Let me see your hand," said Montal, popping out from under the glowing greenery.

Benji held out his hand.

Montal grabbed his thumb and yanked him forward.

"See this?" said Montal as he twisted Benji's thumb toward his face.

"Ow!"

"Shake it off," said the water fairy.

Montal rubbed the pad of Benji's thumb with his hand. "This…" he said jabbing his own finger at the thumbprint, "is your family's mark. This is your ticket inside."

Benji looked at his thumbprint, something he couldn't ever remember doing. Two overlapping circles wrapped their way over the pad of his thumb. He jerked his hand up close to his face and Montal stumbled off. Benji looked at his thumb closer then examined each of his other fingers. They all had the same pattern etched on them, tiny but discernible.

"I can't believe I've never noticed that before."

"I couldn't tell you what mine look like either. Not something most of us pay attention to is it?"

"No, I guess not."

"Put your hand inside. Feel around for a handprint. Match your hand to the indentation and then…"

Benji looked at him waiting for more.

"What?" said Montal.

"And then?" asked Benji.

"I don't remember. A door opens? The flowers part? A tunnel appears?"

"Nothing's going to grab my hand or attack us is it?"

"No. That'd be funny though," said Montal.

Benji raised his eyebrows and then shook head. "You have an interesting sense of humor."

"Nothing we couldn't handle, pup. You'd laugh if it was me. It's always funny as long as it happens to someone else."

"Here goes." Benji parted the flowers with both hands looking for the handprint. "They're too thick."

"Just put your hand in there and feel around," said Montal.

Benji pursed his lips and did as Montal suggested. He pulled his head back and slipped his right hand in. The flowers went quickly by his wrist then edged up to his elbow. They touched his bicep before his fingertips brushed the surface of the wall.

Montal watched intently. "There yet?"

"I just hit the wall."

"Don't worry. Those flowers might tickle you, but they aren't going to hurt you."

"I got some grooves."

"That's it, then. Fit your hand in them and let's get going."

Benji pushed his hand against the wall and adjusted his fingers to slide into the grooves. He jerked his body and Montal jumped.

"What was that?" said Montal.

"The stone felt like it was getting warmer. It stopped though."

"Flower pee," said Montal.

Benji looked disgusted.

"Gotcha," said Montal grabbing his sides laughing.

Suddenly a giant rumble filled the cave. Benji and Montal both floated away from the flowers. A hole gradually expanded until it was ten feet across and ten feet tall. A faint light from within beckoned them forward.

"Have you ever been inside?" asked Benji.

"Yeah. Thirteen years ago," said Montal.

Montal moved forward, and Benji followed behind him.

"What were they like?" said Benji, looking around at the entrance to the lair as they swam inside.

"Who?" said Montal.

"My parents," said Benji.

"Oh, yeah. Good Aquarien. Your mother, Kila, was a sweetheart. Fierce. She was a warrior at heart, but most Aquarien never saw that side of her. Most Aquarien knew her as a healer. Some would swear just being in her presence healed them. I saw her place her hands on a blind pup once, eyes cloudy as the sky before a hurricane. Ten minutes later the pup had normal looking eyes that worked just as well as mine or yours. Things like that were routine for her. It was amazing to be around.

"Your parents were what we call a match made in Tootiki," said Montal.

"Too - who?"

"The Topsiders call it heaven."

"Sometimes they'd make you uncomfortable if you were around them and they locked eyes. Nothing inappropriate, but sparks flew when they gazed into each other's eyes. A lot of Aquarien, cachazi especially, were jealous of that, but you can't replace that gaze with another. Two souls like that don't come together very often.

"Your father was quiet, but in a reflective, powerful way," said Montal.

"What was his name?"

"Boone. He enjoyed his time alone or with your mother. In the company of others you'd never know he preferred being alone. He wasn't outgoing or overbearing or schmoozy. He had one of those smiles and something about him that attracted people to him. He rallied a lot of Aquarien behind him in his effort to propose some treaties with the Topsiders. Most Aquarien trusted him and expected him to make things happen, but most also distrusted the Topsiders, so when Gouguon threw his weight behind a rebellion to try and force your father out of the way, that fear... that fear of fear took over and won Aquari back over to Gouguon's side.

"My money would have been on your father to get things done, but in the end, he never had his chance. Gouguon made sure of that. Thankfully, you were already born. You weren't but a few days old when they attacked. How your mom slid you by without getting a scratch on that head of yours is a mystery to me, but you came out alright, and that's what matters," said Montal.

"And I'm all that's left?"

"There may be few Mystiqs left. In fact, I know there are, but they are in hiding. The majority of them took off Topside around the time your dad and Gouguon were verbally battling it out.

"Most of them didn't want to wait around and see any further damage done to Aquari and Sanjowqua by the Topsiders. Kind of an 'if you can't beat 'em, join 'em' mentality, I guess. Don't bother yourself with them. If they were worth the trouble, we'd be looking for them, but they left, so they got no fight in 'em. Those aren't Aquarien you want to be surrounded by right now," said Montal.

"You got a point," said Benji.

The two of them moved forward into the tunnel. Benji blew a few bubbles and watched them collect on the ceiling. Three of them bounced around in the grooves above him and eventually came together to form a larger bubble. Benji looked up and caught sight of his reflection smiling back at him.

Montal, swimming along on his back, stuck his tongue out at the reflection it cast back at Benji and kept swimming.

"Topside, we can yell in a cave like this and hear an echo," said Benji.

"Thanks for the fun trivia," said Montal.

"Just saying," said Benji.

"Here you can't," said Montal. "Just saying."

"So what's in here?" asked Benji.

"Your father's gunga galunga."

"Excuse me?"

"It's a bubble room."

"What's a bubble room?"

"If you had to take a wild stab at it, what do you think a bubble room would be?"

"Let's see," said Benji rubbing his chin. "A room filled with bubbles?"

"You are today's grand champion winner. What do we have for our contestant, Johnny? Well Montal, today's lucky contestant gets an all-expense paid trip to the end of the tunnel where he'll find the bubble room… hopefully."

"OK. You just made it official. You are my worst nightmare."

"How so?"

"If I could give a form to my conscience, and give it the ability to talk, I'm pretty sure it would be a sarcastic, little…"

BAM!

A flash of light buzzed Benji's eyes, then both his nostrils stretched so hard he thought his nose had been ripped off his face. Benji ended up on his back staring up at the ceiling of the cave. He felt a knot already forming on the back of his head where he hit the rocky bottom.

"That's getting off easy," said Montal jumping up and down on Benji's chin with both his fist balled up and swirling around. "I warned you back at the boat."

"I forgot," said Benji.

"Won't do it again, will you?" said Montal.

"That'd be a safe bet." Benji popped a bubble out of his mouth, and they both watched it lollygag up to the top of the cave and bobble in the grooves of the ceiling before settling into a nice spot to rest. "Man, you're quick."

"Don't forget it."

Mystiq Punglo

(mystiq lair)

BENJI FLOATED OFF the floor and brushed himself off. He glanced at Montal who still had a smug look on his face. Montal pumped his head toward Benji causing him to jerk back.

"Woah!"

"Come on, pup." Montal grinned and waved him toward the dim light coming from the opposite end the tunnel.

Silver streaks flickered past them as a dozen bar jacks made their way into the cave. The crevices in the tunnel made the passage look like the digestive tract of a rather large beast.

"This looks familiar," said Montal as they rounded the corner and floated in front of a lit entranceway.

Shards of pale white light reached down to the floor giving them a reverent look at the bubble room. The illumination came from a skylight at the end of a long recess that extended fifty feet from the center of the room. Two large doorways showcased the open space. A large pedestal stood in the middle of the room. On top of the pedestal sat a large bowl that resembled a clear, crystal pinecone with the top third missing. The beam entering from the skylight collected in the bowl and deflected onto hundreds of infinity symbols lining drawers around the circular enclosure.

Upon closer inspection, there was one very large doorway that stretched ten feet wide and fifteen feet high. What appeared as a column in the middle was actually a humongous strawberry vase coral, the top spread almost four feet in diameter and nearly reached the upper casing of the doorway. The sides of the doorways were covered in rose lace coral and yellow pencil coral. White and black, and blue and yellow damsels danced in and out of the coral. A blue angelfish corkscrewed its way around the vase coral in the middle of the doorway.

Benji crossed the threshold before Montal could reach him. As soon as Benji entered the room, the water rushed out and dropped him on his backside. Montal, reaching for Benji, got pulled into the room as the water rushed out through vents in the floor.

Benji shed his tail and stood up. Montal fluttered up around Benji's shoulder.

Benji walked over to the doorway and put his hand up against a wall of water that now separated the circular room from the tunnel. He pushed against the water wall. It gave, but only by a few inches.

"That's freaky," said Benji. "It's like Jello."

"Who?"

"It's a snack they eat Topside."

Benji pushed his hand against it once more and looked out into the hall. The reflection of his head morphed and changed with the moving water.

"Stop goofing around," snapped Montal.

"So what is this place?" said Benji.

"This is your father's bubble room. It looks like the bubble room from Sanjowqua. Spitting image actually. In Sanjowqua, there are drawers all around the room. Each one is filled with a collection of bubbles. The bubbles are logs; they're thoughts, experiences, and feelings from generations past. Boone did the same thing here."

Benji walked over to the curved wall and ran his fingers along the symbols etched in the drawers. Infinity symbols lined the wall from the ceiling all the way down to his ankles. The floor of the room glowed with an electric blue light emanating from the translucent etchings on the drawers. Benji recognized other markings sketched above the infinity symbols.

"I've seen these before on the globe from the ship."

"Yeah, they're dates. One slash is one. Two diagonally down equals two. The triangle is…"

"…three. Meena taught me," said Benji bending over and putting his hands on his knees as he took a closer look. "They're all upside down."

"What do you mean?"

"The numbers are upside down."

"That's weird," said Montal buzzing over Benji's shoulder.

Looking at the drawers to the right of the water wall, Benji walked a few paces, picked a random drawer about knee height, and placed his thumbprint over the infinity engraving. A small click preceded the drawer separating from the wall. Benji pulled it out, and water splashed on his feet. White anemones lined the inside. Benji brushed his hand over their stubby tentacles and shook his head. "Hmm."

"What's the matter?" said Montal, sitting atop the pine cone-shaped bowl.

"There's nothing in here. Just some anemones."

"Pick another one."

Benji slid his hand up and unlocked another drawer. It slid open, and the white anemones greeted him again. "Déjà vu. You think someone's been in here?"

"Doubtful anyone could make it through what we have," said Montal. "Unless you have a twin I didn't know about."

Benji shrugged. He looked around the room with his hands on his hips. He had started opening the drawers at the bottom, closest to the water wall, and worked his way up diagonally. After coming up empty half a dozen times, he took a step back and looked at his work. "Stairs," he mumbled. "Is there anything up at the surface?"

"A whole lot of nothing. We're maybe a couple hundred yards from the mouth of the cave. I can't ever recall going past this point on the surface, but if I had to guess, I'm sticking with my original assumption: Nothing. Nada. Kapanaka," said Montal.

"Kapanaka?"

"Aquarien for nothing."

"Yeah, that's a fun one. Kapanaka. Maybe someone snuck in here from the surface. I'm going up for a look."

Benji maneuvered up the circular wall opening drawers as he went to create more stairs. He ran out of drawers a few feet from the recess that led to the surface.

"There are some hand and foot holds in here. Sketchy, but looks like I can shimmy up this tunnel." Benji glanced down at Montal. "Who would my father have wanted to keep out of here?"

"That's a long list, my friend. You could add pretty much every Aquariens' name in each of the four oceans at one point or another."

"Why add this recess, though? I mean, someone could go down from wherever this comes out. From the looks of the empty drawers, it looks like they already have."

"Unless there *is* land up there. That would keep anybody out who wasn't a Mystiq or who wasn't a Topsider. How much further you got?"

"Well, there's no elevator, and I don't see any signs for what floor I'm at right now, so I'm going with I'll be there when I get there."

"Fair enough. Anything of interest up there?"

"Not unless you like crawling up tight spaces. I'm not a fan myself. I'd much prefer your vantage point."

"Yeah, climbing's not really my thing. You're making good progress, or the light is playing tricks on my eyes."

"I'm close to the top."

Benji inched toward the top, and when he went to reach up through the light, he stumped the tips of his fingers on a layer of water glass similar to what had formed in the doorway of room below. He ran his hand around the edge and found an infinity symbol. When he touched it, the water skylight evaporated, and he slowly poked his head up above the surface.

"Woah."

"What's, 'Woah'?"

"This tunnel is surrounded by a reef. There's a little island in the middle. Looks like a mirage; a pitcher's mound of sand with a coconut tree in the middle. About as typically marooned as you can get. It's missing a bearded old man with rags, a cane pole, and a few bottles with 'help me' messages surrounding him."

"What are you waiting for?"

"Huh?"

"Get out there and check it out. Can you swim?"

"I've been known to get my feet wet."

"HA! You're starting to come around, pup. Keep 'em coming. Makes life much more fun."

Benji smiled. "No. It's a shallow reef as far as I can see. Looks like the circumference of a hundred yards of nothing but coral. The island looks like it's dead center. I'm halfway between the island and the outer edge of the reef."

Benji stepped out onto the sharp, rocky reef. "Ow!"

"What's the matter?"

"I have to walk across this reef to get to the island, and it hurts my feet."

"Toughen 'em up, twinkle toes."

"Yeah, I'll just change..." Benji looked down at his toes. He imagined a tougher skin on his feet. Just below his knees, the skin turned grey. The color inched down his legs until it disappeared past his toenails. Benji reached down and ran his hand over a tougher layer of skin now covering his lower extremities. "Awesome!" he said, marching out across the reef. He got halfway to the island and looked back at the hole. "Can you still hear me?"

A small splash of water echoed up through the skylight. Montal had nodded off on the rim of the crystal pine cone. Benji startled him awake, and the water fairy plopped back into the bowl full of water.

"Uh, yeah. Let me know when you get out there and tell me what you see," said Montal.

Benji made his way across the coral. A shark's fin slid through the water past the reef on the other side of the island. He was pretty sure they hadn't been followed, but now that he thought about it, he hadn't paid that much attention. He'd been following Montal. The fin disappeared in the water heading back out to sea.

Sharks live in the sea. Not all of them are after me.

"Nope. Remember that, pup. I wouldn't go trying to make friends with every one of them I see, but…"

Benji took one last step on the rock and leapt a few feet onto the sandy island. The whole island tipped heavy to one side, and Montal started yelling up a storm. A ripe coconut dislodged itself from the top of the tree nearly taking out Benji's head on the way down.

"WOAH! WOAH! WOAH!! What was that?!! What'd you just do?!!" yelled Montal.

"I jumped on the island. It almost flipped over," said Benji.

"The walls started rotating. See if you can flip it."

"Excuse me?"

"Flip the island."

"Flip the island says the guy in the bubble room. Sure. I'll just flip the island. That's just a normal thing to do on any normal day when you find out you're a merman and your best friend is a water fairy. Yeah, flip the island, and magic golden coins will start falling from the sky," muttered Benji.

"That's stupid! Whoever heard of gold falling from the sky?" said Montal.

Benji snorted. *Exactly.*

Benji looked up. The tree stood twenty feet tall.

"Why not?" He threw his hands around and clamped his thighs to the trunk. When he reached the top, he leaned back and pulled with everything he had. The tree dipped toward the water, and the little sandy island below began to sway. After a few minutes, he had the trunk nearly parallel with the water.

"Whatever you're doing, keep doing it," yelled Montal while floating on his back with his head resting in his hands in the crystal bowl.

The reef on the eastern and western side of the island extended out twenty feet; long enough to squeeze a coconut tree through. When the top of the tree kissed the water, Benji held on with both hands and dropped his feet in. As soon as his waist was wet, he switched to his tail. He kept one arm snug on the tree and swam down as hard as he could. He got halfway down before the tree started pulling him back to the surface.

Next go around, I got it.

The island turned upright, and the tree dipped in the water on the other side. Benji changed his tail and pulled it the rest of the way until the tree pointed directly below, the island now completely turned over. Bits of sand drifted through the water glimmering off the afternoon sun.

Benji surfaced and called out to Montal, "And?"

"We're in business. Bring those prints of yours in here, and let's get to work," hollered Montal.

Benji made his way back over the reef. When he got to the tunnel, Montal waited with his arms hung over the side like he was lounging in a tub.

Benji looked him over with a smirk. "Thanks for the help. What happened in there?"

Montal peeked around Benji at the island in the distance. "Where's the tree?"

"It's on the other side."

"Of?"

"The island."

"That island's barely big enough to hold the two of us. How's it on the other side?"

"You're looking at the top."

"And?"

"It's on the bottom."

"That's interesting," said Montal scratching his head.

"I thought so, too. So what happened in there?"

"Whatever you did, flipped the walls and caused the water to rush back in. My guess is you were looking at the underside of what you wanted to see earlier. Let's go find out if I'm right."

Montal slid back into the tunnel and zipped down to the main room before Benji got his foot over the lip.

"Leave it open. You'll be wanting to do the opposite of whatever you did out there once we're finished. If Boone hid things, it's a good idea we put them back that way," said Montal.

Benji slid into the water, donned his tail, and swam back down into the main room with Montal.

The entire outer wall had flipped a hundred and eighty degrees. The drawers Benji opened to climb the tunnel now sat secure in their holes. Looking at the infinity signs, Benji couldn't tell anything had changed because the symmetrical symbols looked the same way up or down. He hovered closer to the wall and confirmed that the dates sketched on the drawers were now right side up.

"When's your birthday?" asked Montal.

"That's a good question," said Benji.

"You don't know your birthday?"

"I know the day I have been celebrating the last thirteen years, but knowing what I know now, I'm pretty sure that's not my birthday."

"What do you mean?"

"Well, I think the day I have been celebrating is the day my dad found me in the turtle shell. You said I was born pretty much around that time, so we have a small window to look at."

"Yes. It would be one of the final dates. It's not like any other bubbles were added after…"

"Yeah. Kind of hard to keep a journal when you're dead."

"Agreed."

"March ninth. Three. Nine." said Benji.

The two of them swam in opposite directions looking for the date.

"Yeah. Here it is," said Benji as he ran his fingers over the numbers.

He hesitated, then put his thumb on the family mark. The drawer clicked and popped away from the wall. Benji peered over the edge and saw the top side of the drawer also covered with anemones. His heart immediately sank when purple tentacles popped out and waved at him with nothing in their grasp.

He slid the drawer all the way out. A small bubble shifted in the back corner. He released his breath with a thankful sigh as he reached back and gently grabbed it. A few anemone tentacles stayed attached but gave way without much effort once he gave a slight tug.

He held it up to the light coming through the hole in the ceiling.

"Hard to believe there's anything in there," said Benji.

Montal whispered from just above his shoulder, "I was thinking the same thing."

"What do we do with it now?" said Benji.

"Plop it in that bowl on the pedestal," said Montal.

Benji swam over to the pedestal. He held his hand out over the lip of the bowl and hesitated. "So what am I going to see here?"

"What do you mean?"

"I mean, are my parents going to pop up? Is there anything I need to prepare myself for?"

"I'd expect to see your father. He put in a lot of effort to build this place for you. His imprint, and your mother's is woven all throughout this place. But as far as what he has to say, your guess is as good as mine."

A small ripple of water massaged its way out of the corner of Benji's eye. The tear didn't roll down his cheek like it would have done Topside. As soon as it materialized, it joined the rest of the tears of the ocean, the tears of joy and sorrow, the tears of pain and ecstasy.

They're all one. We're all one.

Even though his parents were gone, he realized at that moment they were a part of him now more than ever.

"What's wrong?" asked Montal

"I've never seen my real parents before, and I just lost the man I knew as my dad. Give me a second."

Montal bowed his head and backed up.

Benji let the bubble slide out of his hand. It floated over the bowl, descending ever so slowly while a gentle but visible current manifested below. Once it dipped beneath the rim, the bubble slid in with a *slurp* and began riding the inside perimeter. Four anxious eyes followed the twirling bubble and every rotation it made. A low hum began echoing throughout the room. As the rotations increased, the sound became more prominent.

Benji looked back at Montal for an answer. Montal stared at the bowl hypnotized.

"This is normal, right?" asked Benji.

"Sure," said Montal shrugging.

The slow moaning sound now filled the entire room, reverberating through the water and vibrating everything it touched. Even the water shook, distorting Benji's vision and making him feel dizzy.

Then it stopped, replaced by complete silence. Nothing moved. The damsels who had woven in and out of the coral in the doorway froze.

Nothing gurgled. All sounds of moving water ceased.

Nothing breathed. Benji's chest seized up, his attention captivated by the silence.

The sound disappeared as fast as the light appeared. A thin ring of light gathered around the bowl and slowly expanded toward Benji, through him, and against the drawers. Once the light hit the wall, it broadened to cover every inch of the room and drowned everything in a heavenly whiteness. Benji's hands fell by his side, and his head fell back. The light lifted his spirit and released the tension in his body. He tried lifting his eyelids, but they felt glued shut, and he was completely OK with that at the moment. A blissful peace fell over him, then the light slowly faded away.

A tiny glimmer sparkled down the entranceway on the other side of the door frame. It started as a faint reflection on the walls and continued until every crevice in the tunnel wall was distinguishable. A tall shadow followed the light and with it a voice that stilled Benji's nerves.

"Welcome home, son," said the voice.

Benji stared at the figure towering in front of him. His mouth gaped open. He thought some words would materialize, but he only looked on in awe.

"My name is Boone. I am your father."

The figure stopped inside the doorway opposite Benji and Montal and bowed toward the water fairy. "Montal."

Montal bowed back. "Boone. Long time, old friend."

"Likewise. Thank you, Montal," said Boone.

"You can pay me back when I get to the other side," said Montal.

"Soon enough," said Boone.

"Woah, now," said Benji. "Montal's been an angel. Albeit, a raunchy, lit…"

Benji froze. Montal floated beside him with his head cocked ready to spring on him. Benji counted to five and continued. "So, let's not get ahead of ourselves," he said, nervously watching Montal out of the corner of his eye.

"I'm a fairy, thank you very little. Angels are a little too holier than thou for my taste." Montal grinned and relaxed. "Don't worry, pup. You're stuck with me for a while longer."

"Angels are real?" said Benji.

"Of course, they are." Montal yawned and stared at Boone. "Let's see what this pup of yours can do. He's a fast learner. Throw in a few lessons, and I think he may just have the makings of a proper Mystiq." Montal looked at Benji and then back at Boone. "He's gonna need it, too. Gouguon has the Mystiq prong. You hid it a little too well."

"It would seem, so," said Boone. "Gouguon's had his heart set on the prong for as long as I can remember, and he's had plenty of time to make his plans."

"He'll use it the first chance he gets. A lot of Aquarien think he's going to head straight for Donquari and build a fortress there to rival Sanjowqua," said Montal.

"What do you think?" asked Boone.

"I think that's a good assumption. I don't think he'd do any harm to Sanjowqua," said Montal.

"He holds a lot of anger toward Sanjowqua," said Boone.

"True, but how much of that would be used to attack the Aquarien living there? His fight is with the Topsiders," said Montal.

"Gouguon's fight is with anyone who gets in his way. I've felt his soul brewing for the last thirteen years. He's not content with sitting idle and watching things happen after simmering for so long in prison," said Boone.

"Why is everyone so worried? I thought the prong could only be used by a Mystiq," said Benji.

Boone looked deep into Benji's eyes. "Gouguon is my brother."

"Which makes him…"

"…a Mystiq," said Montal. "Oh, and your uncle."

"Interesting bit of family history. Why hasn't anyone told me? This is a little bigger than something stuck in my teeth or hanging out of my nose."

"No one else knows, Benji," said Boone. "Gouguon is my half-brother.

We have the same father which makes him half-Mystiq. But make no mistake, he's dangerous.

My father was based in Sanjowqua. He was a powerful Mystiq and a very influential Aquarien in his days. He sat on the security council in Sanjowqua and pushed to establish direct relations with the Topsiders.

"He visited Donquari, the eastern ocean, on multiple occasions and tried convincing them to do the same. The Donquarien have never trusted the Mystiqs, and my father's words fell flat.

"Gouguon's mother sat on the security council in Donquari and had a soft spot for father and the Mystiqs. Apparently, their relationship went further than mere discussions about the Topsiders," said Boone.

"What about Maylani? asked Montal.

"I don't feel she's a threat," said Boone.

Benji looked at Montal and then back at his father. "So, if Gouguon's a Mystiq, too, then I got my work cut out for me."

"Gouguon is half-Mystiq. He's also never been instructed. However, he spent the last thirteen years in prison. The things he has learned while locked up are impressive and are direct indications that he has some grasp on his powers. How much is yet to be seen," said Boone.

"But he has the Mystiq prong now, so that's like a big magnifier, right?" said Benji.

"Gouguon can do the damage he wants," said Boone nodding his head.

"Let's get started," chirped Benji.

Boone waved his hand toward the wall behind Benji. "The dates do not matter."

As Benji turned his head, several rows of drawers next to each of the doorways disappeared into the wall, freeing up space for the others as they started shifting left, right, up, and down.

"I've placed a meditative lesson in drawers with dates that add up to the number twenty-three."

"Why twenty-three?"

"That's how old your mother was when you were conceived. Once you locate the drawers with dates that add up to twenty-three, you can choose one of the meditations to open your abilities. I will not be there to help you once you unlock one of your abilities."

"How do I learn how to use these 'skills'?"

"Awareness and practice, Benji. That falls on you now."

"So I have to go around adding up all these numbers to find the number twenty-three and then choose one to help me?"

"Benji, you're a Mystiq. You are not bound by physical actions. There are many things I wish I could have been there to teach you, but your survival was the most important consideration."

"I understand."

"Skip the actions. Save yourself the energy. Use your thoughts."

Benji scratched his head. *Think. How do I solve this?*

"Don't ask. Command! What do you want? State your intention."

"I want the drawers with dates that add up to twenty-three to show themselves, so I can find what I am looking for."

The lights on all the drawers went dim.

Benji turned around the room, his eyes darting in different directions as the infinity symbols on dozens of drawers began popping out of the darkness one by one.

Benji nodded his head and crossed his arms in front of him. "I want the drawer with the bubble that will help me reclaim the Mystiq prong."

All of the symbols went dim again except for two on opposite ends of the room.

"What next?"

"That choice is yours, Benji," said Boone.

"I don't know what I am doing."

Benji's nose felt like it was being peeled off his face. In a flash, he found himself on his back again. He looked up through the recess in the ceiling. A white puffy cloud in the shape of a box turtle scurried across the sky.

"What the…?"

"Two things you never say," said Montal bouncing up and down on Benji's chin.

"Two?" said Boone.

"Yeah. First is the 'L' word," said Montal.

"Ah. I almost forgot," chuckled Boone.

"What's the other?" asked Benji.

"I don't know," said Montal.

"Then why did you toss me on the floor again?" asked Benji rubbing the back of his head.

"That's it. I don't know," insisted Montal.

"So you have some crazy impulse to slam me on the floor that pops out every once in awhile like some nervous tick?" said Benji.

Boone spoke up. "You do know, Benji. The answer is always within you. You always know. Before you think you don't, stop and look inside. You'll find it."

"I know," whispered Benji. "I know."

Montal smiled at Boone. "I told you he was a fast learner."

"What if I'm wrong?" asked Benji.

"That'll never happen," joked Montal.

"What you think is wrong, is never the case. Wrong equals a lesson you need to learn. Wrong equals a learning opportunity," said Boone.

"I hope wrong is less painful than getting nasal slammed on the floor," said Benji.

Montal flexed his bicep at Benji.

"Sometimes it is. Sometimes it isn't," said Boone.

Boone held out both of his arms and pointed at the drawers on the opposite sides of the room. "The choice is now yours, Benji. Good luck, son."

Benji's eyes followed his father's left arm to one of the lit drawers. The numbers under the infinity symbol began to get brighter. *Two. One. Six. Five. One. Eight.*

"Sixty-five eighteen? What year is it?" asked Benji.

"The current year is ninety-three seventy-six. We started our dates based on the year Poseidon bestowed the trident upon us and gave us the protective sanctuary that is now Sanjowqua," said Boone.

Benji followed his father's right hand to the other wall. *Three. Four. Three. Nine. Four. Zero.*

Benji looked at his father for help. Boone nodded. "Close your eyes. See the drawer. See inside. See the answer. What does it tell you?"

Benji closed his eyes and pictured the numbers: *Two. One. Six. Five. One. Eight.*

He floated up in the water letting his mind take over. The first drawer gave him an empty feeling in his stomach.

He opened his eyes and looked deep into those of his father and nodded his head.

He closed his eyes again, picturing the second set of numbers in his head: *Three. Four. Three. Nine. Four. Zero.*

I know, he thought.

Benji drifted over to the second drawer. He paused for a second to reconfirm his feeling. *I know.*

He placed his thumb on the infinity symbol. The drawer unlocked, sliding out a few inches. Benji tilted his head and peered through the crack then grabbed the drawer and slid it open. Two egg-sized bubbles bobbled in the center of the drawer. He looked over his shoulder at his father. "Both of them, or do I choose?"

"That's for you to decide, Benji. Ask yourself."

Benji looked back at Montal who shrugged his shoulders, then he turned back and scooped up both of the bubbles. He closed the drawer and swam over to the bowl in the middle of the room.

As he held his hand over the bowl, he noticed the strawberry vase sponge moving. With the walls flipped, the top of the vase now hovered six inches from the floor.

The bubbles slid out of his hand, floating just above the rim of the bowl. As they passed the lip, the slurping sound sucked them in and twirled them around. The strawberry vase sponge parted like a cape down the center, revealing a cushiony space big enough for Benji.

"Will I see you again?" asked Benji.

"When you're ready," said Boone.

The gentle hum of the bubbles going around the bowl echoed all throughout the room. Benji's eyes drooped. His skin tingled from the inside out. He flicked his tail twice and slid across the room into the awaiting open flaps of the vase coral.

He didn't know how he knew what he was doing. He only followed his feelings.

As he turned around and settled in, the two halves of the sponge wrapped themselves around him, holding him snug within its cushiony folds.

The hum of the bubbles circulating in the bowl massaged into every inch of his skin. It worked its magic between his bones and muscles, then moved out further between his muscles and his skin. The process repeated again and again until it rattled him from head to toe and everywhere in between indiscriminately and simultaneously.

His mind began racing. Images and short clips flashed inside his skull; some like lightning, others hanging around for a few seconds longer like rolling thunder after a strike.

He saw Joe and the fishing boat. He sat on Joe's lap in the captain's chair steering out into the big, blue ocean.

Charlie Goodstone popped in his head with the stinging splat of a spitball.

Octavius, Mai, Eeke, and Zeeke popped out of the water underneath him and begged him to join them.

He looked down and saw the tip of his surfboard cruising over the waves. Miss Wendy waved from the shore.

He saw kids in his school mocking his height and the 'scars' on his neck.

One by one, memories flashed in his head. The pleasant ones faded with a gentle smile. The painful memories stuck, forcing him to relive every aspect of them.

A slow-motion clip of Charley Goodstone pushing Benji on the pier wandered into his head. Along with it, a sense of anxiety, pain, and anger flooded into him.

The memory stood still, and Benji hovered above it. He had a three hundred and sixty degree view of the entire event. When he looked back from Charley's perspective, he saw the great white shark exploding through the water, splintering the dock, and missing his leg by inches. He saw his legs fly into the air under the exploding wood and Octavius' outstretched tentacles yanking him into the water so Meena and Jaylon could tow him to safety.

If Charley hadn't pushed me, that shark would have had me for lunch, he thought.

The darkness around the memory lightened. Benji looked up and saw the clouds in the sky, the sunlight kissing the water with its golden rays, the seagulls dive bombing the bait ball at the end of the canal. Bright white light flooded the now frozen clip and Benji's mind emptied. His body floated securely in the strawberry vase sponge with only a few inches of water around him. The sponge shook gently causing the water between the two of them to cushion Benji with the most comforting embrace he'd ever felt.

Another clip popped into his head. This time the kids at school teased him about his height. "Hey, string bean," they called. "Hey, too tall," they yelled. One of them poked fun at the scars on his neck. "Look! Fishboy is here," they taunted.

The memory started the same. A dark, swirling cloud surrounded the clip. Benji hovered over each of the kids and noticed fear on a few of their faces. He noticed the unmistakable mask of one of them looking for approval from another as he hurled an insult.

Benji's mind and his attention floated down to his pulsating gills and smiled. With that smile, the black cloud around the clip grew gray. His mind went further down his body to his long, lean, powerful tail. Benji smiled again, this time with his entire body. The gray cloud turned white, then disappeared, surrounding him and penetrating him with bright white light.

He felt his pulse. *Thump. Thump. Thump.* It coincided with the white light flowing into his body. The thump was a pump, a pump of healing energy.

Benji's mind repeated these scenes over and over. Each time, the dark clouds faded and the white light got more intense. Each time he conquered a painful memory, he felt peace wash over him.

As the white light drenched Benji's body, his attention shifted to his forehead. The light rushed out of his head again, but it wasn't a darkness that consumed him. He quickly realized he stood behind a closed door. A door with no handle. The light he had become accustomed to seeing shone through the cracks around the frame. It was there. Benji had not lost it. He simply needed to open the door.

His eyes traced the doorframe. The edges illuminated by a thin spectrum seeping out of the crease. He pulled on the no-handled door with his mind, and a tsunami of white light came rushing through the hole. It washed over him then through him.

Benji took a deep breath letting it pour down into his lungs, filling his blood vessels, coursing through every cell in his body.

Benji floated in the white light with his arms and legs spread. He didn't want to leave. It comforted him. It cleansed him. It supported him. It educated him. It provided for and nurtured him.

A figure came from the distance. There were no shadows, only areas where the light didn't penetrate. The figure spoke to Benji softly. Asking, not demanding or begging, merely requesting that he follow, knowing full well he would, when he was ready. Time did not matter in the light. Nothing mattered or was required other than existing. Benji followed. He did so in the most blissful state he had ever felt.

"You're healed," said the angelic female voice. "It's time, Benji."

"Already?" said Benji.

"You're ready," she said.

"Are you sure?" said Benji.

"Yes."

"Who are you?"

"I am the healer."

The light disappeared, leaving Benji disoriented and cramped in the tiny cocoon of the sponge. "No! Wait!"

Benji had questions, but they fell to the rear as a sharp wail pierced his head. Not a soft low hum like the bubbles in the crystal bowl. This was a sound of pain, of anguish. Someone had been hurt and not just one someone. Many souls cried out at once.

The pain they felt didn't last long. It was there and gone in a flash. The mass realization of bodies separated from souls. The unexpected end of life shocked them all; immediately cut off from those they loved, bodies they had grown used to, places they'd called home.

Benji felt like a giant vacuum cleaner had been placed over his heart and turned on high, like his feelings and emotions were sucked from his chest. His head bobbled on his neck, bouncing from side to side. The longer it pulled on his heart, the more he drooped.

Outside the sponge, the bubbles in the pine cone-shaped vase kicked into high gear. The gentle humming of the spheres rimming the interior of the vase flicked at Benji's ears. He caught the sound, and it lifted his spirit. He lost it and started caving in on himself again. He wrestled with both feelings over and over again until the humming finally drowned out the despair that had invaded his space.

Benji's mind went dark, and he floated inside his skull in nothingness. Up. Down. Left. Right. Nothing surrounded him but complete darkness. He no longer relied on his eyes to give him direction. He sat back in the middle of his head, his own cockpit, staring into the darkness.

Suddenly, the bubble room came into his view. He looked down from the top of the ceiling. Montal sat propped up against the crystal bowl letting the humming of the circulating bubbles massage his back; eyes closed, index finger halfway up his nose.

Benji swung down in front of Montal and silently thanked the water fairy.

Montal's eyes shot open and darted to either side. "You can see me, can't you, pup? You're here, aren't you?" said Montal.

Benji smiled. *I can see.*

Benji turned around and went out of the bubble room, down the tunnel, and out through the entrance of the cave. He surfaced. A crescent moon shined down on him. Mars and Venus shone brightly over the moon forming a smiley face in the cloudless evening sky.

Benji lifted himself above the water until he floated ten feet in the air. He wasn't sure which way he had come, but he knew the way back. He knew everything he needed to know when he needed to know it.

He flew over the water. The fresh ocean air whipped through his hair. The cosmic evening twinkle reflected off the waves sandwiching him between heaven and earth.

A group of barrier islands in front of him caught his attention. He slowed down and dipped closer to the water.

Where's the Fringe? He zipped over and around the island.

This one's part of the inner rings. I must have rushed past the Fringe.

He dipped down into the water. Sure enough, the coral on this island was more lively than the Fringe.

He poked around the exterior of the reef, ears primed, listening for any sounds. It was late at night, but a few creatures stirred under the island. Benji heard several sniffles and a stern voice up ahead. He moved closer and settled a couple of feet from a queen angelfish lecturing a couple of juvenile squirrelfish.

"And you think running off into the open water is going to bring him back? NO! NO! NO, little fries. The Fringe has fallen. And those that lived there are gone along with it," said the elder fish.

"It's not fair," chirped one of the squirrelfish.

"It's life, little fry. That's what it is," said the angelfish.

"We can't just do nothing," squeaked the other squirrelfish.

"Running off on your own isn't going to solve anything," said the angelfish.

"Uncle Cardy would have…"

"Your uncle was a good, brave fish. He'll surely be missed… along with all the others, but I can tell you this: he'd definitely not approve of any rogue behavior from a couple of fries. Do you plan on taking on Gouguon yourselves?" said the angelfish.

"Well, no, but we have to do something. We need to find the Mystiq. He's the one that can stop Gouguon," said one of the squirrelfish.

"He's half Topsider. Do you trust him to make the right decisions for Sanjowqua? I'm not sure I do," said the angelfish.

I'll do right by everyone.

The queen angelfish jerked around and scuttled out a few feet, swimming right through where Benji had set up to listen. Having seen nothing, she hustled back around and shooed the little fish home.

"Swim along now. It's late. Get a good night rest. Tomorrow's a new day," said the angelfish.

The Fringe has fallen. Benji blinked, and his consciousness slammed back into his body, into the space it occupied in the strawberry vase sponge.

He pushed against the walls of the sponge with his elbows. Nothing happened. He shoved the sponge with his hands and used his back as leverage. The soft interior absorbed all his energy. He slowed down and took several deep breaths. Then, he closed his eyes and pulled his hands to his sides.

I need to leave. A sliver of moonlight raced in from the bottom as the sponge parted down the middle. Benji sauntered out.

Montal sat on the pedestal staring into his eyes. "Welcome back, sleeping beauty. What's wrong?"

"The Fringe has fallen."

Miziwu

(ghost)

"COME ON," PROTESTED Benji. "We've got to do something."

"Has the memory of that fishing lesson with Meena worn off?" asked Montal.

"You were spying on me there, too, huh?"

"Guilty. You remember what happened?"

"I don't need a reminder," said Benji unconsciously rubbing his ribs.

"Good. Slow down. You've been in the sponge for a while now, Benji."

"What? An hour, right?"

Montal snorted. "How do you feel?"

"I feel good. I feel…" Benji closed his eyes. "I feel clear."

"Some things have changed."

"In an hour?"

"First of all, you're right. The Fringe fell. Gouguon brought down the Fringe. The power of the Shequarien prong that guards Sanjowqua is now being used to hold up the rest of the archipelago. The field that protects Sanjowqua doesn't expand any further than the eighth ring of islands."

"What does that mean?"

"The field kept Sanjowqua off the radar. The field kept ships and planes and any other means of intrusion from the outside away from Sanjowqua.

That field has been reduced to only cover the islands which means people will start stumbling closer and closer to Sanjowqua."

"How did all this happen? How long was I in there?"

"A month."

"A MONTH?! Thirty days of my life just disappeared in that fat, red sponge? You've got to be kidding me."

"I'm not."

Benji rubbed his chin. "Did I grow a beard? Is my hair white?"

"No, and yeah."

"What?" said Benji pulling his bangs out in front of his forehead.

"You don't have a beard or white hair. You're still thirteen, going on fourteen," said Montal. "Are you ready?"

"That's what I've been told. Hey, how did you know all of that?"

"The ocean is alive, Benji. The coral talks. The animals of Aquari relay the messages. We're all connected."

"I feel it now. Those bubbles must have cleared away some blocks I had."

"They did. What you are capable of is more a result of the limitations you put on yourself than the limitations that actually exist. Come on. Let's close up shop and send you off."

"Where's my father? Will I ever see him again?"

"He imparted his wisdom throughout the memories left in this room. And if you keep progressing, there's no limit to when you can see him, your mother, or Joe."

Benji nodded his head in acceptance. "I never got to see my mother."

"Part of her was with you... is always with you, whether you realize it or not."

"I felt her," said Benji as he floated up the tunnel. He put his hands on the edge of the skylight to pull himself up and tromp across the reef back to the island.

Montal cleared his throat.

"What is it?" asked Benji staring back down the tunnel at Montal.

"This place is organic, not mechanic. It's part of you. It recognizes you now."

"Interesting," said Benji scrunching up his face processing Montal's statement. Benji looked at the bare island across the reef and closed his eyes.

There should be a coconut tree on top of that island.

The island flipped over.

"AHHHHHHHH!" shouted a crab who had been scurrying across the sand and got catapulted out into the middle of the reef.

A huge wall of water arched across the reef as the coconut tree surged out of the ocean and snapped straight in the air. One of the coconuts launched from the plumage. Benji and Montal watched the coconut clear the reef, skip twice, and plop down into the clear, blue water with a splash.

Benji grabbed the edge of the skylight as the water rushed down his waist and out of the room.

I'd like the water back in the room.

The walls of the room continued to flip upside down. The water stopped draining and began pumping back into the room.

"Nice work, pup," said Montal, hovering beside Benji.

Benji closed the top, drifted down the tunnel, and hovered in the room taking stock of everything around him. The strawberry vase sponge stood straight upright. Benji ran his fingers along the wall. The symbols on each drawer lit up as his hand waved over them. The numbers were now flipped upside down again.

"That's a wrap," said Benji. "You ready?"

Benji fluttered out of the room and down the tunnel toward the cave.

"Montal, let's go. I need your light out here."

Montal didn't answer. Benji turned back toward the bubble room.

"Montal. Hey. Let's go!"

Benji poked his head into the room and looked on at Montal sitting on the pedestal with his back against the crystal bowl, his head drooping. The fairy's chin touched his chest and then bounced back up.

Benji rushed over. "Hey, man. This is no time for a nap. We need to get going."

Montal lifted his weary eyes and gave Benji a shake of the head before his chin bounced off his chest again. "I can't go with you."

"What are you talking about? You just gonna camp out here? Come on."

"I used my last bit of energy getting you here. I don't have much left, pup."

"Are you sick? What can I do? Hang on. I'll go get some help."

"Benji, I'm not sick. I'm done."

"What does that mean? Come on now. Stop playing around."

"I'm a water fairy…"

"Breaking news," said Benji with a forced chuckle.

The corners of Montal's mouth edged up slightly. "Keep it up, pup."

Montal took a heavy breath that looked like it took more energy than it was worth. "Your father and I were a team. We do that, water fairies and Mystiqs, you know? Our powers magnify each others'. I helped your father hone his skills as a Mystiq, and your family's powers gave me the extra energy I needed to carry out my duty to help you. I don't have much left."

"What are you saying?"

"I died with your parents the day Gouguon attacked. I was right in the middle of the fight with your mother. We held them off for the longest time. If the reinforcements had shown up a few minutes earlier, we could have saved your mother. Your father got separated from us. They took him down first, but not before he took several Donquarien with him. Boone made sure I stayed with your mother.

"She fought toward the end. They overwhelmed us, but not before she could pass on part of her energy to me. Her energy kept my spirit here even after my body was torn apart by the Donquarien sharks. Your mother was a world class healer.

"I have been waiting for you, to show you the way home, to help you on your journey, to prepare you. Now you're ready to have your own partner. And I am free to join your mother and father and those who left Aquari before me to continue the cycle."

"I'm on my own again? You can't leave me. Not now."

"I'd stay for a while longer if I could, pup. I'd like to keep doing this, but my energy isn't going to hold up much more. Don't worry. I'll still be watching you. We all will."

Benji slumped down against the strawberry vase sponge. He folded his arms over his tail and let out a sigh.

"Water fairies and Mystiqs have been partnering together for ages, Benji. You'll have another."

"I don't want another," mumbled Benji.

Montal jerked his head up. "Hey! Look at me. Don't say that! I got stock in your next partner. I expect great things from the two of you."

"Who is it?"

"You'll meet when the time is right for both of you. That's all I can say."

Benji bowed his head. He shook it back and forth slowly. "I'm scared."

"Good!"

Benji raised his eyebrows, eyes darting up in their sockets toward Montal. "Good? Really? You enjoy torturing me, don't you?"

"Keeps you on your toes. As long as it doesn't paralyze you, a little fear is a good thing. Keeps you aware. Keeps your mind sharp. A little fear goes a long way... if you use it to your advantage."

"If you and my dad were a team, why didn't you tell me about the prong. Why didn't you help me find it before Gouguon?"

"There are rules to what I can and can't do. I can't influence the future."

"Just showing yourself to me influenced the future."

"True and the more I do, the more energy it costs me until I'm out. Getting you this far, cost me, but it was why I was here in the first place."

"Wouldn't retrieving the prong be the most important?"

"Helping you retrieve the prong was more important. Helping you find your powers to do more good in the future was the most important. Believe it or not, you are more important to the future of Sanjowqua and all of Aquari, for that matter, than the prong."

"Woohoo! I'm special," said Benji, twirling his finger above his head.

Montal snorted. "Don't forget about this place, pup. You need to come back. You only scratched the surface this time."

"That's comforting, knowing I'm off to try to recover the prong from Gouguon."

"You have what you need. You always will. You won't be alone, Benji. You have never been alone. There's someone always looking out for you, even when you think you're alone."

"How will I know what to do? I mean, I'm not sure what happened in there," Benji said, pointing toward the vase sponge. "Do I shoot lasers out of my eyes now? Can I fly? Am I like an expert water kung fu master?"

"You already know. Close your eyes and ask. You'll get your answer." Montal paused. "Where's Sanjowqua?"

"I don't ..."

Montal jerked forward.

Benji threw his hands over his nose. "Sorry! Sorry!"

Benji closed his eyes. His head spun as his mind exited the room, shot out the cave, and barrelled through the ocean. "Woah! South. I see it."

Montal held out his hand, his two middle fingers against his palm. Benji stuck out his index finger. Montal grasped it with the Aquari shake, winked, and faded out of site.

"Really? Just like that, huh?" said Benji.

He looked around the room again. The early morning light from the tunnel above spread evenly throughout, giving everything a healthy glow.

Benji rolled his eyes. "You know, I could be on my surfboard right now, or on the boat with Dad. Even getting razed by Charlie wouldn't be so bad right about now, but NO… someone had to go talking to strangers, like octopus and dolphin strangers… I'm not even getting into how weird that sounds… and after a short conversation about his roots as a mermaid/merman/mermaidman, whatever I am, decided it was a good idea to join the club. 'Hey, just toss that gold coin in the water and life will be just honky dory, peaches and cream, chocolate sundaes with whipped cream and cherries on top.' Yeah! Doesn't that sound like a good idea? Let's do it again!"

Benji shook his head; his lips rolled into his mouth.

Snap out of it.

"Right, then." He took off down the tunnel out into the cave. "Need some light, guys."

The water flowers unfurled and lit up the entire cave within seconds. Benji threw his hands over his eyes, half-blinded. "Woah. Woah! Down a notch."

The bioluminescence in the flowers dimmed. He turned back toward the tunnel leading to the bubble room.

"Anybody in there that doesn't want to stay in there for a little while?"

A few bar jacks darted out and buzzed the water flowers around the entrance.

"Anymore? Last call!"

A yellow moray eel slithered out of the door amongst the water flowers.

"That's it, guys and gals."

Benji stood in front of the door like a conductor. He waved both hands together, and the boulder-sized doors to the cave slammed shut. He ducked his head as a few rocks whistled their way down from the top of the cave.

"A little easier next time. No need to break things."

Benji looked around at the water flowers. "You guys light the way for me on the way out, please. I guess you can go back to sleep or do whatever it is you do when I'm gone. Keep the place safe for me. I'll be back."

He headed up and out of the cave, occasionally looking down past his tail. As he passed the flowers, they slowly dimmed and then went dark again. The light from the surface showed itself after a few minutes and the coral, anemones, and fish started visibly dotting the walls and bottom of the cave.

He busted straight for the surface, completing a backflip once he broke the water. The sun was a quarter of the way across the sky. A mid-morning shimmer of sunlight reflected off the tiny ripples in the mostly calm Caribbean waters surrounding him.

"OK. I take back what I said about seeing Charlie."

Benji cupped his hand over his eyes and peered back toward the direction of the cave.

No island.

No reef.

No coconut tree.

He scanned the horizon until he completed a three hundred and sixty degree turn.

Kapanaka.

Benji looked up at the sky once more to get his bearings.

"Here we go."

He slipped down into the water, pushed his hands by his sides, and shot off toward Sanjowqua.

Wohlundi

(intruders)

BENJI ALTERNATED BETWEEN the waves and sand. When he surfaced, he looked for hints of land. Underwater, he skirted across the bottom, ducked past schools of fish, and listened for anything that would tell him he was getting closer.

It started as a speck. He wasn't quite sure what to make of it at first, but the closer he got, he realized he was closing in on the pirate ship that had brought him to Sanjowqua, oh, so many months ago.

From a distance, it looked larger than he remembered. The wide hull slowly split into two separate ships the closer he got. The one on the left, the pirate ship he had arrived in, was covered in a protective shell of coral and algae. A whole colony of fish, invertebrates, turtles, and a few reef sharks kept the vessel's exterior as busy as the galley on his voyage home.

The ship to the right looked new or at least newly sunken. The junk ship sat proud and distinctive beside the other pirate ship. The three sectioned orange sails looked like the dorsal fins of a seahorse. The hull was much slimmer than that of the Sanjowqua pirate ship. The junk boat had two stories built toward the rear whereas the Sanjowqua ship had just one, giving it an elegant curve from bow to stern like a woman's high heel shoe.

Benji pulled up beside the junk boat and sailed over the deck. A blue crab scurried down the center mast. A pair of barracuda swam into the captain's quarters. Benji poked his head in behind them. As soon as he did, one of the snaggle-tooth fish did an about-face scaring Benji halfway across the main deck.

He circled the boats then forged ahead. As he moved on, his heart pulled down in his chest. A heavy feeling seeped down to his bones. He knew where he was going, but part of him felt lost. Stumbling across the first bit of carnage triggered the realization of why he felt so sad.

The crumbled rock and dead coral from the Fringe littered the ocean floor. Initially, it was just a few scattered white rocks and pieces of coral trying desperately to blend into the sandy floor. The energy from the life that once inhabited it still hung heavy in the water.

A straw hat waved from atop a pile of rocks. The edge of it wedged between debris waving in the current. Topsider castaways, fish, coral, and anything else residing on the barrier islands now lay crushed under the remains at the bottom of the ocean. Benji cleared his throat and plucked the straw hat out of the rubble.

A solid line of destruction littered the floor as far as he could see. Several coconut trees jutted out awkwardly from the devastation into the middle of the ocean.

Benji absentmindedly swirled the straw hat on his index finger as he stared at the ruins. He scanned a stand of rocks until his vision blurred and his mind blanked out. The current pushed a few rocks off the top of the pile. They bumbled down and pinned a palm branch to the sand that had been lazily undulating in the water.

His mind repeated this game again and again as he floated over the remnants of the Fringe. Benji moped along over a pile of snow-white coral covered in black dirt from the surface. The soil settled deep into the crevices of the coral giving it an old musty look. He bent down closer and waved his hand over the coral. The black earth swirled into a cloud then resettled further down the mound.

A steady hum reverberated through the water and jerked him back into the now. Benji raised his eyebrows. The rest of his body froze. The straw hat he had been twirling on his fingertip hovered in the water for a few seconds before spiraling back down to the mess below.

That's a boat.

Benji closed his eyes and pushed everything else out of his mind. He focused on the humming noise in the distance.

That's a big boat. Fishing boat for sure.

The more he focused, the more information trickled into his mind.

That's close to the next ring of islands. Montal was right.

He locked on the sound and tuned out the engine. Nearly drowned by the hum of the engine, Benji barely made out the cries for help. They were in one area. Whoever was in trouble, they were in it together.

Benji forced himself past the remnants of the Fringe until he reached the white sand again. He pressed his body against the floor and extended his arms in front of him.

A family of garden eels popped their heads out of their holes, one of them right between Benji's outstretched forearms. The slender fish looked down and then slowly turned to face Benji.

"DA!" he yelled and disappeared back into his hole.

"Sorry." Benji looked out at his arms and changed the coloration and pattern of his skin to match the sandy white floor.

The garden eel poked his eyes and snout back out of his hole and stared at Benji's arms.

"Not bad," he said. "Good luck."

"Thanks," nodded Benji and he began moving toward the next ring of islands.

He tried to block out the yells and focus on the sound of the engine. They were both tied together. He hated the idea of what might be happening to the Shequarien in trouble.

Benji moved at a quick even pace. He dared not go too fast and risk kicking up sand. The dull hum of the motor grew louder with each swipe of his tail.

Midway between him and the next set of islands, Benji spotted the shadows of a fishing trawler and the long dragnet it pulled behind. Benji pulled up behind a large rock, resting his arms on top and his head on his forearms.

From the shape and size of the contents within, Benji could tell the boat had a full catch. There were another six to ten shapes outside of the net, circling, prodding, and yelling at the captives inside.

Most of the noise he heard was jumbled. The boat worked hard to winch in the prize behind it. The fish and the Shequarien proved more weight than it usually hauled. Benji imagined the look on the sailors' faces when they dropped the net, and ten to twenty mermaids and mermen came flopping out on the deck. Half the fishermen would stand in awe. The others would start decrying the ocean's luck was against them and make all sorts of outlandish predictions about the rest of their voyage. That's what Joe's men would have done. But Joe's men wouldn't be doing that anymore, not on one of his boats, at least.

A tear welled up in Benji's eye. He twisted his jaw and bit the inside of his lip to stop any more from forming.

Half a dozen Donquarien with spears circled the net. Several more circled behind them shouting orders.

Benji's mouth dropped when he saw one of the Donquarien thrust a spear through the net. The Shequarien on the other end shook then balled up to contain the pain. Another Shequarien rushed over and scooped up the injured pup in her arms. Benji recognized the cloud of black hair waving back at him through the fish and blood. It silhouetted the head of Lin and part of Yuri's crumpled, limp body in her arms.

Benji slithered closer to the boat while fumbling around the sea-floor looking for something he could use to cut the netting. He spotted a group of rocks a hundred feet away. Benji slid between the rocks and broke off an oyster shell.

He looked up and spotted several streams of blood flowing from the net. A handful of bull sharks circled the action.

This is gonna be tricky.

Benji leaned against the rock and changed his skin color. When he was satisfied, he peeled away and shifted to a shimmering silvery-blue color that hid him in the water. He slipped back to the bottom and blended in the with the sand. He repeated this several times until he could switch the color and pattern of his skin as quick as snapping his fingers.

He lay on his back, staring up and watched for a few minutes. A Donquarien thrust her spear into the net and pulled it back out creating another stream of blood. Benji took a deep breath, cupped the oyster shell in his hand, and moved up toward the boat. Once he reached the hull, he changed his skin to match the blue coating of paint underneath. He faced the stern looking at the net.

"Catch of a lifetime, Skipper," hollered one fisherman, his voice echoing from the hull.

"Either we got a whale or enough for me to take a nice vacation this summer," shouted another.

The tow lines strained on the long booms hanging out over the water. The turn of the winch screamed and squealed.

Benji slid down the hull then jutted out toward the tow line. Once he reached the line, he pumped his tail as fast as he could to reach the net. He looked down at his arms and quickly changed his coloration to match the netting. His heart raced and thudded against his chest almost as loud as the humming engine and the squeaking and squawking of the winch. He held on tight, looking around to make sure no one had seen him.

Lin, Yuri, and most of the Shequarien lay at the top of the heap. Lin looked alright, but Yuri had been stabbed, and the others either looked to be injured or frozen from shock.

"Lin. Can you hear me?" said Benji.

Yuri's head lay cradled in the crook of her armpit, his mouth slightly open. As soon as she heard Benji, Lin bolted upright. Yuri's head rolled over facing the rear.

"Lin. It's Benji."

"Benji?! Where are you?"

Yuri tried to lift his eyes. His head bobbed up, "Huh?"

"Lin. Only to me. Keep your voice to me," said Benji.

One of the Donquarien came racing to the side of the net. "Quiet in there. Give it up, pup. You're on your way to the canning factory."

Another Donquarien came up behind Benji. Benji slipped down a few feet before the Donquarien grabbed the net where Benji's head had rested. He shook his spear and yelled into the net. "You're only a few feet away from a nice home in an aquarium."

"Or a laboratory," laughed another on the opposite side shaking the net.

Benji put the oyster shell in his mouth and used both his hands to move as carefully as possible to get closer to Lin.

"Lin," said Benji.

"Benji, what are you doing here? Where have you been?" said Lin.

"We don't have time for that. I'll fill you in later," said Benji.

"Later? Are you sure about that?" said Lin.

"Don't talk like that. Of course, I'm sure. I'm headed to the rear. I'm going to cut a few strands. I want you and everyone else in there to rest up for a few minutes. When I tell you, I want you to give it everything you've got toward the back of the net."

"No one has much left, Benji," said Lin.

"Take what those Donquarien just said and turn that over in your head a few times. That should give you enough motivation to push out of here when the time comes," said Benji.

"OK," muttered Lin. Her webbed hand stuck through the net.

Benji briefly grabbed it and squeezed. "You're gonna be alright."

Once he reached the back of the net, Benji pulled the oyster shell out of his mouth and began hacking away.

Come on, man! Step on an oyster shell, and it'll rip your foot in half, he thought as he hacked and hacked on the nylon net.

One!

A pair of fish wriggled their heads out, both getting stuck in the process.

Come on! A few more.

Benji moved a few feet to the side and looked toward the boat. The angle of the line began moving up as the net got closer to the surface. He shifted back and hacked away.

Two. Three.

A bulge formed at the end of the net where the nylon filaments began to snap. Three of the fish poked through the hole, battered Benji's stomach, and swam through the Donquarien guard. One of them made it to safety. The others ended up in the bellies of the hungry bull sharks.

Halfway through the next filament, a Donquarien net came crashing over Benji's back. Benji pushed away from the spot he had been hacking and twisted himself right into the awaiting hands of the Donquarien behind him. He watched helplessly as the oyster shell fell from his hands and wobbled down to the ocean floor.

"Now, Lin! Get everyone to the end of the net. Now!" said Benji.

"Well. Well. Well," said the Donquarien staring through the twisted strands digging into Benji's face. "We were just out for some fun today. We weren't trophy hunting, but if I'm not mistaken, this here is a Mystiq."

"Boss is gonna be happy tonight," said another of the Donquarien over his shoulder.

"If he makes it that far," said another. "I hear they're pretty tasty."

"I can't! I don't have any left in me," squeaked Lin.

"Tell the others to push! Follow behind them," grimaced Benji as he faced Donquarien.

The fishing net slowly began raising out of the water. Benji's Donquarien captors kept him bundled up just under the rising bunch of nylon, fish, and tangled Shequarien.

Sys, the lead Donquarien, slithered in circles around Benji and the pair holding him. Sys was much smaller than Gouguon, although so was every other Aquarien that Benji had seen so far. The Donquarien wore his hair similar to Jaylon's, tied back with a streaming piece of seaweed a shade darker than his emerald green hair.

Sys's narrow head and slender frame fit with his streamlined light gray tail. His tail fin looked more like a harvesting sickle than an actual fin and spread a good four feet from tip to tip. His dorsal fin sat further back on his spine and stood closer to a ninety-degree angle than the others' who had longer sloping ones.

"You could have lived a long, healthy life, pup. The boss called off the search for you about a month ago. Seems that the prong works fine in his possession and your services aren't needed anymore.

"It's a shame you had to show up, for your sake, anyway. And what for? This looks like a pretty sorry lot. Not a thing in here I'd risk my neck for, except maybe that cutie with the black hair. She might've made a decent companion one day," said Sys.

"That ain't happening now, though," snapped one of the other Donquarien.

"Now, Lin," pleaded Benji.

Lin passed the message along to the other Shequarien in the net. A few of them began stirring. They pushed their way toward the back of the net which was quickly becoming the bottom. The fish in their way woke up with new vigor and began flapping their tails as hard as they could.

The top of the fishing net cleared the water. All the weight moved back to the mangled hole Benji created with the broken oyster shell. The booms on the fishing boat groaned as the rope tugged on the salty wheels of the winch.

Within the tangled mess of the net, several sets of Shequarien eyes shot open, realizing the weight was a big hurdle for the fishing boat. Each one spread their arms, gathering a mass of fish and swung their tails as hard as they could manage.

Another strand snapped behind Benji's head. "Keep going. It's working, Lin."

Snap. Snap. Snap.

"The net! The net is ripping." Sys pushed past Benji reaching for the ragged ends trying desperately to keep it intact.

The mass of Shequarien and fish pushed feverishly. The net sagged deeper into the water, and the bottom opened up like a zipper. Sys's wrist got wrapped up and tangled, and the Donquarien leader swung out to the side of the exploding net.

The school of fish and Shequarien barreled out of the end like a shotgun blast, overwhelming the Donquarien behind them. The sharks raced in from the sides and pulled out a few injured fish. Most of the Shequarien were spared except for one whose tail fin got nicked by one of the sharks. In the chaos, the injury went unnoticed. Once the shock wore off, she'd need to have Doc take care of it.

Benji took several blows to the back. The massive exit of everyone in the fishing net sent the two Donquarien holding Benji spinning off to the side.

The fish rushed out of the net in hundreds of different trajectories.

They pummeled the Donquarien out from behind the net straight down to the bottom.

Benji unraveled himself from the Donquarien net and tossed it aside. Several of the fish from the dragnet swam right into it and clumsily carried it away before freeing themselves.

Benji flailed his arms and looked around, taking assessment of the situation. A few of the Shequarien floated in the middle of the ocean not sure what had just happened. Most had sense enough to escape and were now on their way to the next chain of islands to seek shelter in Sanjowqua.

Maybe they'll bring help.

"Don't count on it," said Lin looking up at him.

Benji followed the voice and spotted Lin and Yuri a little further down. They had been at the top of the net and had been the last to get out. Lin still held Yuri close to her. Yuri grimaced when she pulled him closer and clenched his side. Yuri clenched his side, and a stream of blood appeared.

Benji swam down to them. "Is it bad?"

Lin nodded. "There were a few in the back who weren't as lucky, though."

The large catch of fish had hidden the other bodies from Benji. As the fish cleared, Benji saw one Shequarien female facing up. Her limp arms dangled in the water. Two other males floated face down in the pile of fish and Donquarien below.

Benji followed Lin's glance up and over his shoulder. Sys hung off to the side unconscious. His body inching closer to the top with the departing fishing net.

"Leave him," said Lin.

"We can't risk any of us being seen," said Benji.

"Leave him!" she insisted.

"*Any* of us being seen," said Benji. "Can you get Yuri out of here?"

"Yeah, I can manage," said Lin.

"Then go. I'll meet you in Sanjowqua," said Benji

Lin shook her head then pulled Yuri against her and took off toward the safety of the next set of islands. Another Shequarien swam up alongside her and took one of Yuri's arms to lighten the load.

Benji watched them for a moment until a flash of light pulled his head down. One of the Donquarien had dropped his spear in the confusion, and the reflection from the sunlight jumped in Benji's eye. He swam down, picked it up, and rushed back to the net.

By the time Benji returned, Sys had woken and was jerking his hand, trying to free himself.

"Captain! The net's busted, but we got a few beasts tangled in there still. Yank it up!" shouted one of the deckhands.

"Stop moving," said Benji.

"What are you doing?" said Sys.

"Getting you out of here," said Benji.

Sys yanked his arm while Benji put everything into slicing the rope. The strands popped and released Sys's arm with a snap.

Sys lunged for Benji as soon as he had his arm back. Benji threw his hands over his face and Sys grabbed Benji's shoulders forcing him toward the bottom as fast the Donquarien could go.

Benji looked over his shoulder and saw a jagged boulder coming straight at his back. At the last minute, Sys released Benji's shoulders, threw his arms around Benji's midsection, and dug his shoulder into Benji's stomach. They changed course immediately, going over then down the backside of the boulder. Sys slammed Benji into the sand and circled back in front of him.

"Thanks," muttered Benji.

Sys inflated his chest and made several sudden moves toward Benji. His conscience held him back.

"Ehhh! Save my life, I don't kill you. The board's clean now."

Sys circled twice more around Benji then took off with a frustrated sigh.

"The board's clean now, pup. We're even!"

"Where'd he go, Sys?" harped one of the Donquarien.

Benji pulled himself along the bottom resting his back against the boulder and changed his skin color to disappear.

"He got away," snapped Sys.

"Which way? There's still a good ways until the next set of islands," said another. "We can get him."

"He's gone. Forget him. He's not our concern anyway. Neither were the others. At least, not right now. They just happened to be in a convenient place to have some fun," said Sys.

"Gouguon wanted the Mystiq!" snapped another.

"Keyword, Jais: want-ed. Past tense. Done. No more. Gouguon want-ed the pup. He thought he needed him to handle the prong. He doesn't. Forget him," snapped Sys.

Jais snorted and pulled back in a semi-circle in front of Sys.

"Come on," snapped Sys. "Gouguon's waiting in the Gulf. You'll have your fun with the Topsiders soon. I promise."

Benji watched them head toward the Donquarien boat. The bull sharks trailed in their wake. He put his hands against the rock ready to push off, and a ten-foot bull shark came cruising around the left side of his hiding spot.

Benji froze.

The pectoral fin missed Benji's nose by an inch. The shark shifted his head in the direction of the others and swished his powerful tail slamming Benji against the rock and knocking the breath out of him.

Benji waited until his breathing returned to normal then peeped around the corner. The fishing boat coasted off into the distance. The grumblings of the unhappy crew and hum of the motor grew fainter by the minute.

The Donquarien boat lifted off the sand and hovered over the bottom slowly picking up speed as it headed west toward the Gulf of Mexico.

That was a delightful welcome home party, Benji thought as he headed back into the interior of Sanjowqua.

Mystiq Kenyabi

(mystiq returns)

"HOW'S YURI?" SAID Benji sliding inside Doc's place.

Yuri lay on a bed in the back room surrounded by Meena, Jaylon, and Lin. Caribbean anemone's covered the surface. The purple matchstick tips of the tentacles swayed and dipped underneath Yuri, rocking him in a peaceful sleep.

Sandival stood on Yuri's chest placing a starfish on a shoulder wound. He rotated one of his beady eyes back when Benji swam into the room.

"Don't take your eyes off your work, Sandival," lectured Doc.

Sandival shifted his eye back in front of him and adjusted the starfish in place. "He'll be OK, señor. He nee's the rest, but will recover complee'ly."

Doc cleared his throat.

"Sorry, señor," chirped Sandival.

"Yes, well… he'll be fine. He needs his rest, but…,"

Benji brushed past the surgeonfish and went to Yuri's side. Yuri's eyes fluttered behind his eyelids.

"Is this the only one?" asked Benji, nodding toward the stab wound in Yuri's shoulder.

"He's…"

Doc cut the shrimp off with a stern look, and Sandival scurried away with a huff. "I'm just a pair of claws. No más."

Doc raised his eyes and shook his whole body as if grabbed by a chill. "He's got another on the lower right side of his back. That one has already been patched up."

"What is that?" said Benji reaching out to touch the starfish on Yuri's shoulder. Doc nipped at his finger before he reached it.

Jalyon kept his eyes fixed on his little brother. "A lucky star. They can read and mimic our emotional frequency. Super helpful little creatures in a fix like this. Doc gives me the lucky star. I think of some happy bro' moments and BAM, good healing energy all day and all night long."

"Cells respond to emotion. Love and gratitude are two of the most powerful," said Doc.

"I think of a few instances where my love for him was really strong, tell myself I am grateful for him, and I throw in a few funny moments for good measure, because laughter lasts the longest, at least it does to me, so…"

"So, he's good?" asked Benji.

"Yes. He'll be fine," said Doc.

Benji looked over at Meena and Jaylon huddled together on the other side of the table. Meena held her arms crossed around Jaylon's neck, her head cradled between his head and his shoulder.

"Thanks, Benji," whispered Meena.

"No problem. I was on my way back in when I heard the noise," said Benji.

"Good thing you didn't rush in when you heard it," said Jaylon.

"I got cautious after seeing an extra boat on the Fringe," said Benji.

They both looked at Benji with an odd stare.

"Sorry. What used to be the Fringe. There were two boats out there. The one we arrived in, and there was another one that I've never seen before. A junk boat."

"That's the Donquarien vessel," said Meena.

"I had no idea. Once I got close enough and realized what was happening, I slowed down. It was the camouflage that got me to where I could help," said Benji.

"No pink this time?" said Jaylon.

"You won't let me live that down will you?" said Benji.

"Not any time soon, pup," said Jaylon.

Benji smiled. "No pink. For some reason, I think that would have tipped the Donquarien off. I just snuck up there and cut away."

"And that's it?" said Lin.

"Yeah, pretty much," shrugged Benji.

"You missed the part where the Donquarien spotted you and netted you. And the part where you rallied me and the rest of us that were tangled up. Oh, and the part where you went back for Sys and cut him loose, too," said Lin.

"Well, I didn't want him to be seen by the Topsiders. That's a good thing, right?"

"It was, Benji, but he could have killed you," said Meena.

Benji chuckled. "It's funny you mention that because he came pretty close." Benji held out his hand turning it over slowly. "Finally stopped shaking. He would have, but his conscience got the better of him."

"I didn't know they had one of those," said Meena.

"I got proof," said Benji.

Yuri shifted in his sleep. The anemones underneath him rocked gently soothing him back into his slumber. Meena put a hand on Yuri's arm. He let out a contented sigh, and a small grin crept across his face.

"Shoo. Shoo. Shoo! All of you," said Doc as he wriggled over Yuri and between everyone else. "He needs some sleep. Go have your social hour outside."

The four of them floated out of the room.

Benji peered back in. He looked down past Yuri's bed and nodded at the other two Shequarien that Sandival attended to.

"What about them, Doc?" said Benji.

"They'll be fine. One is a little more roughed up than Yuri. The other about the same. They'll both make it, though. Sandival is cleaning up the minor cuts and scrapes now. All three of them need some rest," said Doc.

"Do the others have anyone to power up their lucky stars?" said Benji.

"No one has come yet. Sandival will help with that. Swim along now. There's nothing more you can do. Rest is what the doctor orders," said Doc.

The second Benji cleared the doorway, his head flew sideways as Lin attacked him with a whale-sized hug around his shoulders.

"I'm sorry, Benji. We both are. We took things too far," said Lin.

Benji shook his head and puffed a strand of Lin's hair out of his eyes.

"It was Yuri and me at the whale cleaning station the day you removed the harpoon," said Lin.

"I thought I recognized that cloud of hair waving in the ravine that morning," said Benji.

"I'm sorry," said Lin.

"Why?" said Benji. "Why did you do it?"

"One prank led to the next, and it shouldn't have. We didn't think." Lin grabbed his shoulders. Then, she pulled him back and wrapped her arms around him one more time.

"Does this mean my initiation is over?" asked Benji.

Lin let go of Benji and floated in front of him. A somber look covered her face. Lin's drooping head pulled her shoulders over. She paused, shaking her head. "We almost died out there today, Benji."

"What were you doing out there to begin with? The Fringe fell. There's no protection out that far anymore," said Benji.

"We were looking for you," said Lin.

"Wow! Thanks," he muttered.

"Thank you, Benji," said Lin.

"How did you know the Fringe fell?" said Meena.

"Yeah, and where have you been?" said Jaylon.

"I felt it," said Benji, remembering the pain that overwhelmed him in the sponge. "It felt like a piece of me withered and died along with it.

"When I left here, I stumbled across my parent's place. They set up a space for me to train. I thought I was gone for a few hours, maybe a day tops," said Benji.

"You were gone a month," said Meena.

"Yeah, a little longer than I thought. When Eeke, Zeeke, and Mai came back with the news, I lost it," said Benji.

"Under the circumstances, I understand," said Jaylon.

Meena and Lin nodded in agreement.

"Speaking of the dolphins, where are they? Or, how are they?" asked Benji.

"Eeke and Zeeke are fine. A few scars, but they're a hundred percent. Mai is still on the mend," said Meena.

"She took the brunt of the punishment from what I remember seeing," said Benji.

"She did. Eeke found her a couple of surfboard fins that we used to sandwich her dorsal fin while the Doc's tonic works its magic. She can manage around the interior fine, but Doc won't clear her for any more than that for at least another month," said Meena.

Meena reached around her back and pulled her pouch in front of her. She dug inside, cupping something in her hand. "Close your eyes, Benji."

Benji looked at Jaylon who nodded his head reassuringly.

"Bend your head down," said Meena.

Benji did as he was told, but looked up at Meena through half-parted eyelids.

"No peeking!" said Meena punching him in the shoulder.

Benji closed his eyes, bent his head, and clasped his hands behind his back.

Meena opened her hands. A small shell laced necklace unfolded. One small but distinctive charm dangled from the center. Meena wrapped her arms around Benji's neck and fastened the chain.

"You have more than earned this," said Meena.

Benji opened his eyes and peered down at the necklace.

"That's not the…"

"…back of the shell we used on the boat when we brought you here," said Meena.

Benji rubbed his thumb over a symbol etched in the shell. "What's this engraving?"

"It's Aquarien for welcome home. Glad to have you back, Benji," said Meena as she grabbed his hand and gave him the Aquarien handshake.

"Welcome home, Benji," said Jaylon shaking his hand.

"Welcome back to Sanjowqua," whispered Lin.

"This is what we used to warn the whales when we were behind them," said Benji.

"Yeah. That's the end of it," said Meena. "Righty-tighty?"

Benji cracked a huge grin. "Lefty-Loosey."

"If you blow in this one, you'll call for help," said Jaylon.

"But it's so small," said Benji.

Jaylon smiled. "Don't let the size fool you, pup. If there are any whales in the area, they'll come see what the fuss is about. The whales are extremely impartial, so don't expect a rescue crew, but if you really need them, they will be there."

"If Gouguon can take down the entire Fringe, we're going to need an army of whales to recover the prong," said Lin.

"Like Jaylon said, the whales mostly keep to themselves. We won't likely get that kind of help from them, Benji," said Meena.

Benji stifled a yawn.

"Looks like we're not getting much more out of you either," said Jaylon.

"The adrenaline is starting to wear off," said Benji as he lifted his necklace again and beamed at it. "This is the best gift I've ever gotten."

"You more than earned it, Benji. It takes a special act of courage and skill for someone to be given a necklace in Sanjowqua. The charms are indicative of a special accomplishment. You don't get one just for showing up, but I think that one is a worthy reward for what you pulled off," said Jaylon.

Benji held the end of the shell in his palm and smiled.

"Come on. I'll swim with you back to your place," said Lin.

She put her hand on the back of Benji's elbow, and they pushed down into the water.

Evening fell fast. Bobbling jars of bioluminescence lit the bungalows floating throughout the inner ring of Sanjowqua.

Benji and Lin swam through the interior and around the tip of Waputa Wamkala. Two turtles wandered around the perimeter of the five dagger-like islands jutting down from the surface. The rest of the reef looked settled in for the evening.

"How are you?" said Lin.

"Tired," yawned Benji.

"I mean, are you OK?" said Lin.

"Yeah. Why?" said Benji.

"You disappeared in a flash. I know it must have been tough losing Joe. I don't remember losing my parents, but I know that not having them around altered my life. I'm not sure how different I'd be if they had been around, but… I mean, it's not that I am unhappy with the way I am now, but I'd be willing to risk the change to have them around," said Lin.

"What happened?"

"They were casualties of Gouguon's last rampage before he went to Muyu Munda."

"What's Muyu Munda? I heard Jaylon mention it before."

"Muyu Munda is the Aquarien prison. It's where Gouguon was before you got back."

"Where is it?"

"Off the southeast tip of Sanjowqua. Off the coast of what you know as Puerto Rico."

"Your parents must have died around the same time as mine."

"They did. They died at the same time."

"Were they with my parents?"

"Yeah. Your father wanted to talk with the Topsiders. Rumor has it he had lined up some pretty influential people Topside that he was talking to about protecting us and protecting or taking better care of the oceans. Your father felt like the Topsiders could be trusted. He believed that disclosing our existence would help them see Aquari less as a resource and more as another environment to be protected along with the billions of other forms of life down here.

"My parents were part of a patrol group your father summoned to help get him and your mother Topside," said Lin.

"Well, that explains some of the responses I've gotten since I've been here," said Benji.

"It wasn't intentional, Benji. I know you had nothing to do with it. I know Meena feels the same way, but she was old enough to remember our parents. It was tougher on her. Meena is all I can ever remember. She's been both a mother and sister to me."

"Thanks," said Benji. "It's interesting how we internalize the events in our lives. Everything that happens affects each of us one way or another. I think about my dad's death and think about losing him, but Uncle Bill lost a brother, and the entire town of Beech Mill lost a friend and one of the best fishermen in the area. Your parents died saving me, and the ripple effect rolls out even further."

"So, are you OK?"

"I'm not going to go running off again if that's what you mean.

"Coming here and finding out there was more than what I grew up knowing has been a lot to swallow. I'm still in awe of what's been happening underneath my surfboard all these years. I feel like, I don't know, like how could I have been so ignorant, but I'm finally here, and now that I am, I've lost the life I knew Topside. I didn't come here to give up what I had, especially my dad. I mean, Joe."

"He was your dad, Benji."

"Yeah, I know."

"He would have been proud. So would your parents."

"Yours would have been, too."

Benji and Lin reached his bungalow.

"Thanks. I feel like I should walk, I mean swim back to your bungalow with you."

"Rescuing me today doesn't make me a princess," said Lin as she punched him in the arm. "We're safe in here. Get some rest," and she swam off.

Benji put his hand on the doorway. A stream of bioluminescence illuminated the rim of the door and ran along the bottom and top edges surrounding his room. He swam inside and plopped down on his bed. The anemones underneath him cushioned the weight of the day.

A clamshell the size of a teacup sat on a table beside his bed. Benji grabbed it and pried it open. 'Midnight snacks. Welcome home, Lin' was inscribed on the inside top of the shell. A seaweed parcel sat in the bottom half. Benji unwrapped it and gulped down the sliced fruit inside.

He lifted his tail up and stretched his arms over his head. As he closed his eyes, a restless feeling crept over his body. He twisted and turned on the bed trying to get comfortable, but he soon realized the unsettling feeling he had was internal and no amount of shifting was going to soothe it. He lifted his head and stared out the door. When his vision would go no more, his mind took over, forcing his eyes shut, and steered him back toward the north side of Waputa Wamkala to the bungalow with the glowing halo on the bottom. Benji crept through the door and made his way back to the room where Yuri and the other two Shequarien who had been stabbed by Gouguon's goons rested.

A pinch to Benji's fin pulled his awareness back into his body. He opened his eyes and stared out the door. A purple-speckled porcelain crab nibbled at his tail. Benji looked down at the crab and shooed the creature away.

That was weird.

A dull, steady pulse throbbed in his palms. He pulled his arms in front of his chest and focused on his hands. His gaze shifted from palm to palm and back again. The jagged dashes and lines of his hands captured his attention and pulled him deeper into the thumping pulse emanating from each extremity. He walked his gaze up each finger, pausing at the infinity symbol clearly, yet so inconspicuously stamped on each of his digits. Each time, the slow throbbing from his palm pulled him back down again.

Benji's mind flashed back to Doc's bungalow and the room with the injured Shequarien.

The thumping in his palms shook his hands and brought him back to his bed.

As he passed his eyeballs from hand to hand, a movement between them caught his attention. He looked at his bobbing tail somewhat annoyed and then his focus adjusted to the water between his out-stretched hands. Benji's mouth slowly crept open at the sight of the minuscule waves rippling off each extremity. They converged in the space between his hands then reverberated up, out, and under causing the water to shake with a distorted blur.

He moved his hands in front of his face then started slowly pulling them apart, watching the distorted water expand. Then, he pushed them closer together and marveled at the energy moving up and out through his palms, out his fingers and the spaces between them. He pulled his hands back apart and held them outstretched with his palms facing the ceiling watching the energy pulsate from them like near invisible flames; the distorted water being the only clue of their existence.

Next, he turned his palms down toward his chest. They hovered two feet above his torso. He felt nothing from that distance but felt inclined to move them closer to his body. Inch by inch, the infinitesimal waves shook their way toward him. A foot from his rib cage, the feeling grabbed his attention. It started as a slight quiver on his skin and made its way into his muscle tissue. The feeling tickled at first but soon soothed him down to his bones. The closer he brought his hands, the deeper the feeling penetrated. Benji rested his hands on his chest and, with his eyes closed, hummed with the vibration now massaging its way through his upper body all the way to the back of his shoulder blades. The vital organs protected by the cage of bone all hummed with him. Benji's lips vibrated along. Small arches appeared in his cheeks as he smiled with the ecstatic feeling his heart, lungs, and the rest of his organs enjoyed. He hummed over and over again until his whole body felt like it glowed, from the top of his head to the tips of each side of his tail fin.

Benji gently floated up from the bed in a trance. His body propelled him forward. He had no conscious plan of where he headed, but deep down he knew exactly where and why he was going. He rounded the tip of Waputa Wamkala, through the bungalows on the north side, and up toward the home with the glowing halo on the bottom. He slid into Doc's office and swam straight toward the back room where Yuri and the other two Shequarien recuperated.

"Oh, my," said Doc. He and Sandival bounced back and forth in the prep room behind the front observation table. "I haven't felt that in ages."

"Sí, Doc? muttered Sandival. "What is it?"

"The Mystiq has returned. Come Sandival. I think you'll want to see this," whispered Doc.

Benji passed the first table and ran his extended hand through the water over Yuri's tail. Yuri took a deep contented breath. His lips pursed together and the corners of his mouth stretched toward his ears.

Benji swam between the other two Shequarien, hovering an outstretched arm above each of their midsections. His own body still hummed and vibrated from the session he performed earlier. He closed his eyes and matched the vibrations he felt shaking through his body to the hum he began building from deep within his belly. As the pressure built, he directed the energy up his windpipe until it hit his vocal chords and reverberated out through his throat.

Sandival clung upside down to the top of the door frame separating the back recovery room. Doc peered under the lip of the frame beside his assistant. Both of them swayed gently to the deep bass hum echoing throughout the room.

"He's doing it," whispered Doc.

"Doing what?" whispered Sandival.

"Waking up," said Doc.

"They nee' the rest, señor," said Sandival.

"He's not waking *them* up, Sandival. He's waking up to his powers. He's healing them," said Doc.

Ever so slightly, the midsection of each Shequarien rose off the table toward Benji's outstretched hands. Benji felt their bodies react and moved his hands closer. They both responded by relaxing against the bed of anemones rocking and caressing them. Between breaths, Benji moved his hands from their midsections up to the center of their chest. As he continued humming, their chests expanded with huge inhales. The dull, grayish-blue color that dominated their torsos was replaced with a glowing, greenish-blue tint. Several sparkles caught Sandival's eyes as the Shequarien's tails shimmered from the dim bioluminescence keeping the room lit well enough for periodic check-ups throughout the night.

Benji finished his deep hum and moved around the tables toward Yuri. He caught sight of Sandival and Doc at the door frame and nodded toward them. He repeated the same routine, but this time he held one hand above Yuri's midsection and one above his chest.

Sandival couldn't help himself. He scurried down and across the room to the table behind Benji and Yuri. He crept across the bed of anemones over the chest of the first sleeping Shequarien. When Sandival reached the lucky star he had put in place earlier that day, he looked back at Doc, then turned to lift the starfish up for inspection. Sandival used both claws to lift the starfish over his head while he danced back and forth across the spot where the spear had pierced the chest. Bone, flesh, and skin were completely healed. Sandival looked at Doc, back at the wound, then back at Doc again pointing two of his front legs at the spot they tended to earlier in the day.

"Looks like we have some help now, Sandival," said Doc, hovering beside his assistant.

"Sí, señor. We may nee' to find new jobs, no?" said Sandival.

Doc smiled. "Not just yet, Sandival."

Benji's humming came to an end. He pulled his hands in front of him and clasped them at his waist. He took a deep breath. The weight of his exhale rolled his shoulders over and his head down.

Benji let out another contented hum and swam out of the recovery room. Doc and Sandival followed closely behind. Benji nodded at the table in the front room. "Do you mind, Doc?"

"Of course, not," scoffed Doc. The surgeonfish darted up to the ceiling. He snatched a green tube and carried it back down between his body and his pectoral fin. He placed it in Benji's hand, nudging it with his head. "Go ahead. Take a few pulls on that."

Benji lifted the tube to his lips and filled his lungs with pure oxygen courtesy of the healing plants growing on the top side of the bungalow. His eyes bounced back and forth behind his eyelids. A wrinkle in his brow that appeared after the last session with Yuri melted into the water around him.

"Your mother would be proud," said Doc.

A slight grin slipped across Benji's lips after another breath from the tube.

"Did you see her work on many others?" asked Benji with a sigh.

"Kila used to come here once a week. After it was evident she was pregnant, I discouraged her from continuing. Some of the healings she performed took a great deal of energy, and I warned her against the effects that might have on the bundle she carried.

"Seeing you in there tonight brought back some old memories," said Doc.

"The first time I came here, you started to talk about her, but another patient came in just when you got started. Tell me more, please," said Benji.

Doc nodded his head, and Sandival settled in beside Benji to listen.

"Your mother could see and manipulate the energy around others. She could push and pull that energy to alleviate blocks in their auric fields. She helped people move past blocks they had constructed in their personal lives that may have affected their work or relationships. That was the more subtle side of the energy work she did. As soon as she saw someone, she could tell if something was wrong with them.

"She could also heal physical ailments, like what you just did. Seeing you swim in here earlier reminded me of her. She was very confident and deliberate with her movements," said Doc.

"I almost felt guided," said Benji. "Like my body knew exactly what to do and I was there as an observer."

"That's the polarity of the energies, of healer and patient, you experienced. The energy you have wants to help, and their energy," said Doc motioning his head toward the back room, "wants to accept it, most of the time. Letting go and trusting that energy is a big part of the process. Many a Mystiq struggled with that part which, in turn, hindered their powers."

"It didn't feel right to ignore that pull," said Benji.

"And that makes you special," said Doc.

"What do you mean they want to accept it 'most of the time'?" asked Benji.

"Not everyone wants to heal, Benji," said Doc.

"Why wouldn't someone want to heal?" asked Benji.

"Sometimes the pain is a reminder that some people don't want to let go of. Sometimes they're tired. They let it consume them and eventually take them away. Sometimes they like the attention they receive. Sometimes they like the crutch it gives them. You'd be surprised," said Doc.

"I want to do more," said Benji.

Doc chuckled. "Slow down, there. You need to rest before you try to heal the rest of Aquari."

Benji took another pull from the oxygen tube. He inflated his chest as far as it would go, held it in for a few seconds, and watched a steady stream of bubbles flow from his nostrils up toward a small hole in the ceiling. One of the Shequarien in the back room let out a contented moan, and Sandival shot off the table to check on the patients.

Benji nodded toward the back room. "What are you going to tell them about their wounds?"

"You mean their old wounds?" said Doc with a wink.

"Oh yeah. I guess they're gone now."

"Yes, they're healed. What do you want me to tell them?"

Benji hadn't thought that far ahead. He shook his head a few times then shrugged his shoulders. "It was all a dream?"

"Tell you what. I'll tell them Sandival had some special mojo he used on the lucky stars along with some new healing cream we've been experimenting with. How's that?"

"Sounds good to me."

"Speaking of dreams, how are your nighttime excursions?"

Benji shrugged again. "They're just dreams."

"Mystiqs are known for their dream work, Benji. Don't discount what you see with your eyes closed."

Benji yawned.

"That's the second time tonight you've yawned at my place, and for the second time, I think you need to go home. This time, I'd recommend a full night's sleep."

Benji pushed himself off the observation table. "This time I'm staying there, Doc."

Matisi Jango

(oil rig)

"I'M TELLING YOU, Mac. There's no one down there. We're on an oil rig in the middle of the Gulf of Mexico. None of the divers are in the water and haven't been all afternoon," said the captain.

"But…"

"And I checked the last time you said there was someone down there and none of the logs showed anyone working in the water or even below the deck."

"I didn't say someone was working down there. I said someone was swimming down there."

"You've been on the rig for six weeks now. It's that time for you. Happens to us all every once in awhile. You're due a shore leave. Water's messing with your eyes and your head."

"I don't think that's it, Captain."

"Well, you don't get paid to think. You get paid to crunch numbers and give me exact figures. Leave the thinking to me. At least, I hope that's what it is because if you're not getting weary from the water, you're going crazy, and I can't have my engineer going kooky on me before we strike this big well. A few more days and we'll be in there. You think you can keep it together until then?"

"I'm not losing it. I'm telling you. I am a facts and figures, numbers and charts guy more than any man on this rig, but something doesn't feel right."

"Guys like you don't get paid based on their feelings, Mac. You get paid to calculate, and your work's almost done. If you're telling me any of those calculations are wrong, then I got something to worry about, but people swimming below the platform twenty miles out at sea when all the crew is on board and accounted for isn't something that I'm worried about because there isn't anyone out there."

"What if you're wrong?"

"Then someone drowns, most likely, but it ain't one of my men, so it doesn't concern me much. If someone got out here in the first place, they're either super-human or a mermaid, and in both those cases, it takes us back to where we started this conversation. Neither of those exists, so ain't *nobody* down there. Got it?"

"What about the fish yesterday?"

"Now you're reaching, Mac."

"That school of fish was shaped like an arrow."

"Yeah? And that cloud right there is shaped like a palm tree. What do you make of that? Do you think we should call NASA and report a palm tree-shaped cloud?"

"But you said that school of fish was acting strange. We both thought it looked like the school was pointing back toward the shore. The way it moved back and forth looked like it was trying to tell us something. You said you'd never seen anything like it before."

"That's true," said the captain scratching his chin, "and now that I think of it, I don't think I've ever seen a palm tree-shaped cloud either. Get out of my face, Mac. You're starting to annoy me. Go take a nap, get a drink, or do whatever you need to do to pull it together, but get it together. I need you here for three more days until the drilling's complete. Don't go getting loopy on me with this little time left on the clock."

Mac walked out of the tower room and heard the captain mutter something under his breath as the door slammed.

"I'm not going crazy. This much time at sea does it to you, right?" Mac drug his feet down the hallway like a kid after a good tongue lashing from his dad. "Glad I didn't mention the voices…"

"Mac! Stop talking to yourself. Get in here. Drill's being fidgety," said Sal.

Mac walked in one of the adjacent control rooms filled with video cameras to keep an eye on the drilling.

"What's the problem?" asked Mac.

"Don't know. That's your job, Mac. Mine's just to tell you that we got one," said Sal as he ran his hand through his greasy hair. "Your parents must not have liked you much to name you that. Kind of a generic name, huh?"

"I'm a generic guy. Just another kid with bad vision, equally bad teeth, no coordination, and a gift for numbers. Stereotypical engineer, Sal. Why not Mac?"

Sal outweighed Mac by a hundred pounds, a quarter of which looked to be in hair gel. He shifted a toothpick to the opposite side of his mouth with one swift motion, shrugged his shoulders, and looked back at the monitor.

"Hey, Mac. What'd you say about... uh... what was that you were muttering as you walked by... about... you know..."

Mac stared at Sal hoping he had finally found an ally.

"...voices?" said Sal, finally working up the courage.

"Fuhgetaboutit," said Mac in his wretched attempt at an Italian accent.

"Nah, see. I heard you and the skipper talking. Strange things in the water. Signs. Things pointing toward land, like we ain't welcome here," said Sal.

"I didn't say anything about voices," said Mac.

"Not in front of the captain, you didn't," sneered Sal.

Mac looked back over his shoulder, then looked into Sal's eyes to make sure the man wasn't making fun of him. He put his arm on the back of Sal's chair and leaned forward.

"It's been difficult to make out. Mostly moaning," said Mac.

"Something like 'Leave...'" said Sal in a haunting voice as he switched the toothpick to the other side of his mouth.

"That's what you heard?" asked Mac.

"I'm just sayin' with all that may or may not have been going on, something like that could have been heard, you know what I'm saying?" fidgeted Sal.

"You heard…"

"That's the only clear thing I may or may not have heard," said Sal.

"What'd you say you heard, Sal?" said Mac.

"Maybe I did and maybe…"

"Yeah. Yeah," said Mac.

Sal broke their eye lock and looked over his shoulder out the door. "Leave…"

"…Aquari," Mac joined in.

Sal's eyes glistened. His heavy eyebrows twitched upward creating a half-dozen trenches of wrinkles on his sweaty forehead.

"It's like a ghost or something, isn't it, Mac? Like it's flowing through the whole joint. Freaks me out. Lately, it's lasting all night long. I can hardly sleep. How come nobody else is saying anything else about it? It's loud and clear, isn't it, Mac?"

Mac took a deep breath and lifted his chest, pulling his hands off his knees and shaking his head.

Sal looked at Mac with his lips puckered in frustration causing his toothpick to stick straight up in the air nearly grazing the overweight man's eyelashes.

"A minute ago you sounded like you were in confession with the captain, who thought you were a crackpot and now I tell you I've been hearing things, and you decide to clam up? Get outta here, Mac!" Sal grabbed a fistful of Mac's white polo shirt and shoved the engineer out of the room.

Mac walked back down the hall with his head hung having been tossed out of the last two rooms he entered.

"Two for two," he mumbled. "If numbers and equations were people, I'd have more friends than I'd know what to do with."

When he finally arrived at his room, he figured he'd take the captain's advice. He had been working around the clock, and the water definitely plays tricks on your eyes when that's the only thing you see for weeks on end. Whitecaps turn into ghosts riding horses. The sun's reflection off a large wave casts a glare that looks like your first girlfriend. The moonlight bounces off the water just right and makes you think the pope is out there giving Halloween candy to dolphins. Mac chuckled again as he kicked off his shoes and stretched out on his bunk.

Three more days until he was on dry land. Mac closed his eyes and threw his hands behind his head. As soon as he got off this bucket of bolts, he was headed to his sister's house to pick up his golden retriever, Buddy.

A loud bang echoed through his cabin. Mac bolted upright. "Yeah?"

Sonny, one of the technicians, cracked the door. "Captain's asking for you. Wants you up in the tower immediately."

"Everything ok?"

"Far as I can tell. Said he has something he wants you to see. Said it would put your mind at ease."

Mac yawned and slipped his shoes on over his heels then pushed himself off his bed. His head grazed the bunk above him where he kept most of his things.

When Mac and Sonny reached the top floor, laughter bellowed down the hall. Sonny cleared his throat once they got close to the door, and Mac heard a few hushes echo down the corridor.

Sonny walked in first. "Here he is, Captain."

The captain welcomed his head engineer with a big grin. "Found your swimmer, Mac."

Sal stood shirtless behind the captain. He had a shell tied over each side of his chest and what looked like a shredded dirty oil rag hanging over his head. The red cap of a whiteboard marker protruded from his front jeans pocket.

"Those are some luscious lips, Sal. I'd lose the toothpick, though," mumbled Mac.

"Sorry, Mac. We couldn't resist," said the captain.

"That sight will haunt my dreams for years. You successfully killed any fantasies I ever had of mermaids," said Mac.

The captain walked over and patted Mac on the back. "I've always subscribed to the belief that laughter is the best medicine."

Mac was still admiring Sal's costume when a blast of water in the distance caught his attention. Mac's eyes narrowed and his gaze shifted out the window.

"The whales are coming for us now, boys," said the captain as he smacked Mac on the back. "Sal, put your mermaid suit away and go pull out your Moby Dick costume."

The room roared, and Mac cracked a grin.

"Yeah. We'll harpoon 'em for threatening the rig, mates," said Mac.

"Jeez, Mac. Nobody said anything about killing anybody. They're just whales. Man, you're cruel," said Sonny.

"OK. So, we're all good. Sal, how's the drill firing?" said the captain.

"Firing on all cylinders, Captain. We're running ahead of schedule. We'll hit the mother lode in t-minus thirty-six hours."

Another blast of water caught the corner of Mac's eye and pulled his attention back toward the ocean.

"Those suckers got us in their sights. They're going to ram us, boys," joked Sonny.

The captain looked out the window. The gap between the horizon and the last blast of water had grown larger. What happened next doubled the size of his eyes. A three hundred foot wall of mist spouted from the water. Fifty whales lined side to side headed toward the rig, all breaching the surface at the same time. As soon as the mist from the first row dissipated, another shot up immediately behind it and another behind that and another, creating a tsunami of water blasts.

The captain's outstretched hand beckoned for the binoculars. Sal rummaged through one of the drawers and plopped them in his hand.

"What'd you say, kid?" belted out the captain as he adjusted the focus on the binoculars.

"Uh. Looks like they're going to ram us?" mumbled Sonny.

"You ain't too far off and from the look of it, neither are they. I've never seen a pod of whales move so fast," said the captain.

"That ain't no pod, Cap. That's a city of whales," stammered Sal, causing his toothpick to quiver.

"Bunch of firsts today's, huh, Captain?" said Mac, somehow hoping this relieved him of the crazy badge he had been given earlier. "Palm tree-shaped clouds, schools of fish making shapes, whales forming drive by gangs. Pigs might fly by soon."

"They're fifty to seventy-five abreast, and there's no end to them in sight. I thought most of those things were endangered," said the captain.

Sal found another pair of binoculars and pressed them as tightly as he could against his eyes without actually popping them into his eye sockets. He scanned the water frantically, not sure what he was looking at nor where to look next when his head stopped suddenly.

"Captain, look at the front of the line. You're not going to believe this," said Sal.

"What is it?" said the captain.

"Don't make me say it, sir," said Sal.

The captain moved his head slightly as he located the front of the pod of whales. He held his head steady for a good minute before he said anything. "We might see pigs fly today, Mac."

Sal let the weight of the binoculars pull them down from his face. Mac walked by and scooped them out of his greasy hands before they tumbled to the floor.

Mac lined the sights with the front of the rig and moved out into the ocean. He didn't need to go far. The whales had closed in quickly. He caught the front of the pod then scanned back and forth.

"Is that a...?" whispered Mac.

"Say it, Mac," said the captain.

"So, you don't think I'm crazy?" asked Mac.

"Say it, Mac. I don't have it in me," said the captain.

"I'll take that for a 'no'," said Mac.

Mac's binoculars zeroed in on the first procession of whales. Twenty yards ahead, an arrow-shaped school of sharks led the charge.

There's a naked man... Mac ran that thought back to himself in slow motion.

There's a naked man with a spear standing on a great white shark in the middle of the ocean.

"Captain, are you still wanting my confirmation," said Mac.

"I don't need details, Mac. Tell me you see... uh... someone out there," said the captain.

"I do. There's a..."

"OK!!! I said I don't need any details," snapped the captain.

Sal yanked the binoculars out of Mac's hands.

"Whoa!" both the captain and Sal moaned at once.

"What's going on?" said Mac.

"The shark-man just dove off in front of the sharks, and he's outswimming the beasts. I think he's got a tail now," whispered Sal.

The men stood there with their faces and binoculars pressed against the window. Mac didn't need the binoculars anymore to witness the scene unfolding outside the rig.

"He's diving," dribbled out of Sal's half-open mouth.

"So are the rest of them," whispered the captain.

Mac hadn't seen the man dive down into the water, but he saw the animals behind moving deeper with each swipe of their tails. The sharks had all but disappeared under the front of the rig. Fan tails were all that Mac saw from the first line of whales and those disappeared soon after.

"This goes down as the strangest day, I've ever…" started Sal.

"You ain't seen nothing today, Sal," said the captain. "Anything you think you may have seen goes in the log, and I'm not signing nothing with anything remotely describing what you may or may not have thought you just saw."

A loud boom echoed through the rig knocking everyone except fat Sall off their feet. The big man swayed away from the window, but never lost his footing, leaving a pair of red lip marks on the glass. His love handles jiggled over his belt with the rocking platform.

The captain hit the control panel behind him and dropped on his rear. The binoculars slammed against the floor, and one of the lenses shattered, sending shards of glass bouncing along like an army of freed circus fleas.

Sal looked down at Mac whose eyes were as wide open as they could be without his eyelids disappearing into his head. "This thing's meant to withstand hurricane-force winds and waves, right, Mac?"

"Yeah, but not repeated direct hits to the pilings," said Mac.

"From a whale? How much damage is a whale gonna do?" stammered Sonny above the emergency sirens as another impact shook the rig.

Another loud boom smacked the left side of the platform followed by one on the right. Sal lost his balance, and his jiggly rump joined the other crew members on the floor. Each jolt and the booming gong echoes that rattled the rig sent shudders up Mac's spine.

The captain, Mac, and Sonny crouched around the central bank of control panels. Sal leaned against the outside wall staring out the floor to ceiling window panes.

Mac watched the color suddenly drain from Sal's cheeks. "Sal?"

A steady pounding on the metal walkway outside reverberated through the control room. Mac and the captain both jerked their heads up toward the windows to see what caused Sal to go silent. There was nothing there. Mac peered down the hallway as shouts from other crew members barreled through the inside door.

A loud bang came from the glass outside the control room. Mac twisted around and caught sight of a towering man moving around the observatory deck.

The man on the shark, if that's what Mac really saw earlier, and the man standing on the other side of the glass looked the same. Judging from the size of him, Mac guessed he stood between seven and eight feet tall. Mac never played sports in school, but he remembered a few kids from his high school basketball team that would have looked like dwarfs next to this guy.

His mane of black hair swept over and around his head like a shiny helmet. His silver skin shimmered under the beads of water rolling down his chest and arms. The skin on his hips and legs bore a hazy striped pattern.

The man lifted his arm and slammed his palm on the window, splintering the inch thick tempered glass. "Open!" A drop of blood slipped off his hand and ran through the crevices of broken glass his palm left behind.

The shark-man locked eyes with Mac. The engineer pointed to the door on the other side of the control room. Both the man and the captain followed Mac's finger.

The captain hissed at Mac, "What are you doing?"

Mac wasn't sure why he did it. He didn't even think about it. He looked helplessly at the captain and let out a snivel.

The man on the outside of the window glided across the steel mesh walkway and was down one side of the control room and around the corner before Mac blinked. The next instant he was at the door.

The shark-man reached for the knob. As soon as he met resistance from the locked door, a high pitch scream streamed out of his mouth sending glass showering towards the opposite wall where Sal sat shaking. The glass flew across the room, bounced off the wall, and rained down on the whimpering fat man. Mac thought the shards of glass would never settle on the floor until he realized the sound was coming from Sal sniffling.

The shark-man stared down at Sal from across the control room. "Leave Aquari!" he said, his lips never parting. The voice boomed into every crevice of Mac's skull.

Another jolt from the pilings sent Mac's head against the control panel behind him, and he let out a gasp of pain. The intruder turned his head toward Mac and smiled as he pointed his baseball bat-sized spear at Sal.

The handle part of the spear was a dark, reddish brown. Several gnarled, black knots formed around the shaft. An angled diamond prong extended eighteen inches out of the top. The glimmering prong shot straight out of the handle ten inches, then zigged once before zagging upward again and triangulating at the tip.

"Please," was all Sal was capable of uttering.

The glow from the tip of the prong expanded as large as the shark man's fist then leapt off the end of the spear and barreled across the room toward Sal.

Mac covered his head and pulled back behind the control panel. A muffled "umpff" escaped from the corner where Sal sought his refuge followed by a flopping and grinding sound.

Mac stuck his head back around the corner to check on his coworker. A giant, marbled-green and yellow grouper flopped in the seat of the size forty-eight jeans now bunched on the floor. Glass from the shattered window ground into the linoleum each time the fish flipped and flapped his body.

Gouguon made a flicking motion with the spear, and Sal the Grouper sailed through the room narrowly missing a woman on the platform.

Mac did a double take. A woman stood on the platform. That's what Mac thought when Sal flew by her, but his rational mind took hold on the second look. This crew didn't have any women on board, and the ones on the last crew all wore clothes. The woman out there now, if that's what she was, didn't.

She had the same grayish-blue skin tone as Gouguon with dark gray stripes running from front to back, starting at her rib cage and running down both legs. She wore her hair short, a few inches above her shoulders. Thick, red stripes intermingled with her jet black hair. She looked much smaller than Gouguon, although Mac couldn't think of anyone who wouldn't.

Gouguon let out an annoyed grunt when he saw her. "I told you to stay in the water, Maylani."

"I wanted to be with you. In case anything…"

"You don't think I can handle myself with these creatures?" demanded Gouguon.

"No, I just wanted to help," she pleaded.

"I don't want anyone knowing you've got Mystiq blood."

"None of the others saw me come up."

"They won't see you going down either," snapped Gouguon.

Mac's open mouth gathered dust, and an errant fly buzzed his lips as he sat there staring.

The woman's eyes squinted. Her face bunched up around her mouth and nose as she stared Gouguon down. "I've waited for you. I've done everything you asked."

"If you had, you wouldn't be standing there right now. I'll deal with you later." Gouguon whipped the spear around. He stopped right between her collarbones. The tip glowed again. The recoil from the blast pushed his shoulder back an inch, and he laughed as a spotted eagle ray took Maylani's place and disappeared over the side of the rig. "Don't question me again!" he bellowed.

Mac and the captain looked at each other. Sweat barreled down the captain's forehead. A new bead popped up on the captain's hairline when the sound of feet crunching over glass approached. Mac watched the drop of water trickle down the captain's face and disappear somewhere between the tip of his nose and the floor.

The footsteps stopped next to Mac.

The voice returned. Gouguon stared the captain down. "I'll let ten of you leave. You have five minutes. Meet me outside on the deck."

Another blast rocked the pilings.

"One of your life rafts is to be deployed..."

"But we have dozens," stumbled the captain.

"This is not a rescue operation! One of your life rafts will be deployed. Bring nothing other than yourselves. Make no attempt to contact the shore. The ten who are here in five minutes leave."

"And those not here?"

"Don't leave. The second hand on the clock across the room says you've already used thirty seconds of your time," said Gouguon.

Mac and the captain sprung up from the control room. Mac echoed the captain's words as soon as he heard them.

"Evacuate the rig!"

"Evacuate the rig!"

Gouguon walked out of the control room and onto the surrounding deck. Men in bright orange life jackets scrambled below him. One of the men stopped and looked up when he saw Gouguon's shadow. The man tilted his yellow hard hat to shield the sun. Gouguon lifted the prong and blasted the man off the deck. A draft of wind swept the worker under the rig. The hard hat rattled on the deck while the former owner got swatted under the tail of a humpback whale as it added another dent to one of the pilings. The rig creaked before stuttering down and to one side a few feet. Several more men slid off the rig, forming a large red pool under the waves where a school of hammerheads greeted them.

"We're here," said the captain through gritted teeth.

Gouguon turned around to meet the captain and his ten men. The captain held a loaded speargun. Sonny stood beside the captain with a flare gun.

"Put your toys away," said Gouguon.

"I'm taking *all* my men off this rig," said the captain as he lowered the speargun at Gouguon.

"So be it," said Gouguon. He shook the prong once and a wall of water formed around him.

The captain and Sonny both fired their weapons. The water

immediately extinguished the flare. The spear shot into the water. Gouguon shifted to the side, reached up, and plucked it out of the water with a smirk. He shook the prong again, and the water wall crashed down on the deck washing the feet of a few of the captain's men out from under them.

Gouguon pointed the prong at the group. The tip illuminated with near-blinding light. Gouguon motioned over his shoulder, and the entire group lifted off the rig and flew out over the waves.

Gouguon walked to the edge of the top platform, laughing at the workers scrambling underneath him. He jumped down to the next level and dented the steel mesh walkway when he landed. Two men stood near one of the life rafts prepping it to drop down into the water. Gouguon grabbed the first one by the collar and hoisted him over the side. He made a motion toward the other man who decided he liked his odds better in his own hands and jumped off the rig.

Gouguon walked around the life raft ripping the winch wires and tie down cables off the boat. Once it was free, he shoved the orange float off the edge. The raft lollygagged down to the water, an oversized orange leaf drifting carelessly through the air marking the end of a season. Gouguon watched the boat settle on the surface then motioned Mac, the captain, and the rest of the dangling men down into the life raft. Two of the men slid off the boat into the turbulent waters surrounding it. The captain grabbed one of the men by the collar of the life jacket. Mac and Sonny grabbed the other man by the arms and yanked him back aboard.

A blue whale rammed the piling underneath Gouguon. The rig shuddered, creaked, and twisted. When the whale surfaced, the life raft full of men stuck to the whale's skin, dragging them away from the destruction.

Two more direct hits buckled the pilings. The platform jerked back and forth several times causing the communications satellite to dislodge and plop into the ocean. The top of the rig angled toward the water, the twisting metal screeched like a cross between a herd of elephants and pack of Tyrannosaurus. Seconds later, the rest of the rig followed, slowly at first, until the momentum shifted, slamming the steel monster into the water. Gouguon rode the rig nearly all the way down before diving off a few feet from impact, a wicked grin plastered on his face.

A series of waves followed the collapse, rocking the men in the boat until a few of them turned green.

Mac watched as his former office bubbled toward the bottom.

The captain surveyed the horizon in each direction. Nothing had changed: no land in sight. Large tail fins lifted from the water around them then came smacking back down on the surface.

Hammerheads darted to and fro nipping the raft with their fins then shooting away again. Reactions in the boat varied from crying, shaking, or staring silently at the water lapping around their ankles.

"Is everyone alright?" spoke the captain with as much confidence as he was able to muster.

"Aye, Cap," bellowed a few of the men.

"Two, four, six, eight, eleven. Eleven out of eighty-eight," whispered the captain with his head bowed.

"We did our best, Cap," said Sonny, patting the captain on the shoulder.

Mac looked out over the water. A few bubbles burped their way to the surface from the sinking rig; everything else stood still except for a solitary fin circling the boat about fifty feet out. Mac watched the fin come closer and closer with each circumference around the raft.

One by one, the heads on the raft started following the fin. One of the men in the center of the boat began to lose it. "He's toying with us. We're doomed."

The captain reached out and put his hand the guy's shaking knee. "We're gonna make it home, Lou."

"Not if that thing keeps getting closer," said Lou with an outstretched shaking finger.

The fin made another circle twenty feet out then submerged.

Lou started scrambling toward the outside. "He's gonna come right through this thing, I tell you."

"Get a hold of yourself, Lou," yelled the captain.

Lou began crying. Sonny smacked him square on the cheek. The nervous little man whimpered as he covered his face with his hands.

Mac looked back in the direction he last saw the fin. Peering over the side of the raft, he noticed a bright glow emanating from below. The light brightened until it illuminated the floor of the boat. A dark shadow swam up the middle of the glare. Gouguon popped out of the water underneath the light. The diamond tip of the prong protruded above the rippling water.

Gouguon took one look at the men in the boat then turned to the captain, "I said ten. This is eleven."

"In all the commotion I must have miscounted," said the captain.

Gouguon shook his head in disappointment.

"We all fit in the raft. We're all safe," said the captain.

The *chop chop chop* of a helicopter blade echoed in the distance. One of the men gasped, and the rest jerked their heads toward the sound.

"They're coming for us," said Sonny.

"Yes. You're all safe now," mocked Gouguon. "When you leave Aquari today, remember what happened. This is the first bit of retribution your kind will suffer for the destruction of our homes and the degradation of our lives in the oceans, seas, rivers, and lakes around the world. Our kind has cowered to your misuse of our home for decades. That stops today. We will no longer be silent. Today we make our voice heard loud and clear. Leave Aquari!"

"Taking lives will not save lives," muttered Mac.

"I'm willing to test that theory of yours." Gouguon drifted over to the side of the boat where Mac sat. He pointed the prong in Mac's direction, and the tip lit up. A bloom of light leapt from the prong to Mac's chest. As the glowing bubble disappeared into Mac's rib cage, the engineer shook. Mac's midsection ballooned followed by his hips and legs. Mac's skin took on a silvery sheen with black speckles. His head sloped back, his hair disappeared, and his glasses slipped off his face. Mac tried speaking, but only a bark escaped his whiskered mouth. The side of the boat dipped into the water, and a gray seal flopped backward into the ocean.

"Now there are ten," said Gouguon. And he slipped below the water as the helicopters closed in on the life raft.

Nichito Pakoozi

(escort duty)

BENJI SAT ON the dock overlooking the inlet. Joe sat beside him with a childlike grin on his face.

"Do it again," said Joe.

Benji snapped his fingers twice, and two splashes of Coke jumped out of the can this time.

"Man, that's cool," said Joe.

Benji caught the splashes back in the can and passed it to Joe. "Here, Dad. Octavius said your great-grandfather was a Mystiq. See if you got any of the juice in you."

Joe looked at Benji with a glimmer in his eyes, then bent over, his forearms resting on his thighs. The can dangled out over the weathered planks of the dock. Joe raised his right hand over it and bit his lip in anticipation. He looked at Benji like a child looks at his father before he takes off on his first bike ride. Joe lifted his right hand over the drink and snapped his fingers. He jerked back and felt the soda swish around.

"I felt it move," said Joe.

Benji laughed. "Go on, Dad. Try it again."

Joe snapped his finger over the can again. Nothing happened. He gritted his teeth, and three wrinkles appeared on his forehead. Joe glanced at Benji, then focused his eyes on the can and snapped. Benji snapped his fingers at the same time as Joe, and a single splash of Coke jumped out. Joe's head followed it up twelve inches, his eyes and mouth both wide open, and back down into the red and white swirled can.

"You did it, Dad," said Benji resting his hand on his dad's shoulder.

"I guess I do have a little of the ole family juice in me after all," said Joe. "Can you do that in the water, son?"

"Yeah. I showed Doc before I went fishing with Meena," said Benji.

"What did he have to say about it?" asked Joe.

"He was impressed. He also told me to practice," said Benji.

"Practice that, Benji."

"Will do, Dad."

Joe stood up and handed Benji the soda can.

"Where you goin', Dad?"

"You got some business to take care of, son."

Benji fumbled with the can then set it down.

Joe walked to the end of the dock, grabbed the ladder, and stepped down until his feet reached the water. Then he turned and started walking out across the inlet, his feet sending rippled disks out until the surface waves eventually lapped them up. Drops of water kicked up off his heels and splattered the backs of his jeans.

"Benji! Benji!" called a stern voice.

Benji lifted his head in search of the voice. The sun still dangled in the sky a couple of hours from ducking beneath the horizon. Benji saw as far as his eyes would let him out over the water, but Topside faded into blackness at the edge of the dock.

Benji stood up and walked to the edge of the dock. "Will I see you again, Dad?" he mumbled.

Joe turned and tipped his hat up, scratching his hairline with the inner rim. He gave Benji a sheepish grin. "I'm always here for you, Benji." Joe slipped his hat back down, adjusted it over his brow, and kept walking.

"Benji!" beckoned the voice again.

The dock faded from beneath Benji's feet, and he threw his hands out to the side with a gasp. A black and blue cleaner wrasse pecked at the inside corners of his eyes. Tan floated in the doorway nearly out of breath.

"I'm here," said Benji, reeling his arms back in as he recognized Tan's big block shoulders taking up the majority of the doorway.

"Benji, welcome back. The Blue is calling for you," said Tan.

"The one we took the harpoon out of?" asked Benji, shooing the wrasse away from his eyes and stifling a yawn.

"The very same," said Tan.

"Is she OK?" asked Benji, scratching his head. His blonde hair fluttered around in the water. A shrimp shot backward out of his nest head and scurried into a pink anemone on the floor.

"She is. She had been down south, but she's been with us for close to a week. She almost gave up on you," said Tan.

"What's up?" said Benji.

"She wants you. Apparently, you made an impression the first time." Tan glanced around the empty bungalow then back at Benji. "Not one to collect stuff are you, pup?"

"I don't feel like I've been in one place long enough to do so," said Benji.

The necklace around Benji's neck caught Tan's attention. "Medals of honor, not furniture, huh?"

Benji rubbed the necklace. "Right place, right time."

"When duty calls. Speaking of which, let's get going. The Blue's waiting. She's anxious, too," said Tan.

Benji popped up off his elbows.

"The last time she was anxious she dropped her tail on one of the separation walls," said Benji as he looked around the room. "You're right. It is pretty empty in here."

Tan made a beeline toward the cleaning station tube. Benji bounced from side to side behind him. Tan looked back underneath him, saw Benji's shadow on the sand, and growled. "You don't have to follow me, show off. You know the way there."

"Oh yeah." Benji took off toward the tube, leaving Tan like he was treading water.

Benji's eyes swelled when he popped out of the tube and saw all the action in the cleaning station. Two humpbacks and a gray whale bumbled around for a place to park. It looked like every grouper from all of Sanjowqua gathered around a small mountain of coral to get a cleaning. Dozens of sea turtles hovered over another sunken island to get their shells polished. A herd of sea cows bumbled into one another while the Shequarien tried to sort them in order.

Benji pulled up and surveyed the scene looking for the best place to approach the Blue. She floated on the outer rim of the cleaning station. She had done a decent job of staying out of the way, but her presence still caused some confusion and more heads to turn than usual.

"Jeez, you're fast," said Tan pulling up beside Benji. "Bit of a mess, eh?"

"Yeah, this place is packed. What's the occasion?" said Benji.

"A lot have come in to check out the damage done to the Fringe. Others are seeking refuge," said Tan.

"Going to the scene of the crime isn't the best place to look for refuge," said Benji.

"The scene of the crime has moved," said Tan.

"Where to?" asked Benji.

"It's following Gouguon. He's north of Cariqua based on the latest news," said Tan.

"Where?" said Benji.

"The Topsiders call it the Gulf of Mexico," said Tan.

The Blue turned her head toward Benji and Tan. She rocked her body in the water gently. A few of the Shequarien rubbing her down shooshed her and waved their arms in an attempt to calm her down.

"How long does it take to get used to her size?" said Benji, looking at her in admiration.

"I've been around them all my life. I'll let you know," said Tan. "Do you need anything?"

"I have no idea," said Benji. "I guess I'll tell you if anything comes up," he said as he stretched out and moved toward her.

The Blue's tail fin nipped the end of Benji's tail. It came close to clipping Tan's face which sent him reeling back. Tan rubbed his nose and finned away.

Benji closed his eyes and swam alongside her body using his touch to guide him. "What's wrong, girl?"

The Blue let out a soft moan. She arched her back and lifted her head to the surface. Her side caved in, and Benji wobbled over. An expulsion of air and water echoed around the cleaning station. Benji looked up at the droplets raining back down on the surface above them. Her lungs filled with air again and her sides expanded pushing Benji back out. A slow bluesy wail haunted the entire area.

The humpbacks and the gray whale closed their eyes and rocked gently near the surface.

The Blue cradled Benji between her pectoral fin and her side. Benji closed his eyes and fell into her embrace. Bubbles began dancing up from behind his eyelids, a steady stream of white water. Millions of bubbles headed toward the surface. Benji looked up, then down. Nothing but bubbles. His chest tightened, and his muscles froze in panic. The Blue's song danced in his head a little louder, and the bubbles parted like a curtain.

Benji stared straight at a ten-foot-long tail fin fanning in front of him. A similar motion off to the left side startled him. He looked right and saw dozens more. A large knobby, white pectoral fin in his peripheral vision helped him realize his consciousness took up residency inside a humpback whale. A crusty bowhead to his left caught his attention, and Benji jumped inside its body. The gray and white blotched side of a gray whale a few feet up called his name, and up he moved again.

Nothing but whales as far as he could see. He'd never seen that many fish in one place, let alone the most massive creatures on the planet all packed together traveling through the water, a sea of gray bodies slicing through the water.

Loud bangs accompanied by explosions shook Benji's eardrums. He found himself in the body of a Sei whale and rode with her to the surface. A burning oil rig a couple of hundred yards away floored him. Small dots leapt from the platform and disappeared with a splash.

Every fifty feet the whales closed in on the rig another series of gongs, crashes, and explosions echoed around him.

The whales around Benji surfaced for a breath of air. The misty spray from their massive exhales clouded his view. Then, they dove toward the pilings holding up the rig.

Benji bounced from whale to whale using the body of each animal to anchor his consciousness. He leapfrogged until finally coming to rest in a stoic humpback with a bruised side from a strike to one of the rig's piles.

The next series of crashes rocked the platform twenty feet back. It stalled on the backswing, wobbled back to center, and caved in on itself, crumpling like an aluminum can. A vacuum of water pulled some of the men in behind the wreckage. A handful looked to have been judged and given a second chance once the mangled steel crashed to the bottom. A billowing plume of water and sand spit them back out only to have a frenzy of sharks finish the job.

A flash of light caught Benji's attention. He followed the sparkle until it led him to a large Donquarien circling the wreckage, the Mystiq prong held firmly in his right hand.

Survivors treaded water until they lost steam. A few dolphins and whales briefly supported them. Gouguon permitted it long enough to give the men hope, then waved the mammals away and gestured for the sharks to cut in and thrash that hope with their razor-sharp teeth.

Benji looked around at the churning, bubbling water and caught sight of a life raft full of survivors. Gouguon circled the raft. His formidable dorsal fin protruded from the sea, toying with fragile minds and the tearful eyes of those huddled inside the rubber vessel.

Gouguon's voice vibrated through the water. "…we make our voice heard loud and clear. Leave Aquari!"

Benji listened to his uncle's speech then watched as a seal flopped out of the boat, twisted playfully in the water, and darted off toward the gurgling wreckage of the oil rig.

The sound of helicopter blades chopping through the air lulled Benji's attention away from the life raft, then the waving hands of the men in the boat pulled his attention back to them again.

A party of Donquarien waited for their leader. Benji recognized several of them from the incident at the Fringe. They finned in a tight group, exchanging congratulatory jokes about the oil rig while it continued whispering its final wails and settled to a new life on the ocean floor.

Gouguon pulled up when he reached the Donquarien. The diamond tip of the Mystiq prong gathered the incoming surface light trickling down through the water and diffracted it back out again as thousands of glimmering shards. Despite the grave circumstances, the prong's beauty mesmerized Benji. The light from the prong danced across the bodies of Gouguon's supporters. Benji followed several of the shafts of light as they danced on different faces until he recognized Sys, the Donquarien he saved from the net.

"What is the status of the Fringe, Sys?" said Gouguon.

"The Fringe is decimated. Anything on the outer rim of Sanjowqua sits at the bottom of the ocean now, in much the same shape as that oil rig behind you."

Gouguon smiled. "And the next ring?"

"We checked its stability before heading here. It's shaky but stable. The Shequarien prong should keep it floating, but the burden of power required to keep the rest of the rings safe decreases the protection the prong can extend out further. The islands used to support each other, but the loss of the Fringe throws off the balance. The islands are now relying on the Shequarien prong to stay afloat. The eighth ring is the new Fringe.

"Boats have already begun encroaching further into the boundaries of Sanjowqua. The closer the Topsiders get to Sanjowqua the more support you will garner from the Shequarien who live there. It's all unfolding just like you said," said Sys.

Gouguon smiled and nodded his head. "We've called attention to ourselves today," yelled Gouguon as he addressed the rest of the group. "Now we let the other's know we mean business. The next rig is a half day's swim west. Gather in front of the whales and lead them behind the sharks and me."

"Gouguon, a number of the whales are injured and even more are exhausted. We'll lose quite a few of them if we move again so soon," said Sys.

Gouguon tilted his head slowly toward the Donquarien. He pulled the prong down by his waist as he contemplated the statement. Benji could see Gouguon's jaw muscles tighten from behind him. Gouguon lifted his shoulders and rolled his neck in a circle. "I'll release them for the evening. We'll give them time to rest and eat. Then, we'll double our efforts tomorrow," snarled Gouguon.

"Why not use the prong and save the whales from the damage?" said Jais.

"The Topsiders need to know, without a doubt, that the damage being inflicted upon them is coming from Aquari and its inhabitants. Using the prong gives them the opportunity to spin the destruction as a natural disaster or freak accident."

Gouguon turned his head and glanced back at the whale Benji inhabited and continued talking.

"Any losses will more than be made up for by the damage we do to these oil extractors. Any deaths incurred on our end will be celebrated for years to come as Aquarien across all the oceans acknowledge their sacrifices."

There are other ways.

Gouguon turned his back on the swirling circle of Donquarien. He cocked his head and slowly approached the humpback whale Benji used to anchor himself. Gouguon swam around the whale once, then stopped inches from the docile creature's large eye.

"Your father felt the same way, pup. And look where it got him. Living with them does not make you one of them. You made your choice. Now, if you don't want to end up like your parents," Gouguon raised the prong and tapped it behind the whale's eye. "Stay out of my way," he whispered.

Benji jerked out of the humpback. His consciousness slammed back into his own body. His arms and tail shot out in different directions. The Blue pulled her fin in, pressing Benji tighter against her side.

Lin raced up beside the Blue, and the mammoth creature let out a loud wail that sent Lin careening backward. Benji dropped his hand on her fin.

"It's alright, girl. She's a friend," said Benji.

The Blue let out an annoyed snort from her blowhole and turned her head slightly away from Lin.

Benji flopped off the Blue's fin. The outer body experience left him feeling light-headed. He held his left hand up against the whale to calm her and keep his balance.

"Are you ok?" asked Lin.

"Yeah," said Benji rubbing his head with his right hand. "How long have you been here?"

"A while. I saw you and Tan take off earlier. I followed to see what was so important. What happened?" said Lin.

"I saw Gouguon. He's leaving nothing in his wake. Sanjowqua is lucky he only dropped the Fringe. He could have done a lot worse," said Benji.

"Jaylon and Meena were talking about that. It's confusing," said Lin.

"Gouguon had a lot of time to plot this all out. He's relying on more incidents like what happened with the fishing boat out on the Fringe to drive support for his actions against the Topsiders. The Shequarien have been afraid of the Fringe falling since the Mystiq prong went missing. Gouguon plans on letting fallout from increased Topsider invasions stir the pot even further," said Benji.

"What are we going to do?" said Lin.

"I need to…"

"You need to drop the 'I' talk," said Lin. "This is serious business, Benji."

Several chirps echoed through the water. Two slick bodies sandwiched Benji from behind and swept him away from the Blue. Benji gripped them both as the dorsal fins of two dolphins lodged into his armpits and the three of them zoomed straight for the surface. When they breached, Eeke and Zeeke tucked and rolled into a front flip, sending Benji off into the air another ten feet before his tail caught the water causing an epic belly flop.

Eeke and Zeeke giggled, squeaked, and whistled underneath him. When the feeling came back into his face, Benji managed a huge smile, and the two dolphins attacked him again, forcing their heads into the crooks of his neck and under his arms.

"Someone's been missed," said Lin. "How come I never get a welcome back greeting like that?"

Mai swam up behind Lin and nuzzled against her hip. Lin stroked the dolphin's head.

Eeke broke away from Benji and snuggled up against Lin's belly causing her to laugh.

"Better than a fishing net, right?" said Eeke.

"I'd say so," managed Lin between giggles.

"You shouldn't have snuck out," said Zeeke with a straight edgy voice. Then he cracked a big grin. "What were you thinking about not asking us to go with you?"

"Haven't you two had enough excitement for the year?" asked Lin.

"Hardly," said Eeke as he nuzzled under her arm. "We're getting stir crazy."

"Yeah, Doc cleared us for activity, but Darmik won't assign us to anything outside the fifth ring," said Zeeke.

"Yeah. Especially after you guys got caught playing hide and seek with that fishing boat. How'd you end up in that net anyway?" said Eeke.

"Let's see, we got curious what it would be like inside of one and..." said Lin shaking her head, her hands on her hips. "The Donquarien corralled us, clamhead. It was either that or a spear. And a few of us got both. Two of us didn't make it," said Lin.

"How's Yuri?" asked Mai.

"Good as new," mumbled a sheepish voice.

They jerked their heads back to see Yuri floating just behind them.

Lin rushed over and hugged his neck. Then she pushed him back as she inspected his shoulder. "How...?"

"Doc told me Jay powered up the lucky stars with some extra good mojo. They also used a new cream they've been experimenting with. It's mystical if you ask me," he said, staring at Benji.

Benji swam over to him and placed a hand on his shoulder. "Thanks for looking for me, Yuri."

"Thank you for visiting me yesterday," said Yuri.

"How do you feel?" asked Lin.

"Feel like I spent yesterday trying to move Waputa Wamkala. Alone. With one arm. I woke up this morning a pretty stiff. Doc wants me to take it easy for the next couple of days," said Yuri.

The Blue let out a long moan. Benji looked under her belly and saw the two humpbacks circling the station where they had gotten their cleaning done. They both sang out, then the larger one rolled on his side and started slapping his pectoral fin on the surface.

"Looks like they're ready to go," said Lin.

"The Blue wants them to stay, but they've got family out there," said Benji.

Benji closed his eyes and remembered the dream he had with Joe. He snapped his fingers and started moving the water between his hands like a potter molds clay on a turntable. Benji breathed in and lowered his eyelids halfway, blocking out his surroundings and companions. After a few snaps of each hand, he had a basketball-sized swirl of water that he massaged between his palms. Benji pumped his arms back and forth expanding them out further after each inward motion. He finned away from the group to keep from sucking anyone inside the swirling bubble of air he conjured up between his fingers.

"That's an interesting trick," said Mai.

Eeke swam up and poked his nose at the bubble.

"Careful, Eeke" snapped Benji, but he was a second too late.

A vacuum of air sucked the curious dolphin inside the bubble sending him spinning around like a merry-go-round. Benji pulled his hands out and away quickly. The pocket of air expanded and popped. A rush of water filled the void. Eeke swirled around in multiple directions until Mai swam up and helped stabilize her brother.

"I told you that you'd get it one of these days for sticking your nose where it doesn't belong," lectured Mai.

Zeeke bounced back and forth behind Mai, giggling at his younger brother. Mai shot Zeeke a sharp glare. He stopped when her icy stare seized his attention but commenced again even louder once she turned back to her dizzy little brother.

Benji swam over to Eeke to put his hand on the dolphin's head.

"Sorry about that," mumbled Benji.

Eeke blinked his eyes several times then bobbed up and down in the water full of energy. "Again!! Do it again!"

Seeing his brother's enthusiasm, Zeeke immediately got jealous and chimed in. "Woah! Me first! Me first!"

Darmik swam up between Lin and Yuri. Benji hadn't seen him since the first day he arrived when the head dolphin slung him out of the water a good twenty feet into the air. Darmik slid his head under Lin's hand and shook his head at the two dolphins bickering with each other. Darmik let out a loud whistle that sent the two younger dolphins straight into an attentive stance. Mai swam up beside them and awaited for Darmik to address them.

"You two have been itching to get out of here, right?" said Darmik.

Eeke and Zeeke looked at each other with eager eyes.

"Uh. Yes, sir," said Zeeke.

"The two humpbacks are ready to go. They need an escort," said Darmik.

"Wait," said Benji.

Darmik cut Benji a quick, cold stare and resumed.

"You're to guide them out to the eighth ring and return immediately," said Darmik.

Benji spoke up again. "Darmik, if you let them out there, they won't be coming back."

Darmik looked at Benji with a tinge of annoyance written on his face.

"I know these two well. Cut-ups and clowns, yes. But they also follow orders. They were trusted to watch you, young Mystiq. I'd give them a little more credit than that," said Darmik.

"That's not what I meant. Gouguon is using the Mystiq prong to control Aquari's mammals. If you send them out there, they'll end up ensnarled in his control."

Darmik eyed Benji from head to toe. "And how's that work on Mystiqs?"

Benji shrugged his shoulders.

Lin spoke up immediately. "Tell the whales to stay here. It's not safe out past Sanjowqua right now."

"This is a cleaning station, Lin. Not a prison," said Darmik.

"But…"

"I'll go," said Benji.

"Not alone. I'm going with you," said Lin.

"Me, too," said Yuri.

"Us, too," said Eeke and Zeeke.

"I'm coming, too," said Mai.

"Mai, you're not cleared to leave the interior. You shouldn't even be out this far. You're staying put." Darmik looked at Yuri with a questionable stare. "I heard you got skewered yesterday by a group of Donquarien. Doesn't look like you got a scratch on you."

"I'm a quick healer," said Yuri.

"Even so, Doc wants him to take it easy for the next couple of days," said Lin.

Yuri threw his hands up in protest then stuck his tongue out at Lin.

Darmik looked around the group then came back to Yuri. "You're staying here with Mai."

Yuri groaned, and Mai swam up beside him, nuzzling her head against his side.

"Thanks a lot, Lin," moaned Yuri.

"The rest of you can take the humpbacks out to the eighth ring. Eeke and Zeeke, I want you stopping inside the seventh ring. Benji and Lin, you're clear to the interior of the eighth ring. Point the whales out and let them do as they please," said Darmik.

"Got it," snapped Eeke and Zeeke in unison.

Mai bowed her head and gave her brothers a jealous look.

"Alright. Eighty tons of whale is ready to move," said Darmik.

Eeke slid underneath the Blue and headed toward the two humpbacks. Benji, Lin, and Zeeke followed. Benji ran his hand under the belly of the Blue as he swam by her. She let out a worried sigh.

The four of them led the humpbacks out of the cleaning station. The humpbacks, normally playful and bumping up against each other's sides, filed in a line. The Blue let out a final cautionary wail. The humpbacks lifted their tail fins out of the water and smacked them on the surface several times to say goodbye.

"Hold on there," called Jaylon. He and Meena swam up alongside the rest of the escorts. "Not so fast."

Benji looked behind him at the whales close on their tails then cut right to start a zig-zag pattern that would slow their progression.

Jaylon and Meena sandwiched Benji and Lin.

"Are these two aware of what they're getting themselves into?" said Jaylon jerking his thumb over his shoulder at the two humpbacks.

Benji and Lin nodded their heads in agreement.

"Yep. The Blue tried to convince them, as well," said Lin.

Jaylon frowned as he broke off from the front to try reasoning with the whales one last time.

Meena ran her hand over the back of Lin's head. "It's not safe out there. We're going with you guys. Even inside the eighth ring, there's a strong pull coming from the Mystiq prong. Gouguon's recruiting everyone he can reach."

"You felt it, too?" asked Lin.

"No, but we saw it. We weren't sure what it was at first. Jaylon and I were out headed out to the old Fringe doing some hunting. Some of the larger schools are coming in closer now that it's gone. Saves us some time but under the circumstances, I'd gladly swim the extra thirty minutes for food to have the Fringe back.

"A small pod of dolphins kept us company. Once we got between the sixth and seventh ring, the dolphins would zone out every once in a while. They'd go from chatty, bubbly to stone cold.

"Once we got outside the seventh ring they started moving further away completely ignoring us until we broke the eighth ring and they disappeared," said Meena.

"They just disappeared?" said Lin.

"No, sis. They swam off in a hurry," said Meena.

Eeeke and Zeeke swam up in front and twirled over and around the rest of them.

Jaylon came up shortly after. "Looks like we're heading back out, Meena. Zeeke, let us know if you start feeling anything strange," said Jaylon.

"Will do," said Zeeke as he and his brother took off in front, teasing and chasing each other.

Midway to the seventh ring, Eeke and Zeeke began inching ahead of the group. Each time they broke away, Meena reeled them back in with an ear screeching whistle. Jaylon swam up alongside them and peppered them with a few questions before letting them take off to herd the rest of the group forward again.

As the seventh ring came into view, Benji let out a bubbly exhale. "I can't believe we're escorting them out there to Gouguon."

"There's not much else we can do, Benji," said Meena.

Benji flipped over backward to have a final word with the humpbacks. They had stopped their dancing and settled into a rhythmic motion behind their escorts. Benji approached the larger female and moved to the side where he could get eye to eye with her.

"There are no real barriers in the eighth ring, so it's pretty much a straight shot after we break the next set of islands. Are you sure you won't stay?" said Benji.

The humpback undulated in the water with no indication she heard or acknowledged Benji's presence. Benji placed his hand on the humpback's side and pleaded once more. The sparkle he had seen in the whale's eye before they left disappeared, leaving a hollow and empty darkness.

Benji swam ahead of the whale pausing in front of her massive head. The creature powered on, moving Benji up and over with a casual flick of her head. Benji crested her back, rolled off, and went to check on the smaller male. Benji reached him and witnessed the same empty look his partner sported. Then, he jerked his attention toward the front of the group.

Meena, Jaylon, and Lin swam ahead wrapped up in a conversation. Eeke and Zeeke led the way in a straight line; their usual bounce left somewhere in the water between the cleaning station and where they now methodically pierced the water.

Benji called out to Meena and Jaylon. "We've lost the whales. Make sure we've still got Eeke and Zeeke with us."

Meena and Jaylon shot forward leaving Lin alone. They swam under the Eeke and Zeeke and clasped their hands on the top of the dolphins' slick heads. Benji watched the two Shequarien trying to fin hard to the side to pull the dolphins away from their course out past the seventh ring. Eeke and Zeeke both resisted the pull. The dolphins tugged Meena and Jaylon forward, eventually shaking them free and began picking up their pace.

Benji panicked when he saw the dolphins throw the pair to the side. He knew how strong Jaylon and Meena were after their acrobatic performance getting him away from the sharks in Beech Mill a few months before. If they couldn't wrestle the dolphins back in, they risked losing the bottlenose brothers to Gouguon.

Benji looked once more at the male humpback then pushed away in pursuit of Eeke and Zeeke.

Meena and Jaylon doubled back and swam alongside the two brothers, asking them questions and whistling to try snapping them out of their trance. Lin followed behind tugging on their tails.

Benji skirted close to the bottom stirring up a stream of sand in his wake. He rolled over on his back and came up facing the dolphins. He looked at Meena and Jaylon's tireless faces as they pleaded with the brothers. Benji placed his palms on the two dolphins snouts and tried slowing them from the front while Lin pulled from the back. The dolphins bucked Lin's grip and flicked Benji's hands away with ease.

Benji looked over his shoulder. The seventh ring grew closer and closer. He could now make out the colors and shapes of the reef fish swimming around the lower portions of the islands.

Lin swam over the top of the dolphins pleading and begging for them to respond. "Zeeke, what about Mai? Your sister. You can't leave her. She's not well, yet."

"Eeke, there's more treasure to find. We're supposed to go out this afternoon for a look at the sunken ship on the eastern edge. Remember?" begged Lin.

Benji moved a few strokes in front of the pack, raised his hands over his chest, and began snapping his fingers. A steady stream of water flowed between his hands in a saucer-sized disc. One more snap and the disc inflated. A bubble as wide as his shoulders materialized between his hands, and he pumped and pumped his arms like he was trying to fly.

"Hurry, Benji!" yelled Lin.

"Whatever you're doing, you got fifty feet before we break the next chain. Now or never!" yelled Meena.

"Three, two…" shouted Jaylon

Benji's bubble now expanded to the end of his wingspan. He looked over his shoulder. A large, reaching piece of fan coral stretched out from the reef toward him. Benji rolled over to his left and came back around placing the bubble right in front of the dolphins and the open path they had out to the next set of islands. Both of the dolphins' snouts hit the bubble at the same time, causing it to cave a few inches.

Benji gasped.

The bubble sucked Zeeke and Eeke inside with a slurp. A twirling, bumbling gray mass spun lifelessly for a long-held breath until several giggles escaped the confounds of the dolphins' wobbly prison. Within seconds, Eeke and Zeeke began teasing each other and grunting as they bounced off one another and the sides of the elastic walls.

A collective breath escaped.

"Heads up!" yelled Jaylon.

The two humpbacks cruised over the group like warships on their way out to sea. The large, sweeping tail of the female came down just above Benji, sending him and his arm full of dolphins thudding onto the bottom. A puff of sand exploded under Benji's backside. He let out a loud grunt and barely managed to hang onto the bubble as it slammed into his chest then tried to ricochet into the open water. Benji lay flat on the sand then let his head fall back in exasperation.

"Hey, how long you planning on keeping us in here?" said Eeke.

"Get off me," said Zeeke.

"Oh, excuse me!" said Eeke.

Benji lifted his head, smiled, then let it fall back down into the sand.

"Jeez, you guys are strong," said Meena as she swam up beside the three of them.

Jaylon and Lin popped up on the other side.

"Mission accomplished," said Jaylon as he shrugged his shoulders.

The rest of them slowly turned their heads and stared at Jaylon.

"What?" said Jaylon.

"That's a successful mission?" said Meena.

"Whales are gone," said Jaylon.

"He's got a point," said Benji. "Not exactly the cleanest way to go about it, but we did get the whales out, and everyone who was supposed to stay is here."

"Any way you can make this thing a little bigger, Benji?" asked Zeeke.

"Yeah, and bring in a little water?" asked Eeke.

"How about a massage and some refreshments?" said Benji.

Eeke and Zeeke looked at each other and grinned. "Two jellies and facials would be nice. We'd prefer the jellies smoked, like at your welcoming party, if you don't mind."

"You know, I think Gouguon may be able to help you with that," said Lin.

"On second thought, it'd be nice to get back to the cleaning station with our minds intact," said Eeke.

"Agreed," said Zeeke.

"I think I can accommodate that," said Benji as he finned off the bottom back to the sixth ring.

Meena and Jaylon flanked Benji while Lin swam next to her sister. Benji caught Meena glancing back through the gap in the seventh ring at the disappearing humpbacks. From where they swam, the whales appeared to be smaller than a couple of dolphins.

"It's sad not hearing them sing while they swim," said Meena. "It's like they've been forced out of their bodies."

A movement on Benji's chest caught his attention, and he looked down at the necklace that Meena gave him. "It's been hanging around my neck this whole time!"

Lin slowed down and peeked over her sister's back. "Well, what do you know? Meena, stay with Benji. I'll take the shell out there and..."

Lin reached toward Benji's chest, but Jaylon pulled her hands away before she could grab the necklace.

"They had every intention of going out there. If it does break their trance, they're just going to head back out. The Blue talked to them, Darmik talked to them, and I talked to them. It's like Darmik said: 'You can't force them to stay,' Lin," said Jaylon.

"Jay's right. That may be the last whale tune in Aquari. You'd do well to hang onto that," piped up a little squeaky voice behind Benji's head.

"Payton! What are you doing out here?" said Jaylon.

"Benji called me," she said.

"I did?" said Benji.

"Yes, you did, Benji. Saving Eeke and Zeeke was your third act as a Mystiq. Our channel as water fairy and Mystiq is now open," said Payton.

"You're Montal's daughter. And now we're partners?" said Benji.

Payton smiled. "How'd you know Montal was my father? He died before you were born," said Payton.

"Actually, he died after I was born. He told me all about the last battle he and my parents had with Gouguon," said Benji.

"You've seen him?" said Payton.

"He took me to my father's bubble room. He got me on the right track," said Benji.

Payton's eyes glistened. "Father loved the tracks. He bet on everything under the sun, but he loved the tracks."

"He was with you that night we first met," said Benji. "By the tracks of the crab races."

"I'm not big on gambling, but I always feel his presence when I am there," said Payton.

She squeezed her hands together under her chin as she smiled. A cloud of purple glowing specks shot out from her wings and showered Benji's head then danced up, down, and around the bubble he balanced between his hands.

Eeke and Zeeke *ooh'ed* and *ahh'ed* as the flecks speckled past them.

"So what were his two other acts as a Mystiq," asked Meena.

Payton looked at Benji. He shrugged his shoulders, so she dished out the details. "He healed Yuri and the other two Shequarien last night."

"That was you?" asked Lin.

"I thought I had some pretty good mojo," said Jaylon.

"You did the heavy lifting, Jaylon. I went in and did a few touch-ups," said Benji.

Jaylon nodded then reached out and patted Benji on the shoulder. "Nice work, pup! Thanks."

"And the first?" said Meena.

"Healing himself in his father's gunga galunga. Benji spent the last thirteen years Topside. He had a tremendous amount of blocks that were keeping him from realizing his potential. I wasn't sure he would be able to shake them when we first met. That's not an easy task," said Payton.

"But I didn't do anything," said Benji. "I just went inside and let the meditations my father prepared for me do the rest."

"Acceptance is the first step in healing, Benji. Many never get past that point," said Payton.

"Everything should be that easy," said Benji.

"Hindsight has that effect," said Payton.

Benji looked at the dolphins then back over his shoulder at the approaching sixth ring of islands. "Finally."

"The joy ride's over?" said Eeke

"Afraid so, guys," said Benji.

They passed through the sixth ring. The fish on the reef darted in and out of the beautiful coral covering the base of the floating island. A queen angelfish skirting the edge stopped and watched as Benji and the bubble full of dolphins bounced past.

"Lazy dolphins. All they do is play and fool around," said the angelfish.

Eeke stuck his tongue out at her.

The angelfish stared as Benji whipped the bubble around and inside the threshold of the sixth ring, then spread his arms wide. The bubble doubled in size before collapsing. A rush of water filled the void causing the dolphins to spin and flip. The pair of them tumbled head over fin hooting and hollering.

The angelfish shook her head then continued her swim around the reef.

Lin and Meena helped stabilize the dolphins, and Jaylon snickered at them swimming sideways.

"You two head back to the cleaning station," said Meena.

"Where are you going?" said Eeke disappointed.

"We've got to get the Mystiq prong," said Meena.

"Gouguon's in the Gulf," said Benji.

"Then we're going to have to take the boat," said Jaylon.

Meena pulled her pouch around in front her and slunk behind Lin. She fumbled with something in her hands and nodded approvingly. Jaylon made it over the top of Lin's head and back down before Meena's hand disappeared back into her bag. He grabbed her wrist and shook it. Meena gritted her teeth and nipped at Jaylon's ear. A palm-sized, rounded box wobbled loose from Meena's hand and bungled toward the bottom. Jaylon scooped it up before it touched the sand.

"I knew it. I knew it. I knew it! Caught you red-handed," said Jaylon, twisting the curved box in his hand, his eyes lighting up as different sections on the contraption rotated back and forth.

"All these years I thought I was a complete moron and you were this mathematical genius who had memorized the rings and tubes and… and… Well, looky looky what ole Jay found." Jaylon held out the yellow and brown box so Benji and Lin could see. "Look familiar, pups?"

Meena bowed her head and scrunched her lips together hiding a devilish grin as she fumbled with her hands in front of her stomach.

"Meena! That's a map of Sanjowqua," said Lin.

Meena smiled shaking her head. "You got me, Jay."

"I feel a tsunami of apologies lining up and headed my way," said Jaylon.

"What for?" said Meena.

"Making me think I was a moron. Pretending like you knew what you were doing," said Jaylon.

"I never said any of that. We always get where we need to be. I don't see why I needed to disclose how I arrived at my directions," said Meena.

Jaylon crossed his arms and rapped his fingers on his forearms seeing his apologies bubble up toward the surface.

"Where'd you get it, Meena?" asked Benji.

"Montal gave it to me when I was a pup. My parents were running some drills with Benji's dad. I overheard where they were going, and I went down to the north side of Waputa Wamkala looking for where they'd be on the replica. Montal zipped by in a hurry, but he saw me fumbling with the map, and he stopped. There was an empty, baby turtle shell on the floor. He spun his finger over the top of it creating a whirlpool that sucked it off the bottom up into his hands. He nodded at the shell and the plates on the back morphed into the same map I had been looking at on the replica. He gave it to me with a wink and told me not to tell anyone. And I never have. Until now. Satisfied?"

"Well, I guess you couldn't say," said Jaylon sulking. He half extended the pint-sized shell to Meena.

She gently pushed his hand back toward him. "I don't see why I can't share now, though, Jay."

Jaylon's eyes glistened. His lips parted looking down at the treasure in his hands.

"Which way, Jay?" asked Lin.

"There's a tube just around the corner of this island," said Jaylon jerking his thumb to the right with a huge grin plastered across his face.

Meena cleared her throat and pointed in the opposite direction.

Jaylon looked back down at the shell then handed it to Meena. "Follow her."

Foo Quifi Noh

(sabotage)

MEENA MOTIONED FOR Benji to go ahead of her.

"Last time I took one of these with you, I ended up rear-ended by you and Octavius. Fool me once. That's on you. Fool me twice? That's on me," said Benji.

"You forgot our fishing trip which, by the way, you botched," said Meena. "I minded my manners then," she said with a devilish grin.

"Cachazi first," said Benji extending his hand and bowing forward.

"Where'd you learn that?" asked Meena.

Benji winked.

"Argue all you want. I'll be waiting on the ship," said Jaylon as he shot between them and disappeared into the tube with a "WOOOOO!"

Meena jumped in behind Jaylon followed by Lin, Payton, and Benji. A sprinkle of purple and gold sparkles drifted off Payton's wings followed by a playful giggle.

Benji shot out of the tube tail first, flipped over backward, and carried on to catch up with the rest of the group. They needed to swim another ten minutes around the island then out to the Fringe to reach the boat.

"Can you imagine all those whales in one place?" asked Lin.

"I don't think I'm able to wrap my head around that," said Jaylon.

"It's the scariest and, at the same time, most awesome thing I've ever witnessed," said Benji.

Their voices trailed off one by one approaching the Fringe. Meena and Lin let their outstretched hands graze chunks of the broken coral that used to be the first line of defense for Sanjowqua. It now sat at the bottom of the ocean, a crumbled tribute to the creatures who called it home. Jaylon and Benji, unbeknownst to each other, entertained thoughts of the feisty squirrelfish who greeted them upon Benji's inaugural trip. Payton floated off to Benji's right; her head bowed in reverence.

"There it is," said Meena.

The ship lay lopsided with sand covering the bottom of the boat up to water line. Gray knobby sea rods, blood-red sea fans, and branching fire coral reached off the hull into the clear blue water. Schools of ballyhoo and sheepshead whirled around the deck. The sunlight glimmered off their scales. Each movement gave the school the appearance of a flickering blob.

They crested the bow and headed straight for the captain's quarters. A few crabs, unhappy about a possible departure, clicked at them from below. The eight-legged creatures scuttled off the ship's deck to the sides where they would remain uninterrupted during the hull split.

Benji and Payton drifted into the captain's quarters behind Jaylon while Meena and Lin brought up the rear. Jaylon touched a spot on one of the coral supports of the domineering globe. Strips of bioluminescence illuminated the top and bottom edges of the entire room.

As the space lit up, the three-dimensional map of Aquari also came alive. Various shades of green covered the land portion of the globe. Toward the coast, sparse lime green colors formed a camouflage pattern with light to medium browns. Deep pine greens ran up a hefty strip a few hundred miles inland on both coasts of what represented North America. The familiar borders and territory markings Benji had grown accustomed to seeing in Geography class bore no relevance from where he now floated.

Payton's reflection in the bubble encasement snagged Benji's attention as she fluttered up behind him and hovered over his right shoulder.

A few fairy sparkles careened off her wings and glittered off the clear orb covering the globe.

"Benji, the Gulf's a big place. Do you remember where you were when you mind surfed those whales?" asked Jaylon as he reached up toward the three-dimensional map.

"That would be pretty helpful right now wouldn't it?" said Benji, rubbing his chin.

"Seeing as how that's where we need to be," said Payton.

"You're definitely Montal's daughter," said Benji.

Payton winked at him and tugged on his ear.

"All I saw was bubbles, a crashing oil rig, and… wait a sec. The life raft. There were some letters on it." Benji closed his eyes shutting out everything around him. "I saw 'AL 1C Rig' on the side," said Benji.

"What's that supposed to mean?" said Lin.

"They're in the Gulf. There are big oil rigs off the coast of Texas, Louisiana, Mississippi, and *Ala-BAMA*. AL is the abbreviation for Alabama," said Benji.

"Sounds like Gouguon didn't waste any time. No need trying to figure out which one to take down first. Just hit the first one you come across," said Meena.

"This is where we are now," said Jaylon, pointing toward the little boat on the globe. "Remember when we brought you home, Benji, and we were all down in the parlor when Octavius came down?"

Benji didn't have to think long. "Of course, I do. I thought we'd crash because no one was steering the ship."

"And what did Octavius tell you," said Jaylon.

"He said something kooky about intention steering the ship," said Benji.

"Not kooky at all. That's how the navigation system works," said Jaylon dragging his finger along the surface of the bubble charting a course through the Bahamas, around the Florida Keys, and straight up to a wildlife preserve off the coast of Florida. A series of silky fan worms popped up on the map as he moved his finger marking the course. "Course set."

"Meena," said Jaylon, waving her beside him. "We'll leave the boat off the coast of Pensacola, Florida."

"I know a few coves where we can hide the boat and get some of the 'gators to keep their eyes on it," said Meena.

"Benji, your turn to send us off," said Jaylon, raising his brow up and down.

Jaylon headed out the captain's quarters to the helm with Benji beside him. Jaylon picked up a brass spike hanging from the main mast and struck it against a barnacle-covered bell the size of his head. A few lobsters and crabs scrambled out from the corners of the boat and disappeared over the railings.

Jaylon hollered out: "Northern Cariqua. Northern Cariqua. Southern coast of Maipai. Any takers? Boat leaves in five."

"Maipai?" asked Benji.

"The U.S.," said Meena.

Jaylon looked over at Benji. "Well, what are you waiting for?"

"What exactly am I supposed to do?"

"Come on, rookie. Slide the plank out."

Benji scratched his head. "Can't they just swim up?"

"It's courtesy, pup. You're a whiz with your Mystiq stuff, but you don't know anything about customer service. Makes 'em feel special. Over there," said Jaylon, pointing to the plank secured against the inside of the railing.

Benji floated over to the side and started sliding the plank up and out of the brackets holding it in place.

Payton landed on his shoulder and tugged his ear. "What are you doing?"

"Jaylon wants this out."

"There's an easier way."

"I'm all ears, or I am until you pull them off."

"They grow back."

"Really?" said Benji as he reached up and rubbed his ears between his fingers.

"Actually, no. Look, you're already using your energy to heal others and manipulate the water. Be creative. You can use your energy to affect the water around you. The water you affect can be used to affect objects you want. Look at that plank."

This is going to take a few, thought Jaylon, then he rang the bell again. "In ten."

Benji looked over his shoulder and caught a wink from Jaylon. "It's your ocean, pup. I'm just swimming in it."

"Ow!" said Benji as Payton jerked his ear and pulled his attention back to the plank.

"Lift the plank from behind the brackets," said Payton.

Benji stared at the plank for a few seconds.

Nothing happened.

He extended his neck out from his body, focusing more intently. He narrowed his focus, taking in the texture and grain of the plank, a dark knot, a knick on the side. He visualized it moving up from behind the brackets, floating above the deck and gently settling down on the sand.

Nothing happened.

Payton thumped him in the back of the head.

Benji rubbed the spot with a wince.

"*Weir-do*. Are you trying to stare it to death? It's a piece of wood. It's already dead."

"I'm trying to move it."

"With your eyelashes?"

"Uh…"

"Exactly," she said, shaking her head with her arms folded. "What'd I tell you?"

"Look at the plank," said Benji.

"I'm gonna need to spell this out, aren't I?" Payton looked over her shoulder at Jaylon. She held up two fingers and then curled them together forming an '0'.

Jaylon rang the bell again. "In twenty," he said, slumping down against the wheel.

"Before that," said Payton.

"Water," said Benji. "That's my medium."

"Yes. You're getting it. Now, get moving."

Benji snapped his fingers, and a swirl of water appeared over his hand.

"You're here," said Payton.

"And?"

"The plank's there."

"Got it."

Benji rotated his hand in the opposite direction and the swirl of water dissipated. His lips puckered as he tinkered with the problem in his head. Payton backed away and watched his wheels spin.

Benji pulled his arm off to the side like he used to do when skipping shells from Joe's pier. He flung his arm forward. Just before it was fully extended, he snapped his fingers. A stream of water gushed from his hand.

Before the flow reached the side of the boat, Benji expanded his palm and spread his fingers out wide. The stream of water broadened in response. He lowered his hand and watched the jet of water slip under the plank. The wood shook between the brackets and the side of the boat. Benji pulled his hand back and up slightly. The board stopped rattling. It hugged the inside of the brackets and inched up from its secured position. As Benji moved backward, the plank cleared the brackets and slid out from the side of the boat.

Payton clapped her little hands under her chin quickly and quietly. Pink and blue sparkles shot off her wings, little firecrackers of fairy joy.

Jaylon lifted one eye then the other. His mouth slipped open slightly. Meena and Lin floated between the doorframe of the captain's quarters with their arms behind each others' back.

One by one, Benji began flicking his fingers, tickling the water, and the board rotated until the flat side faced up.

"Now, move it into position," said Payton.

Benji maneuvered his hand left and right, back and forth, but couldn't get the board to rotate like he needed. "I don't kn…"

"Don't you even *think* that again," snapped Payton cutting him off.

Benji's eyebrows shot up remembering the last nasal slam Montal had given him for saying he didn't know.

"You have two hands last time I looked," said Payton.

Benji steadied the plank above his head while he pulled his left arm back and slung it upward with a snap at the end. Another current of water extended from his left hand. He expanded his fingers, let the current wrap around the wooden board, and used both hands to guide it over the side of the boat, letting it down with a little puff of powdery sand at the bottom.

Lin swam over and patted Benji on the back.

A long exhale rolled out from between Benji's cheeks, causing his lips to sputter in the water. A mouthful of bubbles broke free on a death race to the surface.

The heads of several seahorses appeared as they led a procession of sea animals up the plank.

"Bloody well took you long enough, didn't it?" said one of the seahorses.

Another shook her head and rolled her eyes at the remark. "Fine job, young Mystiq."

"You taking on Gouguon with that trick?" laughed a spiky horseshoe crab. "I'm getting front row seats for this beat down."

A gray and black grouper half as long as Benji came up the plank next. Two scarlet skunk cleaner shrimp bumbled around the interior of his gaping mouth.

A peppermint shrimp on the grouper's brow shouted out odds. "We got the new pup at twenty to one odds. Twenty to one, folks. Betting starts when we pull anchor and stops upon arrival in Cariqua. Place your bets before it's too late."

"Thanks," mumbled Benji.

The shrimp looked Benji up and down. "Nothing personal, pup. I'm sure you're a great Mystiq. Just business."

The procession of animals filed past Benji into the captain's quarters and made their way into the parlor below.

Jaylon gave the wheel a quarter turn. The exterior shell of rock, coral, and algae split down the middle.

"Let's get this show on the road," hollered Jaylon. "Last call. Northern Cariqua. Pulling anchor. Benji, do your thing on that plank. Meena. Lin. Pull the anchor as soon as he secures it."

Benji lowered the plank back into position in half the time it took him to raise it. Jaylon whistled at Lin and Meena as soon as Benji secured it behind the brackets. The boat creaked then floated up ten feet from the bottom. Benji made his way to the stern and peered over the rail. As soon as the hull cleared the coral, the exoskeleton folded back onto itself creating a seamless structure as solid looking as the one Benji looked out from.

"Benji, get down here," called Meena. "We're taking off."

Jaylon closed the door to the captain's quarters behind them as they took off. Benji had one of the coral supports of the globe in his grip. The sudden explosive shot forward shook him free. He nearly bumped into Lin who caught him by the shoulders.

"Over here, you two," said Meena, motioning over toward the wall.

Jaylon unfolded a table from the wall, unlatched the legs, and secured it on the floor. Meena opened a nearby closet and pulled out four chairs.

"Sorry, Payton. This is the only size," said Meena nodding to the last chair she handed Benji.

"I got a seat right here," she said hovering down on Benji's shoulder and patting it with her hand. She grabbed his ear to scoot herself around and get comfortable.

"Benji, I've been thinking about this a bit. You're just getting familiar with your capabilities as a Mystiq. Going up against Gouguon or trying to fight him for the prong is not going to serve you well. And since you don't have to be Mystiq to handle it, Meena and I are going after Gouguon," said Jaylon.

"Who says you don't have to be a Mystiq to handle the prong?" said Benji.

"Gouguon's been using it since he found it on Joe's boat. We've seen him bring down the Fringe, and you witnessed him controlling all those whales. If he can handle it, we can, too," said Jaylon.

"But you're not a Mystiq," said Benji.

"Neither is Gouguon," said Meena.

"Says who," said Benji.

"Benji, everyone knows Gouguon is not a Mystiq. He either hunted them down or ran them out of Aquari. Your parents and ours were his last victims. He spent the last twelve years in Muyu Munda for their deaths," said Lin.

Benji looked around the table then turned his eyes sideways at Payton. "Gouguon's my uncle."

Meena pursed her lips and looked at Jaylon.

Jaylon folded his arms over the table with his hands clasped in front. He took turns rubbing each palm with the opposite thumb for a few seconds. Then, he used his hands to pull himself back and stretch as he stared at the ceiling. "Hmmm. That's a rather interesting development."

Lin fixed a blank stare on Benji. All the color ran out of her face. She hoped there was more to come... an *Oh, I'm just joking,* or ...*but he's on my mother's side, and the Mystiq powers skip the males.* Anything. Nothing followed.

Payton lifted her knees to her chest, rocking back and forth on her rear. "That's a pretty interesting lineage."

"Why did he go after Mystiqs if he's one himself?" said Lin.

All eyes fell on Benji, thirsty for answers.

"My grandfather met Gouguon's mother during a visit to Donquari. He never acknowledged Gouguon as his son. When Gouguon got older, he went looking for him. He wanted answers to some of the things going on in his life. My grandfather rejected him. And that's why I think he went rogue like he did.

"Aside from that bit of family history, I don't know too much more," said Benji.

Benji alternated glances between the four of them.

"Plan B?" asked Meena.

"That was," said Jaylon.

"Benji's gonna get the prong back," said Payton.

"You think so?" said Jaylon as he scooted the seat back and floated up.

Jaylon swam around the table. A two-inch border surrounded the table inlaid with white and red triangles. Inside the border, a painting of a group of mermaids with spears followed a large ship. The ship's sails billowed in the wind. A stormy sea tossed the boat about on ten-foot waves.

Jaylon grabbed a small bass knob extending from the end of the table, twisted it, and pulled. The picture in the center portion of the tabletop edged out of the frame into Jaylon's hands. He floated over to the wall and ran his finger over dozens of other little round knobs that matched the one attached to the wooden slab dangling from his hand. He pulled on one of them, slid it out halfway, then pushed it back in. He slid out the next one beside it, then filled the hole in the wall with the centerpiece he had pulled from the table top. The insert he removed from the wall slid into the table, then Jaylon moved back around to his seat and settled in.

Benji recognized the outline of the southern states of the U.S. and the east coast of Mexico that framed the Gulf. The crooked reach of Cuba's island paradise looked ready to scratch an itch on Mexico's Yucatan Peninsula.

"Payton, can we get some animation on this?" said Jaylon.

"As you wish."

Payton scooted off Benji's shoulder. She waltzed to the center of the picture, cradled the arch of her right foot snuggly against the curve of her left calf, and used her left wing to spin around. A dusting of blue, pink, and yellow sparkles sprinkled around her like someone had wiped their hand across the top of an old bookshelf. The sparkles hung in the water for a few seconds before fluttering down. Each glittery touchdown created a slow-motion light drop, an illuminated version of a water drop, which bounced ever so slightly off the map and disappeared into the terrain under Payton's feet.

The blues of the ocean deepened and darkened. The murky soil rich water of the mighty Mississippi tainted the ocean water brown at the mouth of the river, the blues of the Gulf eventually swallowing it. Clear patches around the northern tip of the Yucatan Peninsula streaked down the coast of Belize creating a flash of pristine clarity.

The texture of the map drew everyone closer. Soon, white-capped waves appeared in the middle of the Caribbean Sea.

Lin gasped. "Oh, my."

"That must be all of them," said Meena.

"You weren't far off, Payton," said Jaylon.

"Right? The Blue and grey back at the cleaning station might be the last two whales in Aquari," she said.

A dark patch the size of Costa Rica hovered in the Gulf about fifty miles offshore from the triangle formed by Pensacola, New Orleans, and the tip of Louisiana.

"That's a disaster waiting to happen," said Meena.

"When Gouguon's ready," said Jaylon.

"Not just with what he's planning to do with them, Jay. Those whales can't sustain themselves for very long like that. No area in the entire ocean is stocked enough to support them all. They'll drain the food supply dry in a matter of days. Then what?" said Meena.

"They'll starve," said Lin.

"Most likely," said Payton.

Jaylon floated out of his chair and checked their position on the globe. "We've made it around the Florida Keys. Another hour."

"This has more repercussions than with just us and the whales. The Topsiders have surely taken notice of this," said Meena.

"I can't believe Gouguon waited to attack the next rig," said Lin.

"That's what he wants. He wants them to notice. He wants them to see it unfold slowly. I think he's going to take down one or two more, then use the attention he'll attract from the Topsiders to broadcast the destruction of the rest with the prong. We've got to get to him before he's ready to use the prong, or his actions are going to cause the Topsiders to attack us," said Benji.

"But we're hidden," said Lin. "Sanjowqua still has protection from the Shequarien prong to keep our location a secret."

"True, but that position has been whittled down to nothing. The Shequarien prong covers the borders of Sanjowqua only. I can only guess, but I would put a high probability on the fact that the Fringe falling registered on some scientific scales the government uses to track earthquakes and tsunamis.

"Once Gouguon uses the prong again, it's not going to take long before they start putting things together: an unchartable area in the Atlantic where ships, airplanes, and people have gone missing for hundreds of years and the recent rumblings that have come from that area, plus the emergence of a water-based threat in the form of a merman with a devastating weapon that can level islands.

"I can see a naval fleet hovering on the outskirts of Sanjowqua within twenty-four hours if Gouguon does what he's planning," said Benji.

A small shadow on the map caught Jaylon's attention. He leaned forward and mumbled to himself. His eyes lit up, then he pushed away from the table and headed back over to the globe.

"What is it?" said Meena.

Jaylon slid his fingers over the globe, correcting their course. "There's a ship up ahead on the edge of that shelf."

"We've passed under dozens of ships since we left," said Lin.

"This one's right in front of us," said Jaylon. "On the bottom."

Meena took a closer look. "That's the Donquarien ship."

"Looks like it," said Jaylon. "We're going to see for sure."

The boat slowed, and Jaylon headed straight for the helm.

"Shouldn't we swing wide past it then swim back in?" asked Benji.

"I got a better idea," said Jaylon. "The ship's on the edge of a shelf running west to east. We're going wide of it on the west side. Then we'll ride the current on the shelf wall. I'll put the ship just below the edge. You and I are going to ride the top of the mast on our way by to get a look."

"Like a periscope on a submarine," said Benji.

"More or less," said Jaylon.

"You want me to take the wheel?" said Benji.

"I got it," said Meena, floating up behind them.

"The currents on the walls can be tricky, Benji. They whip around pretty fast. Meena's done this a time or two," said Jaylon.

"Remember that time we rode the current on the wall south of Sanjowqua looking for Donquarien that had been reported near Muyu Munda?" said Meena.

Jaylon boogied in the water like an electric shock went up his spine. "That trip almost lost me my lunch. We got whipped around like we were coming out of one of your bubbles, Benji."

"What happened?" said Benji.

"We got called in to check out a report of Donquarien near the prison. Rumors were popping up inside that Gouguon was orchestrating something. Meena and I, plus Darmik and a few of his team, got called up to check it out. It turned out to be a false alarm. Just a couple of hammerheads.

"Anyway, Darmik warned me about the wall. The current on that shelf is notoriously wicked. I was younger..."

"Dumber," said Meena.

Jaylon coughed. "I prefer less experienced."

Meena turned her head away from him with a *whatever* look on her face.

"As I was saying, I wanted to get there quickly. I dipped down from the shelf and rode the wall current. I had control of it for a while."

Meena looked up at him through the top of her eye sockets.

"OK, as soon as I dropped below the shelf line the currents swept us away. We hung pretty tight to the wall for a few seconds. The wall over there is anything but straight. They should call it a jagged, jacked-up line, not a wall if you ask me. And that's pretty much how we traveled. After I got bucked from the wheel, we lost the bowsprit and half the railing on the starboard side. Somehow, during all the commotion, Meena got her hand on the wheel and..."

"I got thrown into the wheel. Luck was on our side that day," said Meena.

"However it happened, she pulled us out of there. We sailed the rest of the way to the prison riding the top of the shelf, got repairs, and returned home with a story to tell," smiled Jaylon.

"And we're riding this wall past the Donquarien ship?" said Benji.

"They're not all like that, Benji," said Meena. "You need to be familiar with the territory. Comparatively, this one's a pup ride."

The dark facade of the wall approached.

"We're about a mile west of the boat. Payton, stand by the globe and give us a heads up when we're getting close.

"Benji, there's a compartment up by the bow. Pull the top and get us two ropes. You and I are going to secure ourselves to the mast in case we get shaken.

"Lin, stick with your sister," said Jaylon.

"Aye- Aye, captain," they barked back at him.

Jaylon puffed his chest out, nodding his head. "I could get used to the sound of that."

"Two hundred yards and closing," hollered Payton.

"Meena get us up a few feet higher," called Jaylon as he checked the knots in the ropes keeping him and Benji secured to the mast.

Meena pulled a lever next to the wheel that attached to a secondary rudder. Pulling it toward her dropped the back end of the wing-like horizontal rudder and pushed them higher in the water.

"Hold it steady," called Jaylon.

Meena put the lever back into neutral position and leveled off. The top of the mast extended five feet above the edge of the shelf wall.

"I see it," said Benji.

"Are my eyes that bad? Nah. Water's murky. You're seeing things, pup," said Jaylon.

"It's there," said Benji, pointing in the distance. The silhouette took shape around his outstretched fingers.

"Impressive. You're coming fishing with me next time," said Jaylon, elbowing Benji in the side.

Benji looked over the starboard side of the boat. The depths beneath them swallowed the surface light like a bottomless pit.

The port side looked similar to the clear water he had grown accustomed to in Sanjowqua. The Donquarien boat sat on the ocean floor about a hundred feet down. Several shadows lurked around the outside of the ship.

"Hammerheads," whispered Jaylon. "They're keeping watch. We ought to be able to sneak by them."

"You're planning on going *in* the ship?" asked Benji.

"Oh, yeah," said Jaylon, grinning and rubbing his hands together. "The ship's dark. Whoever brought it here isn't in there."

After a slow pass by the Donquarien ship, Jaylon told Meena to move the boat down current. They sailed for another ten minutes along the deep water side of the wall then pulled up on the shallow side to drop the anchor.

"I don't know how the Donquarien boat got all the way out here on its own," said Jaylon winking. "The only thing I can think of, to keep a clear conscience, is to return it to them."

"I'm not sure, but I got a good feeling I'm liking what you're thinking," said Meena.

"You're gonna like this one. Follow me," said Jaylon.

They came up twenty yards short of the boat and watched behind a piece of brain coral as large as a minivan. A giant clam on the backside of the coral sat cracked open, filtering the water for microscopic-sized snacks.

Two hammerheads patrolled the perimeter of the Donquarien vessel. One of them, the largest, whistled a broken tune. The other yelled at him every other lap around.

"You're driving me nuts, with that busted tune, Leni," said Jos, the smaller hammerhead. "Being the biggest doesn't give you the right to be the most annoying."

Payton swam up behind the stern and waited. Leni rounded the port side and stopped whistling immediately.

"Finally," said Jos. "Hey, Leni. I'm getting hun..."

Jos rounded the back of the ship and caught Leni's tail on the bridge of his elongated nose. Jos bounced back, shook his head, and moved around Leni's side to see what was going on.

Payton floated in front of Leni's head. Her delicate hand stretched out gently tickling the underside of the shark's horizontal head. Leni's eyes rolled back in his head, and his tongue hung halfway out of his mouth. Jos rounded his big-bellied friend then froze when he saw Payton.

"Whatchew doing out here, lil' fairy girl?" asked Jos.

"Looking for a few friends of mine," said Payton.

"That's not what that looks like," said Jos.

Leni rolled his head over at his friend, his eyes lollygagging in their sockets. "You're ruining the moment, Jos."

"That's what I was saying the entire last hour you've been whistling," said Jos, keeping his eyes on Payton. "So, who are these friends of yours?"

"Come on. Payton's got them occupied," said Jaylon as he waved the rest of them onto the boat.

They snuck over the starboard side. Benji swam inside the captain's quarters beside Jaylon; the door was twice as wide as its counterpart anchored a few minutes swim away to compensate for Gouguon's frame.

A four-foot wide bunch of vibrant blue and electric green bonsai coral extended three-feet from the floor and ceiling. Blood red fan coral sprouted from behind the bonsai coral wrapping itself around a crystal clear bubble as tall and wide as Benji's wingspan. The fan coral created a latticework overlaying the Donquarien navigation globe.

"And what's your special plan for this boat?" asked Lin, bringing up the rear.

"Come here, and I'll show you," said Jaylon.

The group peered over Jaylon's shoulder as he pointed at the map.

"Something tells me the Donquarien need a little extra exercise." Jaylon held his finger over the tiny boat on the surface of the globe. Jaylon smiled from ear to ear as he set a course for the little ship down around the tip of South America, through the Pacific, and finally coming to rest off the southeast coast of Guam.

"Oh wow," said Lin.

"That will definitely get them in shape," said Payton.

"Where is that?" asked Benji.

"Home," said Lin. "That's where Donquari is. Off the coast of Guam near the Mariana Trench."

"We're just returning it," said Jaylon.

Everyone looked around at each other smiling and nodding their heads. Meena patted Jaylon on the back. Lin stifled a giggle.

"Shh," said Jaylon. "We still got to get off the boat. Benji, do you think you can get the anchor up from the behind the brain coral?"

"I should be able to. It may take a little longer, but…"

"I bet you can," said Jaylon. "Come on."

Jaylon escorted them out of the captain's quarters and shooed them toward the bow. He swam up to the poop deck and stuck his head over the railing looking down at Payton working her charm on the two hammerheads. She had them both splayed out in the water completely under the spell of her delicate fingertips. Leni's tail faced the starboard side while Jos faced the opposite direction.

Jaylon peered back to the bow and waved Meena, Benji, and Lin off the boat. Jaylon glanced back down at Payton with his hand held out over the railing. He held up five fingers. Payton nodded and gestured for Jaylon to take off after the rest of them.

"Alright, Benji. Do your thing," said Jaylon as he came around the mound of coral.

"It's farther than I realized," said Benji.

"You got this," said Lin.

Benji snapped his fingers and hurled the current through the water. The displaced water sped through the void. A jangle of chains ran up the anchor line. Benji looked to the rear where the two sharks floated.

Meena grabbed the top of his head and twisted it back toward the anchor. "Keep your focus."

The clattering chains startled both sharks.

Lin held her breath.

"Woah," said Jaylon.

Payton kept twirling her fingers under the shark's snouts and managed to keep them pacified.

Benji twirled his fingers as well, sending the current of water spiraling up the chain. Sand above the buried anchor bulged, but the flukes remained dug into the bottom. The anchor line extended at a forty-five-degree angle from the boat. The tightening chain pulled the ship away from Payton and her twirling mobile of dangling sharks until the bow hung directly over the anchor.

"It's in there tight," said Benji.

"You got two hands, right?" said Meena.

Benji smiled and looked over expecting to see Payton. Realizing Meena was right, he snapped the fingers on his other hand and sent a second jet of water whirling toward the line. The front of the boat swayed a few feet when the current hit the chain. Benji twirled the fingers on his left hand and sent the second stream up the rope. A puff of sand shot up into the water with the anchor quickly following behind. With the flukes of the anchor dislodged from the seabed, the ship began to rise, steadying ten feet above the sand. Benji closed his hands, killing the streams of current and the anchor settled on the bow.

Jaylon held up an OK sign to Payton. She nodded her head, pulled her hands to her sides, and streaked around the opposite side of the boat. Benji felt a tug on his ear when she settled down on his shoulder.

"Nice work," said Benji, holding up his hand.

Payton smacked his hand. "Touché."

They crouched behind the mound of coral watching the boat. The ship floated motionless for a minute before the rudder creaked. The Donquarien vessel made an arching turn to the right that brought the port side around the back of the coral. Five giggling faces followed the boat around and out past the shelf wall. The ship gently picked up speed, and the dark water swallowed it whole.

With the ship gone, the two floating hammerheads stood out like a couple of pink cows in the middle of the ocean.

Benji giggled. "How long…?"

"Give or take ten minutes. I gave them a little extra juice before I left them," said Payton.

"Jay, we passed an overhang out on the shelf wall before we got to the Donquarien ship. I say we skip Pensacola and hide the ship there," said Meena.

"I agree. If the Donquarien left their ship here, we're not too far from the action," said Jaylon.

Natoowi Yana

(tag)

"STEADY. STEADY. A little to the left," said Jaylon as he relayed directions back to the helm.

Meena steered beneath an oyster shell shaped overhang half a mile from where they last saw the Donquarien ship.

Benji sat on the railing of the port side with a rope in hand waiting for instructions from Jaylon. Lin floated beside Benji and cushioned the boat against the wall, making sure they didn't crush any of the coral.

"Bow's secure. Go ahead and tie off the stern, Lin," said Jaylon.

"Aye, Aye!" Lin swam to the rear of the boat, picked up a large rope with a knot in the end, and wedged the knot in a hole in the coral wall.

"Anywhere you can sink that knot in, Benji? We don't want this thing swinging out," called Jaylon.

A lime green moray eel stuck his head out of a hole in front of Benji. "What's a bunch of Shequarien doing out this way?"

"Sorry to bother you. We've come for the whales. Gouguon's taken control of them," said Jaylon swimming up beside Benji.

"Craziest thing I've ever seen," said the eel.

"You saw them?" said Benji.

"Either that or it was a hurricane," said the eel.

"No hurricanes out here right now," said Jaylon.

"Then it was the whales. They blanketed the whole place for hours on end. I thought it was clouds at first. Poked my head out to see what was going on and they just kept rollin' and rollin' and rollin'. The thought of it still gives me the creeps," said the eel over a shiver.

"I bet so," said Jaylon.

"As far as the eye could see. I got to thinking they'd never stop.

"The strangest part was they were all silent. Not a single note from the whole lot of them. I've never seen a whale and not heard them, too, much less thousands of them. A dream. That thought went through my head more than once. But sure enough as I saw them, they kept on coming. Blues, humpbacks, fins. Oh, and orcas, too. Heard a few stories, but never seen one in the blubber. Can check them off my list now."

Benji held up his hand with the knot in it. "Anywhere I can lodge this to keep the boat secure?"

"Let me see. My cousin, Enna, left for the week. My name's Ennis, by the way."

"I'm Jaylon. This is Benji."

"Yeah, well, Enna's visiting some family a few holes down from here. I don't think she'd mind. Let me check and see if her place is small enough to keep that knot snug."

The eel swam out of his home and slithered into another one a few feet away. As soon as the tip of his tail disappeared into the hole, he started grunting.

"She's a hoarder," said the eel, poking his head back out. "Saves everything that floats by here she can't get in her belly, but there's enough room to hold that knot while you're gone," said Ennis.

"Thanks," said Jaylon and Benji.

"No problem. Give me that thing, and I'll stuff it in here for you."

The eel grunted and groaned as he lodged the knot in the hole with his snout. He backed out, surveyed his work, then slithered against the wall into his own home.

"Hey, how long you gonna be, anyway?" asked Ennis.

Benji shrugged his shoulders and looked at Jaylon.

"A day. Two tops," said Jaylon.

"Any longer than that, and we'll have to talk payment," said Ennis. "My cousin'll be back by then."

Meena had her hand in her pouch as she made her way over. She brushed between Benji and Jaylon with an "Excuse me."

The eel's face lit up when he saw the coin in Meena's hand. "That's a Sanjowqua coin."

"And it's all yours. Or yours and your cousin's. Thank you and her in advance for the trouble," said Meena, extending the coin to the eel.

"Much appreciated. You're welcome here anytime," said Ennis, carefully accepting the coin. He used his large underbite to flip it up in front of his face and study the engraving. "Sure enough. Anytime," he mumbled over the mouth full of gold.

"Benji, you said Gouguon was going to give the whales a break," said Meena.

"That's what he said. He wasn't excited about it, but he knew the whales needed it. The physical stress from all the traveling they've done plus the bumps and bruises from slamming the first oil rig brought them to a halt."

"The Donquarien will be herding the whales, to some degree," said Meena.

"We should split the pod," said Lin.

"Go right up the middle of thousands of whales?" said Jaylon.

"Sure. Why not?" asked Lin.

"We'd cut our risk of detection, increase our safety, and we might even be able to communicate with some of the whales," said Meena.

"The whales are pretty locked on the prong," said Benji.

"I like it. We're faster and quicker than the Donquarien. In tight quarters, we'd have no problem if they spot us," said Jaylon.

"We need to hide the boat a little better before we leave. We don't want any Donquarien stumbling upon it," said Meena. "Are we all secure here?"

Jaylon tugged on the line Ennis sunk into the wall. "We're not going anywhere."

"Let's get our passengers out of here and get to work," nodded Meena.

Benji looked at the plank and back at Meena. "There's nowhere to put it down."

"Jay, you and Lin let the gallery know we're as far as we're going," said Meena.

"Lucked out this time, pup," said Jaylon on his way to the captain's quarters.

"Benji, you and Payton are going to help me camo the boat. We're pretty well hidden, but I don't want to take any chances," said Meena as she reached back into her pouch. She pulled out a small purple bottle and held it in her hand like it was made of paper-thin crystal. The dark color clouded her face as she swirled it in front of her eyes.

"What's that?" asked Benji.

"Coral eggs," said Meena.

"And?"

"That's it."

"I mean, what's it for?"

"I'm gonna trigger a coral spawn by sprinkling this along the wall. You're going to fan those babies against the boat, and Payton's going to use her magic touch to help them grow big and strong."

"I'll get those little cuties growing so healthy we may lose the boat before we leave," said Payton.

Meena swam over the starboard railing and then under the hull.

Benji looked over at Payton who was preening her wings over her shoulders. Several sparkles launched into the water as she let go and they snapped back into position.

"Oh, yeah!" she said to no one in particular.

A five-foot gap separated the boat from the wall. Meena swam up a few feet above the keel line. She pulled the top and gently tapped on the little bottle in her hands while humming a soothing tune that Benji thought a mother might use to put a newborn child to sleep.

Meena looked back at Benji holding her free hand up toward him, palm out and fingers extended. "Wait."

She hadn't made it three feet before a milky, white cloud began spewing from the wall.

"OK. Now, fan it toward the boat, Benji, but be gentle," said Meena.

Benji swam under the cloud, turned upside down, and began fanning it all over the side of the boat. Halfway to the front, little flashes of light danced in Benji's peripheral vision as Payton bounced between each new polyp that had attached itself to the ship. She skirted down the side of the hull with her arms spread wide. Her little fingers illuminated each piece of coral she touched with a dose of fairy love.

Once Benji reached the front, the cloud died out. He swam under the mermaid carved in the bowsprit. Maneuvering past the figurehead, he thought he almost saw a smile creep onto the face of the wooden carving from all the pampering they were handing the vessel.

Meena hovered above the boat, a few feet below the coral overhang. She called out to Benji before she got started again. "This should cover the rest," she said tapping the bottle in her hand. "Fan what falls over the starboard side same as you just did."

"Got it," said Benji as he glanced out over the deck.

Jaylon laid the ramp out so it rested on the port side railing. The wooden walkway stretched nearly across the entire deck. Lin stood in the door frame of the captain's quarters watching over the stream of passengers parading out the door and across the plank.

Meena began twirling the bottle toward the coral hanging down from the ceiling. She swam in a zig-zag pattern; one full swipe, turned, then moved diagonally toward the rear.

"I'm gonna wait until this stuff settles. Come back once you fan everything down to the stern. I'm gonna need you to make one more pass. There's a quicker way to do this," said Payton, giving Benji a cheeky wink.

Benji started at the bow and began a steady swim toward the rear of the boat, fanning the coral spawn against the side. When he reached the stern, he popped his head over the poop deck.

"Alright, blondy. One more run," called Payton as she waved for Benji to return.

Payton swirled up the main mast stopping a few feet below the overhang that hid the ship. She stretched her arms out wide and started fanning one of her wings until she began spinning. A few sparkles arched off her wings. Each one rocketed off then slowed as it descended through the water. The display started like popcorn. One blue sparkle popped out. A few seconds later a red one shot in the opposite direction. Benji felt like he was looking for shooting stars until the sparkles multiplied into a shower. A hundred sparklers would have paled in comparison to the extravaganza coming off Payton's wings. Pink, purple, blue, green, red, orange, neon colors, pale colors, and deep, dark bold ones blanketed the boat. Benji caught himself staring at the specks of light now streaking down like the long droopy branches of a weeping willow tree. Hundreds of the glowing speckles zipped down past his body before Payton pulled him out of his trance. "Get going, Benji," she snapped.

Benji fanned the glowing dots against the side of the boat. The coral bits they touched sparkled with appreciation. Once he reached the end, he curled around the back and carefully splayed the light dots against the stern, as well, letting his momentum carry him around the side they already covered. His eyes shot open when he saw some of the coral on the port side already as big as his hand.

Benji made his way back up to the deck. A few sparkles still made their way through the water. Payton beat the last of them down. She landed on Benji's shoulder, crossed her arms, and nodded in appreciation.

"Not bad," she said, tugging Benji's ear.

"Rest time," said Jaylon.

Jaylon swam into the captain's quarters, rummaged around in a closet, and came back out with four hammocks. Six pack rings fastened together formed the clear mesh pattern in each. Jaylon strung his up from the center mast to the starboard side railing, climbed in, and let out a satisfied gasp of bubbles that floated up into the overhang and sloshed around like upside down puddles of silver.

Benji followed suit and set up next to Jaylon.

"Hey, Jay. Why didn't you say anything about Gouguon and the prong to the eel?" said Benji.

"Gouguon has a lot of sympathizers still floating around in the ocean, Benji. Especially, in these parts. New oil rigs pop up all the time, and there's a spill more often than not.

"The whales, though. They're regarded. Highly. Size does that. They're the gentle giants and anyone, and I mean anyone who goes against the whales, be they Topsider or Aquarien will make more than a few enemies down here," said Jaylon.

"You should be a politician," said Benji.

"I'll leave that stuff to Octavius. Plus, I prefer the nets," said Jaylon.

Lin set up her hammock beside Benji while Meena strung hers on the other side of Jaylon. Benji looked up the main mast. Little purple and green branches of coral already reached out into the water.

A loud snore broke through the water. Jaylon's lips shook along with the water shooting out of his mouth.

"Well, he's out," said Meena, peering over Jaylon's chest. "I figure we can squeeze in six hours before we head out. If we follow Lin's suggestion and split the pod, we should be able to come out right in the thick of things. We'll figure out a way to distract Gouguon while, Benji, you swipe the prong."

Payton came up from the side of the boat with an empty conch shell filled to the brim with sand. She stuck the pointed end of it through Benji's hammock then disappeared over the railing again.

"What's that all about?" asked Benji.

"Alarm," said Lin.

"Like an intruder alarm?" asked Benji.

"We need to leave in the middle of the night. Payton's fixing up an alarm to make sure we do," said Meena.

Payton reappeared with a dozen empty clamshells stacked on her head ranging in size from a silver dollar to a teacup saucer.

Benji threw his arms over the side of his hammock, rested his chin on his forearms, and watched Payton work her magic.

Payton fluttered back and forth building a stack of the clamshells underneath the conch she shoved through Benji's hammock. The open side of a clamshell stuck out in every direction spiraling up twelve inches. The tower wobbled slightly. Payton stuck her hand out and steadied it once more while she held her breath. She backed away slowly admiring her work. Then, she swam under the conch shell, spun like a tornado, and came out of the cyclone with a karate chop to the pointy end of the conch shell. The bottom point sliced off clean. It toppled end over end, landing with a thud on the deck. Sand began flowing out of the conch and collected in the bottom shell of Payton's alarm tower.

Payton swam over Benji's hammock. She floated down onto his tail, put her hands behind her head, and wrapped her wings tightly around her body.

Benji watched the sand slowly pile up in the first shell. A miniature mountain peak formed like the drip castles he made as a kid on the beach. Once the tip got too pointy, sand slid down the sides, filled the shell, and began overflowing into the one above it. Benji's eyelids followed the movement of the sand up into the next shell until he fell asleep.

"Benji."

Benji looked down at his feet planted squarely on Joe's dock. He wriggled his toes then flicked a dried up clump of seagull poop into the water with his big toe. His eyes followed the little ripples in the water out a few inches then continued up across the inlet. The marsh grass on the other side swayed in the warm summer breeze.

The boards of the pier creaked as Joe walked up and placed his hand on Benji's shoulder. Benji twitched from the surprise. He looked up and smiled at his dad.

"Hey, stranger," said Joe.

"Hey, Dad."

"What's on your mind, son?"

Benji pushed his hands into the pockets of his jeans and scuffed his bare feet on the deck.

"Nervous?"

"Yeah. I am pretty nervous, to be honest," said Benji.

"Nothing wrong with that. Nerves are a good thing. They keep us on our toes."

"Did you ever get nervous?"

"Of course, I did. You didn't think I was a robot did you?" Joe moved his arms in a jerky up and down motion then turned his head toward Benji in the same fashion.

Benji nicked his dad on the shoulder and grinned.

"How'd you handle it when you got nervous?" asked Benji.

"Try to stop thinking."

"My mind's going a million miles a minute. I need to slow it down before I even attempt to stop it," said Benji.

"You're thinking about the future, son. That's something you can't control. What you can control is the present. You're in complete control of who you are, where you are, and what you're doing at this moment. When you control that, you control the future without having to worry about it.

"Focus on where you are. The future doesn't exist. Consider it invisible. Let it melt into the present, and you'll create it with what you're doing right now. If you don't like where you're at, then change what you're doing and the future, when it comes, will reflect that," said Joe.

Benji scrunched his lips together and nodded his head. "That helps, but it doesn't. I mean, how am I supposed to get the Mystiq prong from Gouguon?"

"That's in the future. That's invisible," said Joe.

Benji shrugged his shoulders. "Thanks, Dad."

"Anytime, son."

Benji looked down at his feet. A monarch butterfly landed on his little toe. She batted her wings against his foot which made him giggle. He closed his eyes. When he opened them again, he looked up at the mast of the Sanjowqua ship. Another tickle on his foot drew his gaze back down where Payton tossed and turned on his tail. Her wings brushed up against his fin. Benji looked over the edge of his hanging bed and saw half the clamshells now filled with sand from the conch wedged in his hammock. He watched the falling stream of sand for a few minutes before drifting back to sleep.

The shells of the tower Payton put together clashed to the deck of the ship after the last one filled with sand and tipped the rest over. Benji kicked his tail then jerked his head up in his hammock. Payton shot off his tail above his head leaving a trail of red, orange, and yellow sparkles in her wake.

"Not cool, Benji!"

"Oops. Sorry," he said followed by a monster yawn.

She shook her wings out then zipped around the deck stopping twice at either side of the captain's door, once at the stern, and once at the bow. With each stop she made, a halo of light appeared and grew steadily brighter until an illuminated area about ten feet wide appeared.

Benji looked around astonished. Coral covered nearly every inch of the ship. In fact, he barely recognized the boat at all. The general shape seemed to be there, but any detail revealing that it was, in fact, a ship lay buried beneath a sea of coral. Bright orange fire coral and canary yellow sea whips dotted the masts. A stand of cream colored brain coral covered the poop deck. Neon blue damsels with yellow tails swarmed above it. Purple sea fans jutted out from the railing. A spotted eagle ray swam beneath large antler-like appendages of Elkhorn coral as large as Benji stationed on the bow. Orange cup coral surrounded the base of the Elkhorn coral. The yellow tentacles of the cup coral swayed furiously as the ray swept over them.

The light on the bow moved up a few feet then zoomed toward Benji, illuminating all the coral beneath its path, then immediately stopped an arm's distance from his face. Thousands of blue bioluminescence glowed inside a lantern Payton held outstretched toward Benji.

"Come on. We don't have all day," she huffed.

"Someone got up on the wrong side of the bed," said Benji.

"No! Someone got catapulted off the wrong side of the bed, Benji," said Payton.

Benji reached out and grabbed the lantern while Payton zoomed around the boat collecting the other lights she had illuminated. Benji looked over the side of his hammock. Meena held another lamp. Jaylon's outstretched hand met Payton above him. He grabbed the light with his eyes still half closed. Payton secured the final lantern for Lin while Meena rocked Jaylon out of his bed. She rolled the hammocks up, stuffed them in the crook of Jaylon's arm, and pushed him toward the captain's quarters. A minute later, Jaylon stuck his lantern out the door, his bulbous chin escorting a whistle. "Get in here."

Jaylon hung the lantern over the table with the inlaid map as he studied the scene ahead of them. Meena and Lin slid up beside him, peering over each of his shoulders. Benji swam over the top of Jaylon's head while Payton settled down on Benji's shoulder.

Before the little water fairy could get too comfortable, Jaylon barked out, "Can you zoom this in, Payton?"

"Tisk. Tisk. Tisk." Payton's head rattled on her shoulders, and she dropped down over the map. She pulled her hands to her stomach and spun. As she rotated and lifted off the map, the image zoomed in.

"Woah!" said Jaylon. "Right there."

Payton came out of her spin with both arms extended. She took a bow and said, "Ta Da."

All eyes focused on the map.

"You're welcome!" The little water fairy threw her hands on her hips and sauntered out the door.

"Thanks," muttered Benji behind her.

"Look at this," said Jaylon, pointing at the mass of whales a few miles away.

"They're not that far off," said Meena.

"What are those other two dots?" asked Lin.

"Yeah, they're moving," said Benji.

"No way," said Meena.

"Yes way," said Jaylon.

"The two humpbacks?" said Benji.

"Wow! They passed us," said Lin.

"Slow and steady wins the race," said Meena.

"Apparently so," said Lin.

"They're not far off. Their arrival should draw attention if the Donquarien are herding the others. We'll keep an eye on those two and slip into the pod once they've monopolized the attention of the Donquarien," said Jaylon.

"You think we'll be able to reach them before they get to the pod?" asked Lin.

"No doubt. We're here," said Jaylon pointing at the map. "A few miles back of them, but they got a ways to go before they reach the main pod. We'll have to set a pretty brisk pace, but we can catch up, for sure."

"Benji can you link in with the whales like you did with the Blue back in Sanjowqua?" asked Meena.

Benji closed his eyes searching for direction. His eyeballs bounced back and forth behind his eyelids. Lin put a hand on his shoulder. Benji slowed his breathing. His attention left the room, skirted around the deck of the ship, then circled the hull. He tried forcing his awareness out past the boat, but each time he pushed, a gentle pull reeled him back in.

"No. I need physical contact with one," said Benji.

"More reason to reach the whales before they get to the pod. Once we reach them, you can see if you can find out where Gouguon is before we get too close," said Meena.

"Are we ready?" Jaylon looked over both shoulders then up at Benji getting a nod at each stop. "Good. Let's move."

Benji went for his lantern, and Jaylon grabbed his tail. "No need. By the time we get there, it will be light, and we won't need these anymore. I'll take this one. That way, if we get spotted, I can divert any pursuers away while you guys get away."

Jaylon led the way out of the captain's quarters.

As Benji cleared the doorway, Ennis poked his head out of his hole. "Good luck."

Benji looked back once more before heading up the wall, marveling at the shell of coral covering the ship. He knew there was a ship under it all, but even so, couldn't believe it.

Benji almost ran into Payton who hovered around the lip of the overhang. "Nice work, Payton."

She smiled at him, snagged his ear, and rode up the wall with him behind the others.

*   *   *   *

A black shadow startled Benji as it skirted beneath them.

"I got an idea. You three stick tight," said Jaylon as he took off after it, the glowing lantern trembling in his fist as he sped through the darkness.

"There goes our light," said Meena.

Payton bounced off Benji's shoulder and fluttered in front of the group. She balled her fists in front of her belly and held her breath like she was about to shoot bubbles out her rear end. Her little cheeks caught fire, and a white-yellow glow popped out around her.

"Thanks, Payton," said Meena.

Payton zoomed in front of Benji and Lin with her hands on her hips.

"Thanks," they said in unison.

The four of them followed Jaylon's lantern below for about fifty feet. Then, he suddenly stopped. The light bumbled in a circle for a minute and returned as fast as it departed.

"Meena, you got another coin?" said Jaylon as he swam back up toward them with a five-foot spotted eagle ray behind him.

"What for?" said Meena.

"This is Maylani. She's going to take the lantern for us. I can't see anything with it right in front of my face. She's headed the same way we are, and she agreed to tote it on her tail for us."

Meena rumbled around in her bag. She pulled out two different bottles and replaced them before she finally produced one of the gold Sanjowqua coins. Jaylon took the money from her and handed it to Maylani. The black and white spotted stingray lifted her head and scooped the coin up into her mouth then fluttered her pectoral fin. The wing-like fin rippled in the water spinning her around in front of Jaylon.

"Be careful back there," said Maylani as Jaylon slid the lantern over her tail.

She lifted her tail slightly to keep the lantern from slipping, then looked back. "Ready?"

Jaylon looked around. Everyone nodded. A gentle pat on the back was all it took for the ray to get moving. Several undulations along the tips of her fins pushed her out in front of the group along with the blue glow of the lamp.

"Much better," said Jaylon.

"I could see fine before," said Meena.

"Much better for me," said Jaylon.

"You ever been to Alabama, Benji?" asked Meena.

"No, I never have. Why?"

"Just curious," said Meena.

"So how big is Topside anyway," said Lin.

"Aquari is two-thirds of the earth's surface. Most of North America, would fit with a little room to spare in the Atlantic in the gap between the east coast of the U.S. and the west coast of Africa," said Benji.

"What's it like where you're from?" asked Lin.

"Beech Mill's a small town. Most of the town is on the water, at least the businesses and stuff are. The ocean's the main draw there. There isn't much else," said Benji.

"How come they trash the ocean then?" asked Lin.

Benji shook his head. "Some of the locals blame it on the tourists. Others point fingers right back at home. Truth is, it's probably some of both. I honestly don't know why. I wish I did. I think there might be something to what my father, Boone, was trying to accomplish," said Benji.

"You mean telling the Topsiders? Working out some treaties with them?" said Meena.

"Yeah, possibly. Awareness helps. Most of the time, people don't think about what they're doing. It's not a case of let's destroy the ocean. It's ignorance and not paying attention more than anything else.

"The Topsiders are concerned more with things. The culture has moved away from nature. No one farms anymore. Only big corporations. Not many people establish a relationship with their surroundings. They're too caught up with their jobs, trying to make more money to buy more things. Materialism deadens their senses. It makes them dull to life and the world around them.

"It's a vicious cycle. People are addicted to things, and those things only bring a temporary smile. Once their 'thing' gets old, which takes days in many instances, the effect wanes and whatever it is they thought they needed to have ends up as waste. The 'things' show up in shiny colors and enticing packaging, touting all these wonderful ways to make their lives simpler. In the end, all they do is tie them down further into a system that thrives by tying them down.

"Small town people still have some relationship with nature. Not a lot, but some of the people, like my dad, still rely on it to provide for them. They're one of the few advocates left for the outdoors."

"Wow. Sounds like you got out just in time," said Lin.

"Yuri is so curious about Topside and all the inventions we hear about through conversations we pick up. You'll give him nightmares if you tell him that story," said Jaylon.

"There's a lot that's still beautiful and untouched up there, and people are starting to come around. They're slowly awakening. Like I said, I think there's something to what my father was trying to do. I think the time is ripe," said Benji.

They swam uninterrupted through the darkness for what seemed like an hour. The lantern, gently swaying back and forth on Maylani's tail, lit a cylinder of light on the sand below them, a lighthouse leading them toward confrontation. They passed dozens of stands of coral, a handful of old tires, and an empty candy vending machine which made Benji do a double take.

Lin shook her head when they passed the vending machine.

"Hurricane or flooding probably," said Meena. "Unless you've got a better explanation."

As twilight crept through the dark waters turning them gray and eventually clear, Maylani slowed her pace, letting Jaylon catch up with her. He took off the lantern, and rubbed her back, then watched her disappear ahead of them.

"We need to pick it up," said Meena.

Within minutes, two blurry forms slowly appeared in the distance.

"Closer than we thought," said Jaylon. "Come on, Benji. Let's get you up there with them so you can find out what's happening."

Benji approached the smaller male from the side. He started off to the whale's left, slightly in front, so the humpback would see him coming. Despite his tactic, the whale showed no notion of acknowledgment. Benji sighed, knowing the loving creature was locked deep below the trance from the Mystiq prong.

He placed his hand on the side of the animal slightly above the left pectoral fin. The whale made a gradual move toward the top, broke the surface with his head, and let out a huge exhale. A massive stream of air shot out creating a flickering rainbow above the calm morning ripples. Another strong push from the whale's tail propelled it another hundred feet on the surface while it took in a deep breath. He pushed down again cruising twenty feet below, a breathing torpedo on a mission to join the war against the oil rigs.

Benji matched the whale's pace easily as he got sucked into the streamline and pulled along. He used his left hand to hold onto the whale's fin. His right arm caressed the side. The gigantic heart, as heavy as Benji, Jaylon, Meena, and Lin combined, thumped methodically behind tons of bone, muscle, and fat.

Ba Bomp. Ba Bomp. Ba Bomp.

Benji closed his eyes. The warm current of water passing down his left side pushed him closer to the whale. Benji slipped out of his body and into the whale's.

Ba Bomp. Ba Bomp. Ba Bomp.

Knowing he was in a search party that would eventually put him near Gouguon with a fight for the Mystiq prong had Benji's nerves buzzing. The added feeling of the strength from an animal as large as an office building almost overwhelmed him, but the steady thump of the heartbeat kept him grounded.

Ba Bomp. Ba Bomp. Ba Bomp.

A large tail appeared in front of him. Off to his right, another materialized. Movements to his left revealed dozens more. He bounced from whale to whale before settling into the smaller body of a juvenile humpback whose adolescence had enough rebellion left in its system to frolick up and down out of the pod's fixed pattern. A fifty-foot dive with the calf gave him a sobering view in every direction. Gray-white lumps littered the surface, ribbed underbellies coasting past him like clouds on a warm spring day. Each wave of bodies that rolled by scrunched the pod closer and closer, squeezing out the light from above, converging like storm clouds.

A black shadow below stole Benji's attention momentarily as a ray sailed just above where the darkness swallowed the light.

Benji rode with the adolescent for a hundred yards then jumped to another when the young animal returned to the surface. Another bounce, then another took him out toward the edge. When he reached a point where no more bodies surrounded his right side, he sat still and waited using the heartbeat to center himself and remain calm.

Ba Bomp. Ba Bomp. Ba Bomp.

A steady line of Donquarien spaced a hundred feet apart, each holding a spear as long as they were, swam alongside the whales. A patrolling

Donquarien looked at Benji's whale, then swam over and prodded it with the blunt end of the spear. "We're almost there. Make Aquari proud."

The Donquarien grunted then swam ahead and prodded the next whale with the same line, and Benji bounced forward through the pod.

He passed several blues, humpbacks, grays, and sperms. He glanced over and saw fin whales and bowheads. The black and white pattern of a couple of dozen orcas stood out in contrast to the predominant large gray masses huddled together. The stark white color and bulbous head of a pair of beluga whales caused Benji to pause in the body of a bottlenose dolphin before continuing his leap to the front of the pod.

The shushing sounds of exhales combined with the sloshing of water as each group of whales surfaced for air sounded like an army of well-oiled machines marching toward battle. When Benji finally reached the front of the group, he settled into a female fin whale.

A school of sharks led the way, a shimmering silver arrow flanked by Donquarien on either side. The largest of the sharks, the great whites lined the outer edges of the formation. Next, came the hammerheads followed by the bull sharks, the striped tiger sharks, and the snaggle-tooth makos.

Gouguon finned in a protective barrier between the tail end of the sharks and the sloped heads of the fin whales, occasionally dipping down while doing a barrel roll to gloat at the size of his forced following.

Gouguon whistled. A Donquarien from either side of the triangular formation promptly rolled under the sharks and came up beside their leader.

"Send out two of the whites. Give me a report on how far we've got to the next rig," said Gouguon.

They both nodded and returned to the outer edge of the sharks. Each of the Donquarien moved up and down the line before choosing one of the larger great whites to send ahead. The sharks nodded their rocket-sized heads before they parted from the group.

Gouguon dove down once more. As he rolled over on his back, he stopped momentarily and stared into the large eyes of the fin whale Benji inhabited. Benji gasped then everything went black.

Suddenly aware of the current running over his body, the powerful fin of the humpback in his grasp, a chill ran through Benji's shoulders, converged in his spine and ran down his back out the tips of his fin. Jaylon, Meena, and Lin swam off to his side. Payton hovered over his shoulder.

"You OK?" asked Payton.

Benji batted his eyes and shook his head. "Yeah. They're on the move."

"You can hear them from here," said Meena. "They're not too far ahead."

"Where's Gouguon? asked Jaylon.

"He's got a front-row seat, between the sharks and whales. That eel was right. There are thousands of them," said Benji.

"We need to get to them before they reach the rig," said Jaylon.

"What are we waiting for?" said Lin.

Benji rubbed his hand on the humpback's side and shoved off. The jetstream pulsing over the gentle giant pushed him back a few feet before he kicked it into gear.

Within minutes, the steady movement of thousands of whales breaching, breathing, and bubbling through the water overwhelmed their eardrums.

"Oh, wow," muttered Lin as they approached the pod.

"You weren't kidding, pup," said Jaylon.

"How deep is the pod," said Meena.

"A couple hundred, more or less," said Benji.

The four of them hovered near the bottom as the humpbacks approached the main pod.

Two Donquarien came in behind the whales and prodded them forward.

"We're sticking together. Benji, you come with me. Lin, go with your sister. I want us on either side of one, no more than two whales. Check in after every other whale we pass. I want us staying above their bellies," said Jaylon.

"I didn't see any Donquarien below the pod," said Benji.

"Doesn't mean there won't be. That's a huge area to cover, Benji. You weren't gone that long," said Meena.

"The Donquarien are busy with the humpbacks," said Lin.

"Let's go," said Jaylon.

If Benji's body wasn't numb from nervousness, he might have giggled from the tingling bubbles pulsating around their bodies as they integrated with the whales.

As soon as they disappeared into the pod, Sys and five other Donquarien emerged from behind a school bus-size stand of coral. An eagle ray swirled around them.

Sys reached out and stroked the ray's back. "Well done. This won't go unnoticed."

"Everyone is to focus on the Mystiq and the Shequarien Jaylon. Leave the two cachazi alone. I want three of us on each of them."

"Take Jaylon out. There's no need for him to be here any longer than necessary. As for the Mystiq, he's to be taken alive. Do whatever you need to do to restrain him, but we're not to hurt him… too bad," said Sys.

Sys split them into two groups then motioned forward.

"What about the other two?" asked one of the Donquarien.

"Focus on the Mystiq. Get him wrapped up and secured quickly. If the other two come into the picture, we may lose the Mystiq. I don't want him, under any circumstances, to get away. If he does, you'll answer to me first, then directly to Gouguon," said Sys.

"And the water fairy?" said Jais.

"Put her in her place. Swat her away. Feed her to one of the sharks. I don't care. She's not our concern," said Sys.

"Got it," they chimed in.

Benji and Jaylon ducked under tail fins and dodged pectoral fins on their way up toward the front. After they passed the first two whales, Jaylon rolled under Benji and looked around the enormous head of a sperm whale. He and Meena met up at the same time, both flashing each other the OK sign. Jaylon winked then rolled back under Benji. "We're running the same pace. Keep moving, pup."

Body surfing the whales turned out to be a lot less effort. The streaming currents coming off each of the whales bucked them from side to side. Every time they dodged one fin, another popped up immediately in front of them.

Payton sat on Benji's shoulder, her fingers wrapped firmly around a handful of hair to steady herself.

Jaylon nudged Benji in the ribs once they came out from under the pectoral fin of a gray whale. "Your turn. Signal Meena we're OK."

Benji doubled up on his kicks and peered around the gray whale's head with his hand extended. Lin met him almost in front of the whale's mouth smacking his open hand with her own before finning back to the other side to cruise past a mighty blue whale. Benji looked over his other shoulder and flashed a smile at Jaylon, but Jaylon wasn't there. Benji dipped down a few feet, barrel rolled, and looked up at nothing but fat white bellies. "Jay! Where'd you…"

Two arms wrapped him up from underneath. Benji kicked and thrashed. As he rolled over, a greenish-brown net engulfed his upper body. Payton shrieked. Her tiny body crushed between the back of Benji's shoulder and the net.

Benji spun around trying to free himself but only ended up tangling himself further.

A hand reached into the net beside his head. Sharp nails scraped his shoulder blade. The webbed hand fumbled for, then snatched Payton and shoved her in a bag. "She'll make a fun pet for my daughter," laughed Jais.

Benji flailed once more and ran out of steam.

"Remember me?" said Sys. "I told you the board was clean. You had a free pass, pup. You didn't have to come all the way out here to see Gouguon. He'll be there soon enough to claim Sanjowqua as his own."

A bag tied to Jais' waist shook furiously. Little fist and foot marks popped out on the leather. A few red sparkles popped out of the top.

Sys seized the front of the net. One of the other Donquarien grabbed the rear. They darted below the whales to the outside edge of the pod where a team of great whites and bull sharks awaited to escort them to the front.

Meena poked her head around the blue whale. Jaylon told them every two, but the blue was every bit of two of the others; three, four, or five in the case of orcas or belugas. She finned in front of the animal for a few seconds before rolling back in beside her sister. "Something's up."

Meena nodded her head to the side, and Lin followed her around the blue's mouth. They emerged on the left side of the blue in a tangle of bubbles coming off the tail fin of an old barnacle encrusted right whale.

Meena pointed toward the rear of the blue then back to the pectoral fin. "Check from here back. Don't go any further."

Lin swam off and returned just as fast. "They're not back there."

"They're not up front either. Stick close, sis," said Meena.

Lin nodded and shot to the surface with her sister. They emerged a few feet in front of the blue's pectoral fin.

"Up top," said Meena.

They kicked themselves on top of the blue's back, behind the blowhole. Meena held her hand up to block out the early sunlight reflecting off the surface. Scanning the pod, she realized they still had a ways to go before reaching the front of the pack. A barely discernible oil rig sat perched on the horizon. From this distance, it looked like a Christmas tree ornament from across the living room.

"We're closer to the east side," said Lin pointing over her sister's shoulder.

"Yep, look there," said Meena, moving her sister's hand a bit forward.

"What is it?" said Lin.

"Hard to make out, but it looks like a group of sharks," said Meena.

"You think that's them?"

"Most likely." Meena surveyed the scene once more.

"What now?" said Lin.

"We'll stay inside. Keep to your plan. Let's move," said Meena.

They slid off the whale and disappeared into the water.

* * * *

Two great whites swam underneath the leading formation, reversed course under the first line of whales, and cruised up beside Gouguon.

"How far?" asked Gouguon.

"Thirty minutes at this pace," snarled one of the sharks.

"Excellent. Take a swim to the end of the pod and back. Keep your eyes open for any unwanted guests. Anything out of the ordinary is to be considered your breakfast."

Sinister grins crept upon the sharks' faces, and they broke off to either side with a pair of snorts.

Gouguon rose to the surface. He allowed the fin whale behind him to sweep him up onto her sloped head. He shed his tail and rose to his feet, surveying the scene. Water sloshed up to his shins, little white patches of foam circled his ankles before trailing off over the whale's back. Satisfied with the report from the great whites and his own observation, he looked to the eastern edge of the pod and smiled. A group of fins approached, black daggers swaggering up the outside of the pod with his newest trophy in tow.

"Let him go," said Gouguon to Sys as the Donquarien pulled in front of the whales with Benji dragging behind them.

Sys and Jais released the bundle of net. It bobbed in the water before washing up over the fin whale's head. Gouguon placed the ball of his foot on Benji's back and gave it a swift shove. Benj rolled over, his arms cramped and tangled around his chest. Gouguon bent down with the prong hovering over Benji's nose. The diamond tip glittered in the sunlight. Benji squinted his eyes. He tried to recoil, but Gouguon's foot on his stomach and the net around his body made any attempt a pitiful effort accompanied by an even more embarrassing grunt.

"Decisions. Decisions. Decisions. They're interesting things, decisions. They can shape our lives into wonderful experiences or doom us to a life of servitude, struggle, and desperation. How do you feel about the ones you've made, Mr. Fisher? That was the name of the man, the fisherman, you called your dad, correct?" said Gouguon.

Benji squirmed in the net for a second until the ropes tightened even further, pinning his shoulders back.

"See what I mean?" said Gouguon with a sneer. "Look out there," he said motioning toward the oil rig. He paused, glancing down at Benji, "Sorry," then he sliced through the net between Benji's nose and upper lip all the way to his ear.

Benji shook his head with the release of pressure. Gouguon slashed another gash in the netting from under Benji's elbow down to the middle of his tail. Benji shook his arms and hands free. He put his palms down on the head of the whale and propped himself up.

Gouguon lowered the prong again with the point inches away from Benji's chest. "Stand up. We get a much better view than the others. We have the best of both worlds, you realize," said Gouguon.

Benji shed his tail. He rolled over on his side and pushed himself to his feet. The rocking whale wobbled him. His feet shifted around several times before he found his balance.

Gouguon waved the prong over the pod. "They'll never see the things we're able to see. They only have fleeting glimpses of horror strangled in nets or impaled on giant harpoons. They can't appreciate what the Topsiders have accomplished with their machinery and their innovations. They have no way to use the internet or play video games.

"But why would they? They live in a world where their senses guide them to beautiful and enriching lives. They, we, live in a world where we see. We feel. We hear. We taste. We live."

Gouguon pointed at the oil rig. He jabbed the prong in the air, stabbing the rig. His lips pulled back across his face. His jaw tightened. The creases of his lips nearly stretched to his ears. His eyebrows dipped. A 'V' appeared on his forehead and pointed down his sharp nose. The veins in his arms began rising above the muscles as he squeezed his grip around the prong. A drop of blood eeked its way out of his fingers, down his palm, and plopped into the water as his fingernails dug into the meat of his clenched fist.

"They do none of those things. They're as blind to their own lives as they are to the pollution they breathe. They're as deaf to the cries of nature to stop defiling her planet as they are to the sound of their pants ripping from too much food. It's not that they are ignorant. Oh no. They know. They turn their backs. They cover their misdeeds with more of the same.

"What did you learn from them for the first thirteen years of your life? What can you take from them to bring to us, to teach us how to live better lives? Is there anything you gained that you can apply to our lives here? Doubtful," said Gouguon.

"Why do you hate them so much?" asked Benji.

Gouguon kept his eyes fixed on the oil rig ahead.

"Hate does not describe my feelings for the Topsiders. There's simply no reason for them to exist anymore. In nature, we all exist for one reason or another. Every organism, every animal, provides balance. We work together. We feed together. We live together. We die together.

Ninety-nine point nine percent of the relationships in nature are a balancing act that keep the cycle going, that promote that cycle, and nurture the cycle, save for one.

"The Topsiders take. They destroy. They feed, and they discard. They consume, and they waste. None of their actions benefit the whole. There's no give and take with the Topsiders, only take. For years they've done their taking Topside. As their resources have dwindled, they now look here. They'll bleed themselves dry, and once they've finished there, they'll come down here to finish us off. It's us or them. You and I are the only two capable of doing what must be done to continue the survival of the oceans. I vote on driving the Topsiders away. Your alliance with the Shequarien tells me you vote on cooperating with them.

"I have the prong. Therefore, my vote carries more weight. But, I'll tell you what." Gouguon looked down his nose at Benji. "You want to carry on Boone's legacy? You want to establish a relationship with them on behalf of Sanjowqua? You want to cooperate with them? Well, to do that, you need to let them know you're the point man. You're the go to. You're in charge of this show. I'll let you do that. The stage is set, young fisher-man. All eyes are on you. The boy from Beech Mill, drowned oh so many months ago, now found surfing whales in the Gulf of Mexico, leading an aquatic revolt on the very people that took you in thirteen years ago."

Gouguon cocked his ear. "And what's that I hear?"

Benji looked out toward the horizon. Several news helicopters buzzed past the rig out toward the pod.

"There's your audience now."

Benji looked down. Sys and Jais swam along either side of the fin whale's head.

"Tie him down," said Gouguon.

Benji's heart jumped. His arms shot away from his body. He crouched, turning his head from side to side.

The Mystiq prong appeared in front of his chest. A sparkle from the diamond tip slammed his left eye shut. His right eye angled down at the crooked tip of the prong pointing up under his chin, a hair below his jawbone.

"I wouldn't plan on going anywhere if I were you." Gouguon grabbed Benji by the shoulder, spun him around, then patted him on the back.

"You'll die a martyr. How's that sound? We'll build a statue of you in the middle of Sanjowqua. We'll tell stories of how you sacrificed your life for the good of Aquari. How you went down in a blaze of glory and a warning to the Topsider's of their intrusion in Aquari. I'll be the one who regained the Mystiq prong and brought its power back to Sanjowqua, establishing a healthy ecosystem once again. I hadn't planned on you showing up, but this is quite a beautiful little story, actually. I'll enjoy recounting it in the years to come. I may even muster a sniffle as I retell the tale. A small one. I'll have to show strength for those I rule, but a little emotion in the right place is endearing."

Benji stared at the oil rig in the distance.

The two choppers thumped their way closer to the pod.

Jais clamped a pair of knots around Benji's wrists, while Sys tied a rope around the whales head and secured Benji's ankles to it.

Payton shoved against the interior of the little leather bag tied to Jais' hip causing it to flop between the Donquarien's body and the whale's head.

"What do you have there?" said Gouguon, pointing the prong at the bag on Jais' hip.

"This?" said Jais, staring down at the flailing bag.

Gouguon stared but didn't answer.

"There was a water fairy with him, Gouguon," said Sys.

Gouguon turned to Benji with a blank face then his face lit up in acknowledgment. "She must be the daughter of the smart mouth fairy that palled around with Boone. He was one of the biggest pests when I eventually caught your parents in the open water. Although, he did go rather quietly in the end, just like the rest of them. She'll make a good pet. Make sure you cage her."

Jais nodded. The bag flipped and flopped against his hip even more violently for a few seconds and died out as Payton ran out of energy.

"Keep an eye on him," said Gouguon, nodding at the two Donquarien off to Benji's sides.

"He's not going anywhere," said Sys.

Gouguon looked down at the knots and nodded in approval.

"Make us proud, pup," said Gouguon.

He patted Benji on the shoulder once more as he walked toward the tip of the whale's mouth then dove into the churning water. His legs morphed back into his powerful striped tail as his arms hit the water. Benji watched the prong glimmer below the surface and disappear beneath him.

Jais and Sys let the current rolling off the whale's head pull them back into the water. They finned off to the side and slithered through the water a few feet out in front, checking over their shoulders every couple of minutes.

A pod of thousands of whales surrounded Benji. He stood tied in place on the head of one of the largest animals on the planet. A school of sharks cut through the water in front of him. They all headed on a collision course with an oil rig in the Gulf of Mexico to take it down with the brute force of thousands of tons of blubber. Benji looked around in complete silence.

The helicopters now scanned the front edge of the pod. The bay doors of one of the news helicopters hung wide open. A wide-eyed, enthusiastic reporter hung halfway out the doors. An oversized pair of headphones covered half his head. He readjusted the clear safety goggles strapped to his face twice with the same hand holding the microphone then pointed at Benji. His other fist was a white-knuckled clamp against the door frame.

Benji hung his head and shook it, half in shame, half in total disbelief. "The future is invisible, huh, Dad? Looks pretty definitive to me."

His chest stopped mid-breath. His eyes focused on his feet, then moved up his legs. He rolled his eyes up into his head and twirled them around in his eye sockets as the wheels in his brain began to spin furiously.

"The future's invisible. Yes! Dad, you're a genius."

Sys and Jais both looked over their shoulders, and Benji flashed them a smile. They looked at each other, shrugged their shoulders, and resumed their forward swim.

Benji wriggled his toes in anticipation as he cruised on the whale's slick body. The pigment of his feet slowly began to darken until both his legs appeared to melt right into the skin of the fin whale. Then, he knelt down and camouflaged the rest of himself.

Mission accomplished.

There was enough give in the rope for Benji to slide his body across the whale's slick skin. Using his arms and legs to scoot himself down the side, Benji slid off the top and around. He hooked his hands into the lip and pulled himself further down. As the color of the whale transitioned from dark grey to white, Benji matched the color change. He used the ribbed throat grooves under the jaw to pull himself under the mouth. Once secured, he lifted his head up and stared directly at Sys and Jais from his upside down position. The two Donquarien fell in behind Gouguon on either side.

Staring past the formation of sharks, Benji barely made out the struts of the oil rig. Gouguon waved the Mystiq prong forward, and the sharks began diving. They split into two groups heading to opposite sides of the oil rig where they planned on waiting for the tumbling Topsiders to plunge into the water. Benji felt their hunger rumbling through the water as they readied themselves for the feast.

A shower of sparkles shot out behind Jais as a tear in the bag at his hip ripped open. Payton's tiny hands forced the rip further apart. She stuck her head out and identified the whale Benji lay strapped to almost immediately. She eased out of the bag, hovering in the water letting the whale come to her.

Gouguon called Sys by his side. "Keep an eye on our celebrity," he said. Then, he followed behind the group of sharks headed to the right side of the oil rig.

"Payton," Benji called, but she clamored on top of the whale before she heard him.

Benji looked in front of him and watched Sys and Jais surface to check on where he was supposed to be. At the same time they surfaced, Payton came walking down the rope with her arms across her chest.

When she reached the end of the rope, she fumbled around his foot then yanked on his pinky toe.

"Ow!"

Payton fluttered up to his head tracing the outline of his body with the tips of her fingers.

"Pretty clever, but what were you planning on doing next?" she said.

"Good question, but if you're gonna help, this might be a good time to do it."

Payton looked over her shoulder. Sys and Jais scrambled toward the whale.

"Oh, yeah," said Payton as she swam up and pulled the knots loose from his wrists.

She fluttered back to his legs and untied the rope around each ankle. As she did, Benji dug his feet into the throat grooves and snapped a bubble between his fingers. He bent at the waist and massaged the bubble as large as he could get it without being completely visible then shed the whale camouflage. The rope slid off and snaked slowly toward the bottom.

Sys and Jais shot down the side of the whale. A second before they reached him, Benji stood and opened his hands as wide as they'd go. The bubble expanded and sucked the two Donquarien inside. Benji pushed off from the whale and slid into his tail with the bubble between his hands.

"Where's Jaylon?" barked Benji.

Sys leapt at the wall of the bubble and bounced off.

Jais swiped at Payton. His hand popped back against his chest.

Payton wagged her finger in front of him with a smug look on her face.

"Where's Jaylon?" repeated Benji.

"Gathering crabs and other bottom feeders, most likely," snarled Jais.

"What should we do with them?" asked Benji.

Payton shrugged her shoulders. "They're out of the way now. Best keep it like that."

Benji shoved the bubble down and back watching it bobble from the current of the passing whales.

"How are we going to get the prong?" asked Benji.

"You can't take on Gouguon alone," said Payton.

"That's a pretty fair assessment," said Benji. "We need to…"

"Getting caught is one way to beat us up here," said Meena as she clamped down on Benji's shoulder.

"Jeez," squealed Benji, nearly jumping out of his skin.

"No wonder you guys got wrapped up the first time," said Lin.

"Where's Jaylon?" said Meena.

Benji and Payton looked at each other then back at Meena, neither able to say a word.

"Don't worry. He's alive," said Meena. "I can feel him."

"Where's Gouguon?" said Lin.

Payton pointed off to the right of the oil rig struts now shadowy columns looming ahead.

"One out of two ain't bad," said Lin.

"Do you mind?" asked Meena, gesturing toward the shell around Benji's neck. "I'm not usually one to take gifts back, but…"

"I'll let you borrow it. Deal?" said Benji.

"Deal," said Meena. "I'm taking this to the left side with Lin. You and Payton get stationed behind Gouguon. When you're ready, Payton fire off some sparkles. I'll call the whales. That should throw off Gouguon enough for you two to get the prong."

Everyone nodded in agreement and split.

Meena stopped. "Benji. Remember our first fishing trip?"

Benji rubbed his ribs. "Yeah, I do."

"Good. Don't rush. Get into position and get comfortable. This may all start before we take action. We may be too late to stop it completely, but if we're lucky, we'll stop the worst of the damage."

"Got it," Benji nodded. He shot down to where the light faded and camouflaged himself dark blue.

The rig pilings sat anchored in a clearing surrounded by what looked like a dilapidated ancient coliseum of rocks and coral. Most of the fish had long since disappeared into the nooks and crannies. Even the color of the coral seemed to retreat from the oncoming herd of giants.

Benji came up and around a crumbled mess of rocks. Gouguon hovered halfway up the embankment with a perfect view of the oil rig. Several Donquarien circled him clockwise above his head. Two more swept below.

"He's pretty well guarded," said Payton as they pulled up behind Gouguon. "How you feeling, Benji?"

Benji pursed his lips, breathing heavy through his nose. Gouguon floated below him twenty yards away. His eyes darted from Gouguon, to the guards, to the rig, to the pod, and back again.

"Nervous," he said.

"Don't be. All you have to do is snatch the prong," said Payton.

Benji's eyes grew twice their size. "It's that easy, huh? What was I so worried about?"

"Look, we used to play a game when I was younger. It's called natoowi yana. We started off with each of us drawing a strand of seaweed. The shortest strand was 'it'. The rest of the group tried to avoid letting the 'it' fairy touch them. If you got touched, you were 'it', and the game kept going."

"We call it tag," said Benji.

"Good. You already know how to play. You just took the short strand of seaweed. You're it. Go tag Gouguon. While you do, snatch the prong, then get away before he tags you. Sound good?"

"Yeah, I like that. I'm faster than Gouguon... I hope."

Payton nodded. "I'm going down below for some bien pow."

"Bien who?"

"Hmmm." Payton rubbed her chin. "Call it visual entertainment. We need to let Meena know we're ready. I'll take care of that. You're ready, right?"

"Yeah, I'm ready."

"Keep your eyes peeled below. My signal's going to alert Meena. It should also attract some of Gouguon's guards. Once Meena blows the horn, there's going to be a mass of confusion. That's when you tag Gouguon."

Tag. Tag. We're playing tag. Just a game of tag. Stay relaxed. Stay calm. Don't jump the gun. Tag. Tag.

Payton smacked Benji in the back of the head so hard his chin nearly hit his chest.

"Calm down! I can hear you thinking." She swam in front of his face and nodded at him. "You got this."

Benji nodded back, and Payton took off behind him.

Crouching behind the stand of rocks, Benji kept his eyes peeled on the area below Gouguon as his uncle watched the carnage about to unfold. The sun disappeared momentarily behind one of the news helicopters. When the light reappeared, Benji shielded his eyes, forcing his attention below. A blur of wings and legs zipped along his peripheral vision. Seconds later, a firework-style display of color and light shot up from the platform of rock and coral beneath Gouguon. Purple and blue streaks shot out of several different bunches of star coral. The flower and tube corals spewed out oranges, yellows, and reds. A three-foot, purple, stove-pipe sponge shot out big canon bursts of white, baseball-sized patterns erupting between Gouguon's top and bottom guards.

Gouguon waved his hands in front of his face swatting at the light bombs soaring past his head. He backed up and yelled at the Donquarien below him. "What is that?"

One of the guards yelled back through his arms over his face. "I don't know."

Gouguon leveled the prong and turned the Donquarien into a crab.

"It would be a good idea if the rest of you stopped it!" yelled Gouguon.

Benji watched the other two take off toward the commotion below. Benji's hands gripped the rock in front of him, half keeping him from going for the prong and half keeping himself from shaking.

The first line of whales breached then dove toward the supports of the oil rig. A ring of sharks circled the water a few feet below the surface. Many of them sliced their fins through the water, an ominous signal to the Topsiders above of their presence.

We're too late, thought Benji.

A low wail crept out from the other side of the oil rig. It started as a noise from a location Benji felt like he could point to if asked of its origin. That lasted until a second wail took over. The second blast worked itself into the amphitheater formation surrounding the oil rig. The whale tune seemed to take on a life of its own as it consumed the interior of the structure. A loose rock near Benji's hand danced with the sound waves. Before the second tune had a chance to settle, another took its place. The rock near Benji's hand bounced up and down like it was headbanging at a heavy metal concert until it partied itself right off the edge.

Gouguon shook his fist in anger while yelling at the guards surrounding him. "What's going on? Where's that whale tune coming from?"

One of the guards looked at Gouguon ready to answer him with an *I don't know* then took off with the rest when Gouguon began lowering the prong in his direction.

The first line of whales locked their sights into the struts holding the rig in place. Benji stared at the whale whom he had ridden briefly and braced himself for impact. Her clouded over eye blinked several times before a twinkle reappeared. She finned hard toward the rig, then banked right at the last second. The whales behind banked with her, some to the right, the other half of the line to the left.

Benji shifted his attention toward Gouguon. As soon as the whales veered off their course, Gouguon lowered the prong toward them. Benji put everything he had into pushing past the rock ledge. It took him three swipes of the tail to reach the prong. He thought he gave it his all to reach Gouguon, but found once he gripped the prong, another burst of energy exploded through his tail. The prong slid out of Gouguon's hand and fell into Benji's.

Sucker.

Benji curved his upper body out toward the rig and kicked hard. A steely grip clamped down on his tail above the fin. He stared at the prong in disbelief and stopped dead in his tracks.

A dip in the sound of the whale tune uncovered a half laugh, half growl. Benji kicked and kicked. He threw both his arms over his head and used his hands to try and pull himself through the water.

Gouguon threw his other hand around Benji's tail and the fight to flee died out like a snuffed candle.

"Close, pup," said Gouguon.

Benji wheeled around. He leveled the prong at Gouguon's chest. A beady-eyed lobster caught his attention behind Gouguon's waist. Benji flicked the prong hoping that was all he needed to do to use it. The water parted as the prong magnified Benji's thought. Gouguon let one hand go and rolled to the side. A rock beside the lobster turned into another lobster, and the two crustaceans sat there staring at one another. As Gouguon rolled, he yanked Benji's tail toward him then swiped for the prong. He came up short of the prong, but his hand seized Benji's wrist and ground the bones together with all his might.

Benji kicked and jerked from side to side. The more he moved, the more determined Gouguon clamped down on him. Benji stopped, motionless, staring up at the clouds for some reprieve or release, maybe an answer, but nothing came.

Gouguon chuckled. "You've got some fight in you, pup. Not as much as your father, but it's different when you're fighting for your family. You've got no one left. Do you?"

Gouguon yanked Benji in front of him. One hand clasped around Benji's wrist. The other slid onto Benji's throat. Gouguon's index finger and thumb dug into the meat of Benji's neck below the jaw bone. The pressure sent lightning bolts of pain through Benji's skull.

Gouguon's other hand grew tighter and tighter around Benji's arm. The tips of Benji's fingers began throbbing as Gouguon's grip strangled the wrist below the Mystiq prong. Benji's pinky finger sprung off the shaft. One down: like the wheel of a combination lock hitting the right number.

Benji's whole body stiffened, solid as the statues he saw when he first entered Sanjowqua. His eyes rolled back in his head. His eyelids wanted to close up shop, but his eyeballs, bouncing between flickerings of light up at the surface, kept them from shutting completely.

Gouguon shook Benji by the neck. One final shake and Benji gave up the fight. His eyeballs dropped in their sockets pulling his eyelids with them. The only tension left in his body remained constrained around the shaft of the Mystiq prong.

"Give it up!" growled Gouguon through gritted teeth as he shook Benji's wrist.

Benji's arms fell to his side, yet his grip remained as if every ounce of his energy migrated to the hand now clasped three fingers and a thumb around the prong.

Darkest before dawn.

The tension eased from his body. He floated… hovering in a space of tranquility. Nothing seemed to matter where he was, wherever he was, not that that mattered either. All the pressures of life, of the body's functions, of the forces around him; gravity, water, temperature… everything vanished except Benji. Whatever he was on the inside, far beneath the Mystiq, beneath the kid from Beech Mill, beneath Joe Fisher's boy or Boone's son, beneath being a boy at all, all of that fell away slowly and effortlessly. All the layers he had padded himself with over the years, the layers of identity he placed on himself and others placed on him as well, they all fell away one by one until nothing was left, just a being in complete darkness completely OK with being in darkness.

Benji floated there for what felt like hours, being. Being whatever was left of the entity aware of the emptiness. In nothingness, nothing matters. It, as in everything, is gone.

A speck of light appeared in the distance, the size of a grain of rice on the other side of a football field. But in darkness, in nothingness, the light shone. Benji started toward the light, or…

… is the light moving toward me?

He couldn't be sure nor could he be bothered. His awareness brought them toward each other.

The light grew brighter, steadily expanding across his field of vision. The closer it got, the more intense the light shined until it was nearly blinding. Benji wanted to shield himself, protect his eyes from the light, but in nothingness, as nothing, there were no arms to keep the light away, no eyelids to help defend him.

The light kept coming, faster and faster. Benji had lost awareness of his heart and all his other bodily functions long ago, but something within what was left of him began to race as the light approached. Something inside him stirred. Faster and faster, the stirring took over until the light stopped coming.

IT ARRIVED!

It arrived with a jolt that shook Benji. His chest pumped. His back arched. Both of his arms shot out beside him. He kicked his tail and shot through the water leaving Gouguon stunned.

An arm hooked under Benji's armpit and dragged him through the water. "Benji! Benji! Talk to me, pup."

"Mom," mumbled Benji.

"Benji! It's me Jaylon."

Jaylon thrashed through the water with Benji laid against his chest. Lin came up from beneath and hooked under Benji's other arm.

Benji's eyes fluttered. A shower of sparkles behind him finally forced his eyelids open all the way as he focused on the commotion he left behind. Payton buzzed in and out from around Gouguon's head assaulting him with an array of hits keeping him confused and disoriented.

Whatever shook Benji back into his body had a similar effect on Gouguon who was half limp in the water, his arms barely swaying around his head to keep Payton away.

After half a dozen swipes at Gouguon, Payton buzzed the semi-conscious Donquarien once more then took off full speed behind Benji. She landed on Benji's chest and walked up to his bobbing head. Payton lifted his head by the chin and stared deep into his eyes. "Benji! Are you OK?"

"I'm..." Benji stared at her for a second then nodded. "...OK."

Movement behind Payton caught Benji's attention. He moved his head to the side.

Payton followed his gaze. "Uh oh."

Gouguon shook himself in the water several times. He moved forward slowly, shook his head, then moved forward a little faster when he zeroed in on the twinkle from the Mystiq prong. His hands clenched into fists. He flexed his shoulders and pulled them back. His massive head jutted out, and his tail swiped with every ounce of power he could muster.

"You two got any more steam in the tanks?" hurried Payton.

Jaylon tugged a little harder under Benji's armpit. Lin grunted to keep up with him.

"That's not gonna do it," said Payton.

"That's all I got," huffed Jaylon. "Benji, you awake yet? Now would be a good time to put your blanket away and get your thumb out of our mouth."

"He's stirring," said Payton.

"Shake him. Stir him. Smack him if you have to," said Lin straining.

"Come on, pup," said Jaylon.

Payton stood on his chest directly below his chin and pulled on his bottom lip. Benji locked eyes with her and nodded his head.

"Got him," said Payton.

Benji swiped his tail accelerating them toward the other side of the rig.

"Keep it up, pup!" yelled Jaylon.

Benji pulled his arms in front of him holding his hands above his stomach. Payton moved around Benji's chest and up onto his shoulder. She gripped his ear and kept her eyes focused on Gouguon.

With his right hand still clenched tight around the Mystiq prong, Benji snapped his left hand. A bubble shot out from his fingers. He moved the bubble between both hands and expanded it until it was as wide as his shoulders.

"Hurry, Benji," squealed Payton as Gouguon closed in on them.

Benji eyed Gouguon thrashing behind them. The two of them snarled at each other. Gouguon kicked it into another gear lunging closer still.

Benji grinned. He moved the bubble over his abdomen with his left hand and touched the edge of it with the Mystiq prong. The bubble barrelled toward Gouguon but he rolled right, and it burst into the wall of coral behind them.

Benji looked over each shoulder. "Jaylon. Lin. Roll to the sides when I say."

"What side?" said Lin.

"Away from each other."

"We're not leaving you, Benji," said Jaylon.

"Yes, you are. Roll!" Benji blew past them and threw his elbows out as he did. They both tumbled away.

Gouguon slowed momentarily at the distraction but kept his sights on the prong.

Payton poked Benji's head. "I hope you got something brewing up there, blondy."

"Hang on," said Benji. He flipped over and zipped between the rig's struts. He kicked it into another gear and wound his way back around and through the supports. Benji shed his tail and planted his feet square on the outside edge of the rig strut perimeter. "Pull me back if I start moving."

Gouguon raced toward the bottom, both his hands balled up ready to rain fists on Benji as soon as he got within striking distance.

Benji took in a huge breath. His eyes rolled up, and he cocked his head back before snapping it forward again. A massive, ear-splitting shriek screamed out of his mouth and caught Gouguon dead center of the pilings. The vibration from Benji's howl sent sound waves smashing through the interior of the coliseum-style enclosure surrounding the rig. The four struts under the rig acted like a giant tuning fork and shook the water underneath with a ferocity that distorted Gouguon to the point he looked like a blue-gray blob of glue.

The vibrations sucked Benji closer.

Payton knew the prong was the last thing he'd let loose, so she grabbed the handle and yanked with everything she had. She fluttered her little fairy wings as fast as the water under the rig shook. Slowly, Benji's feet drug along the sandy ocean floor away from the vibrating oil platform.

Benji stopped his siren. His body relaxed and his head followed another whale tune echoing throughout the enclosure. Line by line of whales peeled away from their course toward the oil rig. A pod of orcas, the sparkle back in the eyes, barrelled through the water just below the surface toward the ring of sharks circling below the platform. Chaos surrounded him, pure chaos, but in the confusion order slowly claimed its territory as harmony reestablished itself.

Payton fluttered onto Benji's shoulder and pumped both her arms as she settled. At the same time, Benji changed his tail and headed up causing Payton to stumbled away. Benji scooped her in his hand. "Gotcha."

Jaylon and Lin came from opposite directions and sandwiched Benji. Jaylon grabbed him by the sides of the head and embraced him forehead to forehead. "What was that?"

A bashful smile and half a laugh stuttered out of Benji's mouth.

Lin attacked Benji from the side. "I had to see that to believe it!"

By the dozens, whales and dolphins chased after their captors. The Donquarien's spears slipped through the water as Gouguon's army lightened their load in an attempt to flee. The tips of the spears glinted in the sunlight until they lodged into the sand, staffs exposed, waving for mercy in the bottom current.

The pilings slowly stopped vibrating, revealing Gouguon barely twitching face down in the water.

"Let's get him contained before it's too late," said Payton.

Benji approached his uncle from the rear, conjured up a bubble, and wrapped Gouguon up for the trip back to Sanjowqua.

Each group of whales surfaced immediately after being freed from the control of the prong to expel the energy that had held them captive. Once they cleared their lungs, they added their own notes to the song Meena blew out through the shell. Soon the entire area hummed and danced from the sounds of freedom.

The men of the oil rig stood cautiously away from the edge watching it all transpire. The struts shook from the noise alone as wave upon wave of whales sang their songs while cruising under the steel city.

The two humpbacks from Sanjowqua brought up the rear, batting a bubble between the two of them like two kids keeping a balloon airborne. Sys and Jais tumbled over with each nudge of the giant creatures' mouths. As they approached, the female nudged the bubble with Sys and Jais into the bubble with Gouguon then turned her attention to Benji. She veered toward him so quickly, Benji didn't have time to react. She scooped him up onto her head and tossed him out of the water.

Benji changed his tail and landed square on her head with his feet planted, the Mystiq prong in his hand, surveying the scene.

The news helicopter buzzed above them. The reporter clung to the side of the door pointing the cameraman toward Benji as he rattled into the microphone as fast as he could go.

"And what are we looking at, Jeff," said the anchor, sitting comfortably in the news studio.

"Well, Rebecca, it appears to be a boy. Possibly a teenager on top of a humpback whale. The whole charge of whales that looked to be on a collision course with the oil rig has diverted. Thousands of them are reversing course out of the Gulf. Believe it or not, this boy looks like he's leading them. He's holding some kind of staff," said the reporter to his live newsdesk.

"Jeff, are those others in the water around the whale. They almost look like…"

"Yes, there are others in the water surrounding the whale, Rebecca. I'm not exactly sure, but they almost look like, like… mermaids."

"And a *DUDE*," snapped Jaylon, shaking his fist up toward the helicopter with his trademark ear to ear grin.

"Mermaids are real," whispered the anchor.

"What we're seeing seems to confirm that, Rebecca," said the reporter.

Benji looked up at the helicopter, smiled, and dove back into the water.

"You didn't want to stay and sign autographs?" asked Lin.

"I think an appearance is sufficient for now," said Benji.

Meena stared Benji down then nodded with a grin. "That's a good start."

"Come on. We've got a long way back carting these goons," said Jaylon, motioning at the two bubbles with Gouguon, Sys and Jais floating inside.

The female humpback circled the bubble containing Sys and Jais, opened her gargantuan mouth, and sucked them inside.

"That solves that," said Meena.

Lin floated beside Gouguon. Meena yanked her sister out of the way before the male humpback did the same to the bubble containing Gouguon.

"*And* that," said Jaylon. "Sanjowqua, here we come."

Chewana Makawindi

(full moon festival)

BENJI SAT DOWN on the dock. The mid-day sun glistened off his damp hair. A bead of sweat popped out on his forehead and trickled down to the tip of his nose. He wiped the straggler off with his finger and flicked it away. The boards of the dock squeaked behind him.

"Redneck security system right there," said Benji and Joe at the same time.

Joe wrestled his hand through Benji's wet hair. Benji shook his head and sprinkled Joe's t-shirt and jeans.

"How you doin', son?"

"Good, Dad."

"You did good."

"How'd you know?"

"Word gets around."

A splash of water pulled their attention towards the end of the dock. Boone stood halfway up the ladder with a proud grin on his face. "Yeah, word gets around."

"This is awkward," said Benji.

"It doesn't have to be," said Boone.

"I have two dads. I guess stranger things have happened," said Benji.

"Joe more than earned that title. Under the circumstances, I don't really have a say in that. I only wanted to keep you safe, son."

"Thanks," said Benji, and he paused to consider what to say next. "So, you know each other?"

"We've had the pleasure of meeting," said Joe as he flashed Boone a thumbs up.

Benji looked at Boone. "What was that light I saw? I saw it in the cave. It hit me when Gouguon grabbed me, too."

"That was you," said Boone.

"Me? It was bright," said Benji.

"So are you, son," said Joe.

Boone nodded. "Yes, that light, that bright light, was you. That was your own healing energy. Joe's right, Benji. Once you learn to harness that, you'll be a very powerful Mystiq."

"Cool. There was a voice," said Benji. "In the cave. A female voice that followed the light."

"Your mom was there. She was guiding you," said Boone.

Benji looked back and forth between the two men. "And, where is she? Why didn't I see her?"

"She's here," said Boone nodding his head around the three of them. "There," he said, gesturing across the inlet to the marsh grass. "There," he said toward a group of pelicans flying overhead.

"Your Mom was a healer, Benji, like you. There's a little of her everywhere. Part of her was with Montal. Her energy kept his consciousness anchored on that side for so long. That's how the healer energy flows once it leaves the body. That's what made her so good and will do the same for you.

"We're all connected, but the healers use that connection to fuse a part of themselves with others, with things, with animals, to pull energy from where it can best help and push it to where it is needed when they heal. It's in their nature to expand when their energy is no longer confined to a physical body.

"That energy is what jolted Gouguon when he grabbed you. Gouguon has a lot of pain, but he's not willing to heal it. Part of him wants that pain. Part of him needs that pain. As soon as your healing energy touched him, he immediately rejected it. And he did so in such a violent manner that it nearly killed him."

"Now that we're here, what about my dreams?" asked Benji.

Joe shrugged and looked at Boone.

"Your dreams are a special place, Benji. Some of your biggest challenges and most important questions can get answered here, where you are right now," said Boone.

"Where do we begin?" asked Benji.

"You've already begun," said Boone.

Something brushed against Benji's leg. He looked down to see a purple cat winding around his leg. It wrapped its tail around Benji's calf and tickled the back of his knee. He reached down to shoo it away and woke up.

"No!" said Benji annoyed.

"What's wrong?" said Octavius, his tentacle wrapped around Benji's tail.

The anemones underneath Benji bobbled him as he rolled over in bed. "I was in the middle of a dream."

"Was she cute?"

"Haha. I was talking with my dad and Boone."

"Ah, that kind. You're progressing nicely, then."

"I was until a purple cat showed up and spoiled it," said Benji, giving Octavius the evil eye.

"I'm not a purple cat," said Octavius.

"You were a few seconds ago."

"How are you feeling?"

Benji stretched his arms over his head and flexed his tail. "I could use a few more hours of sleep," he said with a yawn.

"There will be plenty of time for that when your time is finished here," said Octavius.

"You put a time limit on my stay?" asked Benji.

"We all have a time limit," chuckled Octavius. "There's nothing even a Mystiq can do about that."

"Oh, you mean 'finished' finished. So, I'm not being shoved out?"

"Far from it. You're home. Care to take a swim?"

"I'd prefer sleep, but you got me up now," said Benji as he pushed off the bed.

Octavius grabbed his shoulder, and Benji looked around the room. Several large vase sponges sat in the corners of the room.

"Where's Payton?" asked Benji.

"I bumped into her on her way out. I like what she's done with the place, by the way. A water fairy's touch is always a welcome one," said Octavius.

Benji nodded his head in agreement.

"She's already out primping the coral this morning. Everyone's prepping for the big party."

"The Fringe is gone. There isn't much to celebrate is there?"

"Life goes on, Benji. Further than you know."

"I got an idea."

"Yes, I suspect you do now."

A buzzing excitement filled his senses as soon as Benji's head parted the doorframe. A group of Shequarien cachazi cleaning the coral turned when they saw Benji, each giggling as he passed.

"Good morning, your excellence," said several blue tangs as they swam by.

Benji shook his head looking at Octavius. "Was that for you?"

Octavius chuckled again. "Yes. There was an emergency meeting of all the elders of Sanjowqua last night. Mumkaza was voted out as head of the Security Council."

"And you were voted in?"

"Yes."

"Well, I feel special. I'm palling around with royalty this morning."

"You have to be born into royalty, young Mystiq. I'm just a humble servant of Sanjowqua."

"Wow! You were born to play this role."

"That's something I've had to practice."

"You had a pretty good hang of it when we met."

Chelli bobbed down from the surface and grimaced at Benji. "Guess you were worth the effort after all, pup."

Benji waved and smiled. "I'll take that as a compliment," he said looking at Octavius.

"Coming from Chelli, that's about as close as you're going to get to one."

"So, what's going to happen to Gouguon?"

"He's on his way back to Muyu Munda along with Jais and Sys. His cohorts will spend a year there. Gouguon's going back in for a while longer. He'll be lucky to get out again.

"Meena and Jaylon left first thing this morning to take them back. They should be back late tomorrow," said Octavius.

"What about the other Donquarien?" asked Benji.

"They're on the way back to Donquari, although it will be a while before they get there based on the fact their boat mysteriously went missing."

Benji looked innocently over both shoulders. "I wonder how that happened?"

"Yes, that's curious. There will be a meeting of all the elders from Sanjowqua, Beiquari, Nanquari, and Donquari before the Full Moon Festival to decide what other actions should be taken against the Donquari."

Peca and another mermaid swam by. Peca blushed then waved as she fluttered down to the coral at the base of Waputa Wamkala.

"When's the party? It must be a big one with all the action going on around here," said Benji as a pair of water fairies buzzed past.

"It's still a few weeks away, and yes, it'll be huge. The biggest you've ever seen. I'll earn my stripes and then some in the coming weeks."

"Everyone's happy to have the Mystiq prong back, then."

"You could say that. The prong has been gone for over thirteen years. There are some here who have never experienced the Full Moon Festival."

"I'm looking forward to that."

"You should. The Full Moon Festival used to be one of the most cherished events in all of Aquari. For one night each month Aquarien could venture Topside within the confounds of Sanjowqua and live another life, a life with legs where they ran, jumped, skipped, climbed trees, hiked to the top of Waputa Wamkala, and did anything they wanted for the entire evening. During certain moons, the force was so strong it allowed them to stay Topside up to three days. That's the longest I ever heard of, though," said Octavius.

"And how long until the next one?"

"Twenty-one days, by my count."

"Why is everyone worried so much about cleaning down here, then?"

"They need to pamper the coral. It's been a long time since the last festival. Everyone will likely need a few days off afterward," smiled Octavius.

"I need to get going then. I don't want to miss that."

"And where is our resident Mystiq headed in such a hurry?"

"I've got an invite to extend Topside," said Benji, pausing to scratch his temple. "Am I allowed to do that?"

"Of course, you are. Who's the lucky recipient?"

"My uncle. He's all I have left up there."

"I'd recommend taking the boat. It's a long way."

Lin and Yuri saw Benji as he and Octavius rounded a bungalow. They changed course and made a beeline toward him.

"I'll need a crew, right?" asked Benji.

Octavius nodded at him. "I think we can scrounge one up for you."

Thank you!

The best part of an adventure is sharing your experience with others. I, for one, would love to hear about your experience with Benji and your thoughts/ideas on his next journey through the deep blue sea.

Please take a minute and post a review on Amazon at
https://amzn.to/2xgcKdo

You can also follow me on my Amazon Author page under Bo Wu.

If you have any suggestions (animals you'd like to read about next, a fun character name, etc.) for the next volume in the journey, please contact me through Goodreads, or the Mermaids Are Real website at
https://www.mermaidsarereal.co

When you send me a message or subscribe to updates on the Mermaids Are Real website, you'll be automatically entered for a drawing to win a free copy of the next book.

Made in the USA
Columbia, SC
18 October 2018